# THE CASE FOR
# ZIONISM

WHY CHRISTIANS SHOULD
SUPPORT ISRAEL

# THOMAS ICE

## What Others Are Saying about *The Case for Zionism* . . .

In *The Case for Zionism,* Dr. Thomas Ice presents a fresh, comprehensive, and engaging analysis of Zionism from a variety of perspectives — historical, political, theological, and ultimately biblical. In the process, he soundly refutes many of the unfounded, and often scurrilous, objections and accusations that have been leveled against both Jewish and Christian Zionism. Demonstrating a clear command of the subject, which stems from many years of Christian ministry and academic research at the highest level, Dr. Ice presents a clear, watertight case for why every true Christian should stand with God's chosen nation, Israel. I highly recommend this well-researched and readable book.

> — Dr. Paul Wilkinson, Minister of Hazel Grove Full
> Gospel Church, Stockport, England, author,
> international conference speaker, and contributor to
> Christian television, radio, and documentary films

I've been waiting for this book for many years. It's needed now more than ever. Tommy is a passionate voice for premillennialism and a future for national Israel. Simply stated, no one is better on this subject than Tommy. I've heard him speak at conferences on Christian Zionism over the last three decades and am thrilled to see his clear, careful research available in one resource. I will read this book carefully and use it again and again as a trusted guide. You should too.

> — Dr. Mark Hitchcock, Senior Pastor, Faith Bible
> Church, Edmond, OK, and Associate Professor of
> Bible Exposition, Dallas Theological Seminary

The Hebrew word "Zion" is used 154 times in the Old Testament — 37 of which are in the Psalms and 46 usages in Isaiah. The New Testament uses the word 7 times. Dr. Thomas Ice has brought to the attention of its readers, a book that clearly presents the case for "Zionism" and urges Christians and Jews alike to support it and defend it. Psalm 87:2 states: "The LORD loveth the gates of ZION more than all the dwellings of Jacob," and in Psalm 99:2 we read: "The LORD is great in ZION; and He is high above all the people." May the God of Israel bless the efforts of this excellent book!"

> — Dr. David Hocking
> HOPE for TODAY Ministries and radio broadcast

The Christian opponents of Zionism, especially the proponents of Christian Palestinianism, are averse to biblical theology; It is their stated nemesis. The very reason they cannot manage it is because it undermines the biblical and historical basis for their belief system — and for this same reason that Dr. Ice's careful biblical and theological presentation of the case for Zionism is so vital to the present debate. With experience and skill, Dr. Ice focuses on the major issues of concern and surfaces the crux of their ancient interpretation and application in the modern context. It was very satisfying to finally see a thorough biblical and historical analysis of the Khazar theory that will dispel any honest reader's thought that this idea ever had currency in historical interpretation. Another excellent contribution is Dr. Ice's tracing of the historical Christian influence on Jewish national Restoration long before the advent of the Zionist movement that reveals Christian ministers and statesmen understood biblical theology and acted upon the conviction that to know God's will is to do God's will. May this fine book find a place on the shelf of every pastor and politician who needs to have a basis for supporting Israel's modern return to the Land and future hope in its Messiah.

— Randall Price, Ph.D.
Distinguished Research Professor, Liberty University

Replacement theology and anti-Semitism have brought much confusion to Christians regarding the nation of Israel. With this important book, Tommy Ice brings much-needed clarity on the issues of Israel's place in the plan of God and how Christians should view and support Israel. This is a must read!"

— Michael J. Vlach
Professor of Theology, The Master's Seminary

*The Case For Zionism* is a cogent, logical presentation focusing on the centrality of the nation of Israel in the plans and purposes of God. Dr. Thomas Ice describes the biblical, historical, and prophetic part that Israel had in the past and the role it plays in the present and future times. This book explains why one should steadfastly support the modern state of Israel.

— Dr. Jeffrey Gutterman, Ariel Ministries, Dallas/Fort Worth Branch Director

Zechariah 12:3 predicts the world turning against the nation of Israel when it says, "It will come about in that day that I will make Jerusalem a heavy stone for all the peoples; all who lift it will be severely injured. And all the nations of the earth will be gathered against it." This end time turning against Israel is the very thing that we see happening today both inside and outside the Church. Thus, there has perhaps never been a more important time for believers to equip themselves concerning God's perspective concerning the nation of Israel. This is why Dr. Thomas Ice's new book *The Case for Zionism* is a timely one. It covers the important and volatile subject of Israel from a biblical, political, legal, and even a spiritual warfare angle. For all who seek to discover the mind of God on the critical subject of Israel, as well as equip themselves to stand against the anti-Israel sentiments that are so prevalent in our day, this book is required reading.

— Dr. Andy Woods, Senior Pastor
Sugar Land Bible Church, Sugar Land, TX

Israel, wars, and violence in the Middle East continuously distress everyone in the world. Many believe the solution to this problem would end the problems with Islam. For many, blame resides with the very existence of the nation Israel. But is this true? How did the Jewish people come to return to their historic homeland? Was the return of the Jewish nation a coincidence of history? Or does God still have a plan for the Jewish people? Are the Jews of today genetic descendants of the biblical Israelites? Is anti-Zionism anti-semitic? Is there a biblical and prophetic significance to the re-establishment of the nation Israel? These are a few of the many questions you will have answered by reading this fascinating biblical and historical analysis by Dr. Thomas Ice. Dr. Ice has spent years researching this vital topic and he brings to light many facts that are commonly ignored or unknown by many politicians. Dr. Ice clearly demonstrates the unequivocal biblical, historical, and legal case for Israel's right to their historic homeland. This easy-to-read book will answer your questions and make you well-informed on the Christian's view on Israel.

— Dr. Robert Dean, Jr.
Pastor, West Houston Bible Church
Faculty, Chafer Theological Seminary

First printing: February 2017

ISBN: 978-0-89221-753-3
Library of Congress Number: 2016963343

Cover by Left Coast Design

Please consider requesting that a copy of this volume be purchased by your local library system.

**Printed in the United States of America**

Please visit our website for other great titles:
www.newleafpress.com

For information regarding author interviews,
please contact the publicity department at (870) 438-5288.

**New Leaf Press**
A Division of New Leaf Publishing Group
www.newleafpress.com

# Contents

# FOREWORD

As a result of the Holocaust, for the next several decades anti-Semitism was viewed as a social negative and many rebelled against such a stereotype. Anti-Semitism did not disappear but it stayed low key, and anti-Semites were careful not to be too obvious. But in more recent times things have changed.

Anti-Semitism has again reared its ugly head in two new more subtle forms — first, as anti-Zionism, claiming that they are not anti-Jewish, but only anti-Zionist or Anti-Israel, equating Zionism with racism. They provide a faulty definition of Zionism and then judge Israel based on such a misconception.

A second subtle form of anti-Semitism is the claim that most Jews today are true descendants of Abraham, Isaac, or Jacob but are the products of the Khazar Kingdom that had converted to Judaism in the Middle Ages. Therefore, there are no "real" Jews and therefore they have no right to the land of Israel (which for them is Palestine).

Dr. Tommy Ice scholarly deals with both of the above issues as well as others that all believers need to know and know well.

Anti-Semitism appears in many forms: racial, ethnic, social, economic, political, and religious, to mention only a few. From a biblical basis, the worst kind is theological anti-Semitism, which has been the true roots of replacement theology in all of its forms. This is not to say that all replacement theologians are anti-Semitic, but the early originators of replacement theology certainly were, as their own writings show. Modern-day anti-Semites would not be attracted to dispensationalism but would be to replacementism. Many evangelical believers believe in replacementism only because that is what they have been taught, and too often never hear the other side. This is exactly where Dr. Ice's book makes a valuable contribution and shows biblically why all Christians should support Israel.

Arnold G. Fruchtenbaum, ThM, Ph.D; Ariel Ministries

# WHAT IS
# GOING ON?

In this conference we continued as Palestinian Christians to challenge Christian Zionism. We have done this in the first conference. We have done this in the second conference, and the third and the fourth, and we will do it again. Because we continue to see that theology as a threat to us, let alone in our opinion, the way we read it is not combatable to the teachings of Jesus. — Munther Isaac, Christ at the Checkpoint, March 10, 2016

Just as historic anti-Semitism has denied individual Jews the right to live as equal members of society, anti-Zionism would deny the collective expression of the Jewish people, the state of Israel, the right to live as an equal member of the family of nations. Israel's policies are thus subjected to criticism that cause it to be singled out when others in similar circumstances escape any criticism at all. Surely if any other country were bleeding from terrorism as Israel is today, there would be no question of its right to defend itself. But Israel's efforts merely to protect its own citizens are routinely portrayed as aggression.[1] — Abraham Foxman, ADL Director

Anti-Semitism has been around for thousands of years, and it is still very much with us today. The world has witnessed, in the last few years, the greatest increase in anti-Semitism since World War II. Danny Danon, currently Israel's United Nations ambassador, has said, "Jew hatred and demonization of Israel are at 'the highest level of our lifetimes.' "[2] Since the founding of the nation of Israel, anti-Semitism has expanded into another strand we call either "anti-Zionism" or "the new anti-Semitism." The new strand of anti-Semitism is expanding throughout the world under the leadership of the Arab Muslim world. Former Palestinian Muslim terrorist Walid Shoebat said, "As it was with the Nazis, the Palestinian schools are terror factories."[3] In essence Islam has become the new Nazis with an agenda to exterminate the nation of Israel and all Jews worldwide, and it appears to be getting worse every year.

God is not going to set up His future millennial kingdom without His chosen people Israel existing in a right relationship with Him. The Bible predicts Israel will reach this relationship at some point during the 70th week of Daniel, often known as the Tribulation. Since the Bible clearly teaches a roadmap concerning the destiny of national Israel, then I as a Bible-believing Christian believe what God says about future Israel. This is why I am a Christian Zionist, or a "Restorationist" as it was known before Zionism became a movement at the end of the 19th century. This book provides many reasons and defenses of Christian Zionism, because there is tremendous support from many different areas for the modern state of Israel.

I believe the battle for Israel and Jerusalem today is more than just human interaction over an issue. Instead, it involves a struggle over God's plan for history and the opposition to that plan from Satan and his angels in the spiritual realm. To be on the wrong side of this issue is to oppose God Himself. This is the advice given by Gamaliel to his fellow Jewish leaders when they were persecuting the early Church. "So in the present case, I say to you, stay away from these men and let them alone, for if this plan or action is of men, it will be overthrown; but if it is of God, you will not be able to overthrow them; or else you may even be found fighting against God" (Acts 5:38–39). If God has decreed it, then there is nothing anyone can do to stop it; not even Satan himself. If God has not decreed it, then it will not be accomplished. This is a book about how God is bringing to pass His plan from before the foundation of the world for Israel. Yes, it does involve men and means, but ultimately God will bring it to pass in history.

## International Assault on Israel

Since Israel is at the center of God's plan of redemption for humanity, it is important that Christians learn of and know how to defend the modern state of Israel. I am currently 65 years old and have been in the church almost every time the doors were open starting nine months before I was born. Yet, when I was in high school, I do not remember even knowing if there was a modern state of Israel. I soon learned that there was a new country called Israel. When we were 21, my wife and I went to Israel on our honeymoon, and we have been learning about ancient Israel and the modern state ever since. Just eight months after our first tour of Israel the Yom Kipper war broke out and Israel was almost overrun by her Arab enemies, but she was not defeated; instead, the nation executed one of the most amazing comebacks in history.

Since her founding as a modern nation, Israel has had many military victories that have enabled her to become one of the most productive and wealthy nations in the world. Yet she is constantly and increasingly under attacks from other people throughout the world. For example, on October 17, 2016, the United Nations Educational, Scientific and Cultural Organization (UNESCO) voted to deny that there has ever been any Jewish or Christian historical connection to the Temple Mount. Instead, they said Islam is the only religion that can make a historical claim to what they call "the Al-Haram Al Sharif" (the Noble Sanctuary). The implication of such a view is that any event recorded in the Old Testament could not have happened, nor could any of the references to Jesus and the early Church in the New Testament be historical as well. The vote for this resolution was 24 for it and 6 against, while 26 abstained and 2 were absent. The United States voted against it, while most European countries abstained, and those voting for it were mainly Islamic countries with a few exceptions.[4]

Such assaults against Israel continue daily, in addition to the military and terrorist activities the citizens of Israel must constantly deal with. The United Nations has for years implemented a constant assault on the young nation. "From 1947 to 1991, there were about 300 anti-Israel General Assembly resolutions against Israel. In 2012, there were 22 GA resolutions specifically against Israel, while there were only four for the rest of the world combined."[5] It appears that the main purpose of the United Nations is to pass resolutions against Israel. The European Union (EU) is constantly pressuring Israel on a variety of issues with which they are unhappy about concerning Israel. No doubt the Obama administration has radically changed the relationship between former best friends — Israel and the United States. Christians need to make sure they know God's viewpoint on these issues as they continue to be very important issues in our day and into the future.

### Islam — the New Nazis

Islamic nations produce the most fervent hatred toward the modern state of Israel. In the last few decades, researchers have come to increasingly understand the relationship between Middle Eastern Islam, Hitler, and the Nazis in the 1930s and 40s. One figure arises as the primary source and instigator of so many of the problems of today — Haj Amin el Husseini, the former Grand Mufti of Jerusalem and the modern father of Arab terrorism. "*Mein Kampf* in Arabic remains a perpetual bestseller in Muslim countries, especially among 'Palestinians,' " contends Dave Hunt. "Hitler was, in fact, a great partner with Haj Amin Mohammed Effendi al-Husseini (great uncle and mentor of Yasser Arafat and still a hero to Muslims), a murderous terrorist, appointed Grand Mufti of Jerusalem by Britain and personally responsible for the concentration camp slaughter of hundred of thousands of Jews."[6] Husseini and Hitler were great friends and spent a significant amount of time together during the late 1930s and the early 40s. Husseini encouraged and advised Hitler on killing Jews, something that Husseini took great interest in planning. Husseini even recruited about "100,000 European Muslims" who "fought for Nazi Germany during the course of the war."[7] Moshe Perlman tells us:

> It has now also been established that the ex-Mufti of Jerusalem, Haj Amin el Husseini, played an active role in that unprecedented massacre of a people. Records found in Nazi achieves and evidence produced at the Nuremberg trial reveal in specific terms that the ex-Mufti was a leading henchman of the SS Obersturmbannfuehrer Eichmann, principal executive officer in the liquidation of European Jewry. It is now established that, but for Haj Amin, the scale of murder might not have been so extensive, and hundreds of thousands of Jewish lives might have been saved.[8]

Nazism may have been crushed in Germany with the defeat of the Third Reich during World War II, but a remnant of its leaders escaped capture by the Allies, and many of them resettled in Arab countries, bringing with them their Nazi aspirations and goals. Toward the end of World War II, Husseini attempted to escape from Germany and was captured by the French at the Swiss border. He was held under house arrest outside of Paris for war crimes. He then escaped and made his way to Cairo, Egypt, where he was welcomed by King Farouk as a welcomed guest of the Egyptian government.[9] Husseini continued to live throughout the Arab world until his death (of natural causes) in the summer of 1974 in Beirut, Lebanon.[10] Husseini did not die until he had passed his legacy of militant terrorism on to other Arab Muslims like Yassir Arafat. In fact, it was because of Husseini that a peaceful relationship between Arabs and Jews never had a chance under the British Mandate for Palestine. Perlman summarizes his career as follows:

> Once upon a time, Arabs and Jews lived peacefully in Palestine. Their leaders walked and planned together. Then came Haj Amin el Husseini, Uncle of Yassir Arafat. He chose fascism and jihad. Moderate leaders had to go, and he dispensed with them by murder and intimidation. His bloody projects were temporarily interrupted by WWII, during which he fled to Germany and cooperated closely with Nazi leaders in plans of extermination and battle. Designated as a war criminal, he escaped Allied hands to continue his work of terror, a work continued by his relatives and associates after his death.[11]

"At the conclusion of World War II, al-Husseini would play a key role in what came to be known as Project Odessa, an operation that provided a pipeline for Nazi war criminals fleeing justice and making their way into Arab and Latin American countries."[12] These veteran Nazi leaders combined with an Arab Muslim's inbred Jew-hatred would produce today's irrational new anti-Semitism that is embraced by today's Islamofascists like the former president of Iran, Mahmoud Ahmadinejad. The current Islamic Nazism was engendered by the "newly arriving Nazi war criminals [that] would be quickly assimilated into Arab military, intelligence, and propaganda services," after World War II. "Many of these former Nazis had no problem converting to Islam, changing their names to Arab names, and assimilating into Arab society."[13] In fact, one such refugee, Nazi Louis Heiden (his Arab name became Louis al-Hadj), translated Hitler's *Mein Kampf* into Arabic. "*Mein Kampf* remains a perennial bestseller and literally a blockbuster in much of the Arab world today. In his preface to *Mein Kampf*, al-Hadj states, 'National Socialism did not die with the death of its herald. Rather, its seeds multiplied under each star.' "[14]

Even though some in the Arab Muslim world were already on the road to Islamofascism there is no doubt that al-Husseini was the catalyst for its actual development. Morse tells us:

> Al-Husseini's unique brand of Nazism, a merge between modern scientific socialistic Nazism and a strain of fundamentalist Islam, would make profound inroads into the Arab world during the war and that influence continues to metastasize today as evidenced by the continuing geno-cidal program against the Jews of Israel. . . . The difference between Hitler's Nazism and that of al-Husseini and his Nazi-Muslims should ultimately be viewed as strictly cosmetic in nature.[15]

There is no doubt that wherever Islam is culturally dominant, Jew-hatred is always present as well, especially in the Arab Muslim world. When speaking about the supremacy of anti-Semitic propaganda in the Arab Muslim world, former Palestinian terrorist Walid Shoebat noted, "As in Nazi Germany, the media throughout the Middle East is plagued with myth."[16] Shoebat continues, "Beginning with our lullabies, Jew-hatred is an integral part of daily life for all Palestinian children and for Muslim children in many countries around the world."[17] Shoebat goes on to document how every phase and aspect of Arab life in the Middle East is immersed with the most extreme forms of virulent anti-Semitism.[18] Jew-hatred is so inbred into the everyday life of the Middle East that it is part of the air that Arabs breathe.

*The Protocols of the Elders of Zion*[19] was released in 1903, and was a book advocating the Jewish world banking theory. It was originally titled *The Jewish Programme to Conquer the World*. Basically, the book argues that there is a worldwide Jewish banking conspiracy by which the Jews run the world. The Jews are said to cause strife and conflict in the world leading to wars so they will eventually be able to take control and rule the world. The Jewish world conspiracy is very popular in the Arab Muslim world. In reality, the *Protocols* were proven to be a fabrication under the tsar of Russia in support of the pogroms he carried out against the Jews. Yet in the Islamic world the *Protocols* are considered the key to understanding current Zionism's supposed attempt to rule the world. For example, Egyptian Muslims created a TV series of 41 episodes on the *Protocols* that ran during Ramadan in 2002.[20] It has since been shown throughout the Arab-speaking world.

### Is It 1938 Again for the Jews?

The October 2003 edition of *Whistleblower* dedicated its entire issue to the theme of "The New Anti-Semitism." Jewish talk-show host Dennis Prager wrote an article in that issue asking the question, "Is It 1938 Again For The Jews?"[21] Why would he ask if it was 1938 again? Prager poses this question because 1938 was a turning point in the rise of Nazi anti-Semitism that prepared the way for the Holocaust. Prager, an American Jew, wonders if we are at a similar key point in history, this time in relation to the Arab anti-Semitism that is gaining momentum in the Middle East. "Even the bulk of Jewry that was not alive in 1938 feels now as if that year of appeasement of evil is being replayed," says Prager. "As in 1938, the world now seems to be divided between those nations that were about to murder Jews and those that would let it happen."[22]

As I assess the geo-political climate of the world, especially the Arab Middle East, it appears that we are on a collision course of some kind similar to the events that led to World War II. We see the buildup of fascism, this time Islamofascism. The overall response from the West is pacifism and appeasement, similar to Neville Chamberlain and the British toward Hitler in the 1930s. Just a decade ago we could say the only major exception to Western pacifism is the United States, which has gone after the Islamofascists. However, the Bush administration was pushed into a corner with the increasing unpopularity of the Iraqi war during the last couple of years of his administration. The Obama administration clearly favors Iran in the Middle East, and now Russia is moving into that area as the strongman, especially the ever-growing alliance between Russia, Iran, and Turkey that appears to be setting the stage for the Gog and Magog invasion of Israel during the last days. These trends will likely open the door to a time of great persecution of Israel, which has been predicted in the Bible to occur during the Tribulation.

Just as a time of pacifism and appeasement preceded and fostered the buildup of Hitler's fascist regime, so also today we see pacifism and appeasement is the perfect environment for the growth of Islamofascism.

Ivy League professor Peter Beinart wrote an interesting article a few years ago when Bill Clinton was president entitled "An Illusion for Our Time: The False Promise of Globalization."[23] Beinart argued the Clinton administration's primary principle in their foreign policy was to no longer interpret international problems as items demanding political and military attention; instead, they viewed problems as relating to trade and commerce. Beinart thinks this is the same kind of policy the British adopted that led to the rise of Nazi fascism. Beinart notes parallels between 1910 and our own day.

On March 20, 1997, *New York Times* columnist Thomas Friedman wrote that we have entered a "new world of globalization — a world in which the integration of financial networks, information and trade is binding the globe together and shifting power from governments to markets." In his December 8, 1996, column, Friedman wondered whether "a country, by integrating with the global economy, opening itself up to foreign investment and empowering its consumers, permanently restricts its capacity for troublemaking and promotes gradual democratization and widening peace." And on February 14, 1996, in a column on the impending Russian elections, he wrote: "Sure, a Communist or radical populist in the Kremlin would be worrying. But their room for maneuver would be constricted — much more than we realize and much, much more than they realize. Russia today is connected with the global economy."

The conventional wisdom about post-cold war American foreign policy is that there is no conventional wisdom — no unifying theory that traces disparate phenomena to a single source. But one candidate for conceptual preeminence may be breaking from the pack, and it is Friedman's candidate, globalization. The idea is that technology has led to unprecedented and irreversible economic integration among countries. The only way governments can survive is to do what global business demands: observe the rule of law at home, and act peacefully abroad. For the United States, that means abiding by the imperatives of the global economy and informing others that they must do the same. It is a foreign policy vision for a world where politics barely matter.[24]

Beinart tells us this view did not originate with the Clinton administration, but it has been around for almost a hundred years now.

"International finance has become so interdependent and so interwoven with trade and industry that . . . political and military power can in reality do nothing. . . . These little recognized facts, mainly the outcome of purely modern conditions (rapidity of communication creating a greater complexity and delicacy of the credit system), have rendered the problems of modern international politics profoundly and essentially different from the ancient." These words come from perhaps the best-selling book on international relations ever written. That book, *The Great Illusion*, sold more than a million copies in seventeen languages. Its author, Norman Angell, was knighted, and won the Nobel Peace Prize. In the years following the book's publication, close to 100 organizations arose to spread its message: that the world had entered a new era in which economic interdependence made war unthinkable. *The Great Illusion* was published in 1910.[25]

It is amazing to think that such a belief dominated the British government a hundred years ago. It would only be a few years until World War I would break out across Europe. Such a mentality fueled the rationale for Chamberlain's passivity and appeasement of Hitler in the 1930s. In short, such a mentality facilitated an international mood that led to the bloodiest century in human history — the 20th century. In 1910 Britain was the most influential global power. Since World War II the United States has occupied that position. Especially in light of similar policies of passivism by the Obama administration for eight years, America appears to be more aliened with

European pacifism and appeasement and ready to abandon any war against Islamofascism. Islamofascist-dominated governments are not ready to join the world community on the basis of economics and trade. So while the West seeks only peace and prosperity, militant Islam is on the rise and on the march.

From a biblical perspective, it appears the stage is being prepared for the events of the Tribulation that will increasingly focus on Israel and her enemies. At some point all the nations of the world will come against Israel in an attempt to wipe her off the face of the earth. However, Israel will have one Person on her side, the Lord God Almighty. The Lord will protect His Chosen People even though the nation will have to go through great testing and persecution before realizing the redemption the Lord will provide.

## Israel's Future

As horrific as Israel's past history has been, they have not yet experienced the greatest time of persecution according to the Bible, both Old and New Testaments. The New Testament predicts there will come a future time of such great persecution of the Jews that many of them will have to leave the city of Jerusalem and Judea and hide away in the wilderness for a three-and-a-half-year period (Matt. 24:15–22; Mark 13:14–20; Rev. 12:6, 12–17). Most likely the Jews will flee to a place in southwest Jordan known as Petra, as I shall show in a later part of the book. A future for Israel, at least the remnant of Israel, is also strongly supported by the Old Testament (Isa. 4:2, 33:13–16, 37:31–32, 41:17–20, 65:8–16; Joel 2:32; Obad. 17; Mic. 2:12).

Revelation 12 is a biblical chapter explaining why the world will hate and persecute Israel during the Tribulation. Ultimately, it is due to the conflict between the seed of the woman and the seed of the serpent as originally prophesied in Genesis 3:15. It is an important chapter for Bible students in our day to understand since it will help explain why the world, especially Arabs in the Middle East, have developed an irrational hatred for the modern state of Israel. "Let every student of this great chapter realize right here that the understanding of this chapter is the key to the understanding of many things," declares commentator Herman Hoyt. "It is the key to correct interpretation of the Book of Revelation, of the Bible, and of history. In this chapter will be found the story of the conflict of the ages. This conflict is not one of the mere abstractions, such as right and wrong or good and evil. This is a conflict of great personalities."[26]

In the previously mentioned article by Dennis Prager, he asked many Jews in Israel why they think so many in the world hate them. About half, mainly the religious Jews, said, "it is ultimately the fate of Jews to be alone . . . this is the burden of being the Chosen People."[27] The other half, who tended to be secular, said "they could not explain Israel's Isolation. One Israeli after another said that the almost universal condemnation of Israel was utterly irrational."[28] The Bible says it is irrational since it is inspired by the demonic, Satan himself as part of the unseen conflict between God and Satan. Through God's revelation of this conflict in Revelation 12, we are able to gain insight, even today, into this irrational hatred.

## "Christian" Replacement Theology

Ever since I have learned about the belief, often found in virtually every form of Christianity, known as replacement theology or supersessionism, I have not been able to justify it in my mind in light of Scripture. I am still puzzled that so many hold such a view, even though I have studied its development and history. The Bible nowhere teaches such a view! Not in the Old Testament. Not in the New Testament. National Israel is part of God's plan from Genesis to Revelation.

I attended the fourth bi-annual Christ at the Checkpoint Conference in Bethlehem, Israel, on March 7–10, 2016. I thought it would be helpful to better understand their view, as they would characterize it. There were about 400 people in attendance, with about 100 of them native Arab Christians. The rest were primarily from the United States and some from Great Britain. About 100 of those were college students.[29] I was surprised to see a classmate of mine from Dallas Seminary in attendance and in full support of the anti-Christian Zionist viewpoint. This year's theme was said to be "The Gospel in the Face of Religious Extremism." Can you guess who the extremists are from their point of view? Yes, I am considered an extremist.

## What They Believe

Their stated purpose for the conference is as follows: "The mission of 'Christ at the Checkpoint' is to challenge Evangelicals to take responsibility to help resolve the conflicts in Israel/Palestine by engaging with the teaching of Jesus on the Kingdom of God."[30] The leaders at Bethlehem Bible College hope to accomplish this via the conference.

The conference will bring Palestinian and international Evangelical leaders, to study and explore the rise of religious extremism within Christianity, Judaism, and Islam and how this impacts the Israel/Palestine conflict. We will also explore what the Bible has to say about religious extremism in any form. Together, we will seek a Biblical response to religious extremism, and find ways that provide an alternative through living out the kingdom of God.[31]

The leaders of the conference claim to be Evangelicals, yet their Manifesto includes the following liberal points:

1. The Kingdom of God has come. Evangelicals must reclaim the prophetic role in bringing peace, justice, and reconciliation in Palestine and Israel.
3. Racial ethnicity alone does not guarantee the benefits of the Abraham Covenant.
5. Any exclusive claim to land of the Bible in the name of God is not in line with the teaching of scripture.
9. For Palestinian Christians, the occupation is the core issue of the conflict.[32]

There are 12 points in the manifesto, but the ones listed above are the ones that jump out at me as errant. In short, their agenda is that of the far left on the matter of the modern state of Israel. They attempt to totally disassociate modern Israel from any biblical connection, past or future. Like liberals, they derive their theology mainly from Jesus, but not based upon what Jesus actually teaches; instead, upon their regurgitated claims they say Jesus taught.

## Speakers

There was a wide array of speakers, primarily leftwing in orientation. For example, Regina Henderson, an American from Duke University, claimed she was NOT an Evangelical, but a moderately conservative liberal. She called Jesus a radical and spoke of how pleased she was that students from Bethlehem Bible College were the first to support Black Lives Matter when things were happening in Ferguson, Missouri. She also said the Bible must be understood, not in its original context, but within our social setting of today.

Another socialist speaker was Lisa Sharon Harper from Washington, DC, who works for *Sojourners* magazine, the socialist organization headed by Jim Wallis. She said Israel was an apartheid state like South Africa used to be. Harper agrees with Obama that colonialism was the evil cause that ripped off the colonies of the world; thus, we now need to redistribute the world's wealth. She said true repentance means resisting the unjust structures. She in essence closed with an altar call as she led the group in singing "We Shall Overcome."

Hank Hanegraaff made an appearance, which is not surprising since he also participated in an anti-Israel conference in Iran a few years ago. He gave his normal replacement theology rant. The promises made to Abraham have already been fulfilled. God only has one chosen people, which were fulfilled in Christ. Hanegraaff accused Israel of ethnic cleansing. He said Abraham was a Zionist, as are modern Jews who reject Christ. He claimed modern Israel has no biblical basis for its existence since Jesus, not Jerusalem, is the fulfillment of the Old Testament. Hanegraaff then went on to provide a preterist/idealist explanation of the Bible's eschatology. He accused dispensationalists of being racists since we believe God has a future plan for national Israel. He closed with an allegorical vision of the millennium and the eternal state, sounding like a postmillennialist.

## Analysis

The first thing that struck me and held true throughout the entire conference was their whole viewpoint was based upon the idea that the current Church Age is really a spiritual form of the millennial kingdom. Many sounded postmillennial, as if they were going to advance the kingdom leading to a time of utopia, if they could only get rid of the so-called Israeli "occupation." Their whole rationale presupposes kingdom building rather than fulfilling the Church's actual calling of the Great Commission (Matt. 28:16–20; Mark 16:14–18; Luke 24:44–48; John 20:19–23; Acts 1:6–8). Because they have misidentified the dispensation in which we currently live, they are pursuing unrealistic dreams they will never be able to implement since the actual kingdom will not arrive until Jesus returns at the Second Coming and set it up not far from Bethlehem, in Jerusalem.[33]

The Christians at Bethlehem Bible College have totally misidentified their real problem and where their opposition really comes from. Their problem is really with their Arab Muslim brethren. Before the Oslo agreement was initiated in 1995, the Arab Christians in Bethlehem and throughout

Judea and Samaria had experienced a slight but steady growth since 1967. It was when local Muslim rule was implemented in 1995 that the Arab Christian community went into steep decline. Actually, the decline started under Jordanian rule from 1948 until 1967. The obvious reason for the separation wall that Israel has erected is due to Arab Islamic terrorism and has nothing to do with Arab Christians, who have not been a threat to Israeli safety. So the real problem is caused by the Arab Muslim domination of the once Arab Christian majority of Bethlehem's population.

Replacement theology in various forms was prominent throughout the conference. It was a dogmatic dictum that the modern state of Israel had no divine right to the land. In order to come to such an errant conclusion they practiced an extreme form of non-literal, allegorical interpretation of many parts of the Bible. This is to be expected since even a cursory reading of the Bible makes it clear God gave that land to Israel, in the past, present, and future. Since God is sovereign and nothing can happen in the world unless He allows it, I wonder how the modern reestablishment of Israel as a contemporary nation could have happened since they say it is certainly not His will for it to have occurred. They repeatedly said Jesus fulfilled the land promises to the Jews so the current state of Israel is a mistake in history caused by the evil colonialism from the West. They further argue that the Arabs are the indigenous people, thus, they are the ones who have a right to the land today. The late Joan Peters has demonstrated in her great work that the overwhelming majority of Arabs had been in Israel less than one generation when Israel became a nation in 1948.[34]

With all their emphasis upon so-called "peacemaking," they displayed no passion for the preaching of the gospel as having a role in the mission of the Church or at Bethlehem Bible College. Isn't that what Christ's last words to the Church were right before His ascension? Yes they were! Instead, they are bringing division within the Body of Christ with their social activism, which is not commanded in Scripture. In order for them to justify their focus they have adopted a liberal social action agenda, while at the same time they call themselves Evangelicals. The historic use of the term "evangelical" is a label for those who focus on preaching the gospel.

## Biblical Teaching

The purpose of this book is to inform Christians about why we should support the modern state of Israel, because it has biblical significance and fits into God's plan for history. Anyone who takes the Bible literally, as God intended, will see when God said "Israel" He meant "Israel" and not something else. In order for the anti-Christian Zionist position to be true, Israel has to mean something else. The notion that God has forever replaced Israel with the Church requires an allegorical interpretation that is totally subjective. It is as if these people really know what the hidden message of Scripture says and means, while those who take it literally just don't have the spiritual insight of the allegories. Even if one rejects the biblical teachings about Israel, as many do, it is important to also know international law totally supports the modern state of Israel and she has a right to all the land west of the Jordan River. However, if the Bible is totally rejected as a source of accurate history, then how would anyone know the Jews and their land of Israel are who they are today? How would someone like Hitler know who the Jews are in order to persecute the chosen people? God's Word is true and will be further demonstrated to be true in the future.

## Endnotes

1. Abraham Foxman, "The New Anti-Semitism," *U. S. News & World Report*, November 3, 2003, p. 44.
2. Danny Danon, quoted in "Israeli UN Envoy: Jew-Hatred At 'Highest Level of Our Lifetimes,' " Breitbart News, Sept. 9, 2016, p. 1, www.breitbart.com/jerusalem/2016/09/08/israeli-un-envoy-jew-hatred-at-all-time-high-anti-semitism-2-0-uses-internet-as-tool-for-hate/.
3. Walid Shoebat, *Why I Left Jihad: The Root of Terrorism and the Rise of Islam* (United States of America: Top Executive Media, 2005), p. 97
4. Tovah Lazaroff, "UNESCO Votes: No Connection between Temple Mount and Judaism" *Jerusalem Post*, October 13, 2016, http://www.jpost.com/printarticle.aspx?id=470050.
5. Eric R. Mandel, "Is the United Nations Anti-Semitic?" *Jerusalem Post*, July 7, 2014, http://www.jpost.com/printarticle.aspx?id=361842.
6. Dave Hunt, *Judgment Day! Islam, Israel and the Nations*, 2nd edition (Bend, OR: The Berean Call, 2006), p. 37–38.
7. Chuck Morse, *The Nazi Connection to Islamic Terrorism: Adolf Hitler and Haj Amin al-Husseini* (New York: iUniverse, 2003), p. 71.
8. Moshe Perlman, *Mufti of Jerusalem: Haj Amin el Husseini, a Father of Jihad* (Philadelphia, PA: Pavilion Press, 2006), p. 86.
9. Perlman, *Mufti of Jerusalem*, p. 10.
10. Morse, *The Nazi Connection to Islamic Terrorism*, p. 92.
11. Perlman, *Mufti of Jerusalem*, back cover statement.
12. Morse, *The Nazi Connection to Islamic Terrorism*, p. 93.
13. Ibid., p. 93–94.
14. Ibid., p. 95.

15. Ibid., p. 108.
16. Shoebat, *Why I Left Jihad*, p. 101.
17. Ibid., p. 100.
18. Ibid., p. 95–125.
19. Matvei Golovinski, *The Protocols of the Meeting of the Learned Elders of Zion* (Russia, 1903).
20. Daniel J. Wakin, "Anti-Semitic 'Elders of Zion' Gets New Life on Egypt TV," *New York Times*, October 26, 2002, http://www.nytimes.com/2002/10/26/world/anti-semitic-elders-of-zion-gets-new-life-on-egypt-tv.html.
21. Dennis Prager, "Is It 1938 Again for the Jews?" *Whistleblower*, vol. 12, no. 10, October 2003, p. 4–6.
22. Ibid., p. 5.
23. Peter Beinart, "An Illusion for Our Time: The False Promise of Globalization," *The New Republic*, Oct. 20, 1997, Internet edition http://www.tnr.com/archive/10/102097/beinart102097.html
24. Ibid.
25. Ibid.
26. Herman A. Hoyt, *Studies in Revelation* (Winona Lake, IN: BMH Books, 1977), p. 80.
27. Prager, "Is It 1938 Again?," p. 5.
28. Ibid., p. 6.
29. These numbers are all estimates.
30. Taken from christatthecheckpoint.com, home page, "About the Conference."
31. Ibid.
32. From christatthecheckpoint.com, "Manifesto."
33. See the article by Charles Clough, "Why the Millennial Kingdom Cannot Come with Leadership of Fallen Man," http://www.pre-trib.org/data/pdf/Clough-WhytheMillennialKing.pdf. Clough's biblical points render the idea of the kingdom in this age impossible.
34. Joan Peters, *From Time Immemorial: The Origins of the Arab-Jewish Conflict Over Palestine* (New York: J. KAP Publishing, 1984). See also another painstaking work that surveys who own what land and when within modern times in Israel. Arieh L. Avneri, *The Claim of Dispossession: Jewish Land-Settlement and the Arabs 1978–1948* (New Brunswick, NJ: Transaction Books, 1984).

CHAPTER I

# What Is Zionism?

Now the LORD said to Abram,
"Go forth from your country,
And from your relatives
And from your father's house,
To the land which I will show you;
And I will make you a great nation,
And I will bless you,
And make your name great;
And so you shall be a blessing;
And I will bless those who bless you,
And the one who curses you I will curse.
And in you all the families of the earth shall be blessed."
— Genesis 12:1–3

David captured the stronghold of Zion, that is the city of David.
— 2 Samuel 5:7

Afew years ago my wife and I hosted some foreign students in our home for Thanksgiving so they would be able to experience the holiday with an American family. Among our guests was a young student from Saudi Arabia. Upon seeing a Christian magazine on our coffee table with a cover story on Israel, he asked if we liked Israel. We said we liked Israel very much; in fact we went there on our honeymoon over 40 years ago. The Saudi student said that he liked Jews but hated Zionists because they plotted to take over the world. I told him that we were Christian Zionists. He was greatly surprised since we are not Jewish. He asked me, "What is a Christian Zionist?" I spent much of the afternoon explaining the gospel and Christian Zionism to him. Interestingly, one of the other student guests was an Arab Palestinian from Ramallah in Israel who mainly listened to our discussion.

In the last couple of decades, the secular and liberal religious communities have basically woken up to the fact that much of the American Evangelical community is very supportive of the modern state of Israel. Guess what? They do not like it one bit! They see an ever-increasing danger and even the possibility that Christian Zionism could bring about World War III. Israel somehow just does not fit into the elite's view of the current world order. They see the modern state of Israel as a threat.

## What Is Zionism?

"Zionism is understood to mean a modern Jewish movement aiming at resettlement in the land of Israel and the revival of an independent Jewish nation."[1] Obviously the word "Zionism" is derived from the biblical word "Zion" used 163 times in the Bible (156 times in the Old Testament and 7 times in the New Testament).[2] Zion is the term used by the Psalmist during the Babylonian exile when longingly remembering the homeland. "By the rivers of Babylon, there we sat down and wept, when we remembered Zion" (Ps. 137:1). Thus, it is not surprising that "Zion" or "Zionism" became the modern Jewish term expressing a desire for the Jewish people's return to Jerusalem and Erez Israel.

"The term Zionism was first used publicly by Nathan Birnbaum at a discussion meeting in Vienna on the evening of January 23, 1892. The history of political Zionism begins with the publication of Herzl's *Judenstaat* (*The Jewish State*) four years later and the first Zionist congress."[3] Birnbaum himself described what he meant by the term in a letter dated November 6, 1891, as the "establishment of an organization of the national-political

Zionist party in juxtaposition to the practically oriented party that existed until now."[4] Birnbaum use of the term "practically" meant philanthropic or non-political. It is recognized that there were previous efforts before Theodore Herzl's (1860–1904) founding of the Zionist movement in 1897 with the First World Zionist Congress in Basel, Switzerland. Even though early Zionism was largely secular and political, over the years it has grown to include religious, Jewish Zionists as well. Today, Zionism encompasses anyone, for any reason desiring to see the nation of Israel continue as a Jewish state and prosper.

## Christian Zionism

"Christian Zionism is a religious belief among some gentiles of the Christian faith that the return of the Jews to the Holy Land and the restoration of a physical Israel is in accordance with biblical prophecy. Furthermore, Christian Zionism is motivated by a biblically based religious conviction that the Jewish people are still God's chosen people and are entitled to possess the land of Israel for all time. This belief is based on a specific interpretation of Scripture."[5] Christian Zionists generally believe Israel's return to their Promised Land is fulfilling dozens of Bible prophecies from the Old Testament. They believe this is an indication that God is setting the stage for the events that will take place during the future seven-year period commonly called the Tribulation. For that time period to take place, Israel must be a nation again and in control of Jerusalem. Since 1967 this has been the case concerning the modern state of Israel.

English scholar Paul Wilkinson says, "Christian Zionism is an umbrella term under which many Christians who support Israel have congregated. . . . I believe that Christian Zionism, properly defined, incorporates the following key elements:

1. A clear, biblical distinction between Israel and the Church.
2. The any moment, pre-Tribulation Rapture of the Church.
3. The return of the Jews to the land.
4. The rebuilding of the Temple.
5. The rise of the Antichrist.
6. A seven-year period known as the Great Tribulation.
7. The national salvation of the Jews.
8. The return of Christ to Jerusalem.
9. The thousand-year reign of Christ on earth."[6]

Wilkinson's description is what American Christian Zionism has become.

In the past, Christian Zionism was known as "Restorationism" and began among English Protestants as early as the late 1500s. From England, Restorationism spread throughout Protestantism in Europe, but the English-speaking world is where it was the most intense. Wherever the spread of the English Bible went, there were those who were able to read Scripture for themselves and thus became aware of the passages that taught a last-day restoration of the Jews to their homeland in Israel. "Since the Reformation, an interest in the restoration of the Jews to their land has been a factor in Anglican and Protestant thought. Among the first English Christian advocates of this restoration were the 17th-century theologians Henry Finch and Thomas Brightman."[7]

Within the English-speaking world, the most pro-Israel element has been American Christianity, starting with Colonial America and up to our present time.[8] The reason appears to be the fact that America was primarily founded, not just by Christians, but by Protestant Christians who were clearly philo-Semitic — the Puritans. Thus, America did not have the centuries of anti-Semitism found throughout the Middle Ages in Catholic Europe as part of their cultural legacy. Yaakov Ariel notes, "Premillennialist messianic convictions were popular among the first generations of English settlers in what was to become the United States. . . . their messianic hopes included the conversion of the Jews to Christianity and the restoration of that people to Palestine."[9] Also, American Christian Zionism is largely built upon dispensationalism, which is the strongest, most consistent expression of Christian Zionism. "The dominant form of Christian Zionism in America is the dispensational variety,"[10] observes Richard Kyle.

### Christian Zionist Influence

Genesis 12:3 records God's promise to bless those who bless Abraham and his descendants (i.e., Israel). The Abrahamic covenant is directed to Abraham, Isaac, Jacob, and their descendants. It is repeated to them 20 times in Genesis (12:1–3, 7–9, 13:14–18, 15:1–18, 17:1–27, 22:15–19, 26:2–6, 24–25, 27:28–29, 38–40, 28:1–4, 10–22, 31:3, 11–13, 32:22–32, 35:9–15, 48:3–4, 10–20, 49:1–28, 50:23–25). Although there are multiple features to the Abrahamic Covenant, it always includes the land promise to Israel. Does this promise still stand, or has it expired? Since these biblical promises are intended by God to be taken literally and they still apply to Israel, and not the Church, it should not be surprising to anyone that such a view leads one to some level of Christian Zionism. If one does not a believe in a future for a redeemed Israel in the land of Israel, it is hard to understand how one could be thought to have a right understanding of God's Word since God's entire plan for history revolves around this passage. I believe it is that clear in the Bible.

An important aspect of Christian Zionism is not just the fact that there are biblical prophecies about Israel's future, but from the very beginning in Genesis 12:3, God has promised: "I will bless those who bless you, and the one who curses you I will curse. And in you all the families of the earth shall be blessed." This pattern is seen throughout the rest of Genesis and Scripture. When one examines Genesis 12:3 closely, it becomes clear that the passage is the foundation for Christian Zionism.

"I will bless" is an imperative stating what God will do since He is the subject. The statement "those who bless you," is in the plural. When contrasted with God's declaration, "the one who curses you I will curse" is in the singular. This indicates God's desire is to bless multiple people; however, the individual who curses Abraham and his descendants God will curse. In the orginal Hebrew the first word translated "curses" means to treat lightly, while the second word translated "curse" is a strong term for curse. Allen Ross explains:

> The two words for "curse" 'arar and qalal, are synonyms and thus overlap in their meanings. But 'arar, the stronger of the two, means to impose a barrier or a ban, a paralysis on movement or other capabilities, or to remove from the place and power of blessing. Qalal, "treat lightly," means to hold in contempt, speak lightly, or curse. Anyone who disrespects and treats Abram and his faith lightly will thus be removed from the place of the blessing. The wording records this threat as a necessary part of the outworking of the promises.[11]

In essence, God tells Abram that He will bless him and his descendants (Israel) in order to then bless the world, ultimately through Jesus the Messiah, who is a descendant of Abraham. While Jesus is the main fulfillment, there are many other sub-issues involved in this covenant. The world will also be cursed if they treat Abram and his descendants (Israel) lightly and attempt to ignore their God. The Abrahamic Covenant is at the core of Christian Zionist theology with the prophetic aspects bolstering this core belief. "Christian Zionists cite the Abrahamic Covenant as the basis of Israel's right to possess the land, claiming that God's promises to Abraham were 'quite specific and unambiguous,'" notes Wilkinson, "having been sealed by an unconditional and everlasting covenant (Gen. 12:1–7, 15:18–21, 17:6–8, 26:3, 28:13–15; Heb. 6:13–17)."[12] Wilkinson continues, "Christian Zionists insist that this unconditional covenant, unlike the 'conditional covenant' of Sinai, has not been abrogated or superseded by the New Covenant."[13] If the Abrahamic promises were superseded or replaced somehow by the New Testament, then what passages teach such a thing? Instead, Romans 9–11 says that even though Israel is in temporary unbelief, it will come to an end one day and God will fulfill all those blessings to Israel and then through Israel will bless the entire world. This will result in the ultimate fulfillment of the Abrahamic promises. The New Testament reveals the progress and fulfillment of Old Testament prophecy and introduces previously hidden aspects of God's single plan for history in a mystery known as the Church. The implementation of the next phase of His plan will deal with Israel's temporary unbelief, which will lead to their national conversion.

## Christian Zionism Under Attack

Back in the spring of 1992, *Christianity Today* did a cover story on Christian Zionism.[14] The article "For the Love of Zion" reflected a generally negative tone toward Christian Zionists, which has become normal for *Christianity Today*. The article argued that evangelical support for Israel is still strong but it has peaked and is declining.[15] Yet today, about 25 years later, the consensus appears to be that Christian Zionism is still very strong, but there is a growing group of Evangelicals who oppose it.

The last decade has seen the rise of a small but vocal and young opposition to Christian Zionism and the modern nation of Israel.[16] We have seen the supporters of an anti-Israel narrative cast Christian Zionists as people whose pro-Israel views will bring about a disaster often called Armageddon. Most of the titles of their books have the word Armageddon in it, as if that is the passion of Christian Zionists. *On the Road to Armageddon: How Evangelicals Became Israel's Best Friend*[17]; *Peace or Armageddon? The Unfolding Drama of the Middle East Peace Accord*[18]; *Anxious for Armageddon: A Call to Partnership for Middle Eastern and Western Christians*[19]; *Christian Zionism: Road-map* to Armageddon?[20]; Allies for Armageddon: The Rise of Christian Zionism[21]; Expecting Armageddon: Essential Readings in Failed Prophecy[22]; Fuse of Armageddon[23]; American Armageddon[24]; Armageddon Now: The Premillenarian Response to Russia and Israel Since 1917[25]; Armageddon Again? A Reply to Hal Lindsey[26]; Skipping towards Armageddon: The Politics and Propaganda of the Left Behind Novels and the LaHaye Empire[27]; Racing Toward Armageddon: The Three Great Religions and the Plot to End the World[28]; and End-Time Visions: The Road to Armageddon?[29] I am certain I did not find them all.

Over the last few years, there have been a number of books and articles that chide those of us who believe the nation and people of Israel have a positive future detailed in Bible prophecy.[30] They think evangelical support for Israel is a bad thing, because, the modern state of Israel is viewed by them as a bad thing, totally unrelated in any way to Bible prophecy. These naysayers often like to blame J.N. Darby and dispensationalism as the modern source of evangelical views. The truth of the matter is that love for Israel was well entrenched by Bible-believing Christians long before 1830.[31]

Earlier in this article I quoted Genesis 12:3, which is God's promise to bless those who bless Abraham and his descendants (i.e., Israel). Does this promise still stand, or has it been changed? If the Bible is to be taken literally and still applies to Israel and not the Church, it should not be surprising to anyone that such a view leads one to the Christian Zionist position.

## Christian Anti-Zionists

Probably for the first time ever since the birth of the Evangelical movement an organized effort appears to be on the rise among Christians (many of whom are Evangelical) who are becoming outspoken anti-Zionists. While there has always been opposition to the pro-Israel views of Evangelicals, they tended not to be aggressive in their disagreement. Knox Theological Seminary, founded and headed by D. James Kennedy (interestingly Dr. Kennedy did not sign the document), has posted a document on their website denouncing those who are supportive of the modern state of Israel as engaged in "a serious misreading of Holy Scripture."[32] Oh, really! Mike Stallard has noted concerning the "Open Letter" the following:

> Taking a cue from the subtitle of the document, the message of its theology is that the people of God should only be defined soteriologically, the geographical land of

biblical Israel is unimportant in the scheme of world history today, and the gospel of Christ is compromised when it is taught that any divine favor rests upon Israel (or any other nation) apart from Christ.[33]

Stephen Sizer is vicar of Christ Church in the London area and has written a couple of books attacking Christian Zionism. First is *Christian Zionism: Road-map to Armageddon?*[34] and then *Zion's Christian Soldiers? The Bible, Israel and the Church.*[35] Sizer's opposition to Christian Zionism went so far as to identify positively with a clear anti-Semitic website in early 2015. "After some deliberation, the Bishop of Guilford placed Rev. Sizer under a cone of silence under which he will 'refrain entirely from writing or speaking on any theme that relates, either directly or indirectly, to the current situation in the Middle East or to its historical backdrop.' He is also barred from attending any conferences related to the subject. He cannot even recruit others to speak on his behalf about issues related to Israel."[36] If he violates his discipline, he could be defrocked from the ministry in the Church of England.

Colin Chapman has written what amounts to an anti-Zionist book in *Whose Promised Land? The Continuing Crisis Over Israel and Palestine.*[37] He attempts throughout his work to downplay the biblical teaching about ethnic Israel's right to the land for the modern state of Israel. "Christian Zionists tend to think about the present Middle East situation primarily and largely in biblical or theological categories. If God has said in the Bible that the land belongs to the Jews forever and that they would return to the land, the only problem for Christian Zionists is to know how to help the Jews to establish and defend themselves in the land."[38] He is right! We Christian Zionists are deeply influenced by what the Bible teaches. How is that wrong, unless one thinks there is some authority higher than God's Word, especially since the Bible speaks directly about this subject?

Gary Burge is a New Testament professor at Wheaton College in Illinois. Burge is very active in his opposition to Christian Zionism and has also written a couple of books articulating his views — *Whose Land? Whose Promise? What Christians Are Not Being Told about Israel and the Palestinians*[39] and *Jesus and the Land: The New Testament Challenge to "Holy Land" Theology.*[40] Burge is active with a number of anti-Christian Zionism organizations, most notably the Christ at the Checkpoint Conference sponsored bi-annually by Bethlehem Bible College in Israel. Burge makes a declaration against Christian Zionism as follows:

> Therefore the New Testament locates in Christ all of the expectations once held for "Sinai and Zion, Bethel and Jerusalem." For a Christian to return to a Jewish territoriality is to deny fundamentally what has transpired in the incarnation. It is to deflect appropriate devotion to the new place where God has appeared in residence, namely, in his Son. This explains why the New Testament applies to the person of Christ religious language formerly devoted to the Holy Land or the Temple. He is the new spatiality, the new locale where God may be met.[41]

Burge is following the new trend in replacement theology that says Jesus fulfills all the land promises and reduces God's plan to spiritual salvation since the Church is the final phase in His plan. Apparently, the land promises to Israel have been dropped out, all in the name of Jesus.

Gary DeMar of American Vision Ministry has for many years exhibited his anti-Zionism via the many incarnations of *Last Days Madness*.[42] In an appendix entitled "'Anti-Semitism' and Eschatology," DeMar quotes from Assembly of God premillennialist Dwight Wilson's *Armageddon Now!* saying that premillennialism fostered anti-Semitism during the Holocaust. Both Wilson and DeMar have made a statement that is ridiculous and cannot be supported from the facts of history. DeMar says, "Wilson maintains that it was the premillennial view of a predicted Jewish persecution prior to the Second Coming that led to a 'hands off' policy when it came to speaking out against virulent 'anti-Semitism.'"[43]

Wilson and subsequently DeMar's interpretation of the premillennial record on this matter is simply wrong. Instead, historian David Rausch is correct when he declared:

> This theory of "Fundamentalist anti-Semitism" is not only biased — it is totally inaccurate. Fundamentalist Protestants are not historically anti-Semitic, nor are they anti-Semitic at the present time. In fact, Fundamentalism is itself a religious movement which grew out of a millennialism which was Zionist. Fundamentalists are ardent supporters of Israel and the Jewish heritage.[44]

Wilson,[45] and therefore DeMar,[46] made a number of mistakes in their characterization of premillennialists in regard to anti-Semitism. Wilson quotes a poem written by a premillennialist entitled "Hands Off" relating to anti-Semitism. The poem is saying that those who have persecuted the Jews would be better off keeping their hands off of God's people because God will judge them for their sin. Wilson characterizes the poem as if the author was advocating a hands-off policy of Christians toward helping the downtrodden Jew. The actual viewpoint of the poem was telling people like Hitler to keep their hands off the Jews, not for Christians to be apathetic toward persecution in Europe.

Contrary to the Wilson/DeMar viewpoint, Rausch argues that premillennialists were involved in fighting anti-Semitism and did not sit back and do nothing. Rausch cites example after example of American and European premillennialists warning against anti-Semitism in Europe (especially in Germany and Russia) during the many Prophetic Conferences convened between 1878 and 1918.[47] Rausch notes that American dispensationalist Arno Gaebelein, a German immigrant, "castigated Gentile Christendom in his lectures and writings for its attacks on the Jew."[48] In 1895, Gaebelein, upon returning to the United States from a trip to Germany, sadly stated, "It is only too true that Protestant Germany is Jew-hating, and we fear, from what we have seen and heard, that sooner or later there will come another disgraceful outbreak."[49]

The fact of the matter is that there were not too many premillennialists in Hitler's Germany since most of Christianity in Germany at that time was of a liberal variety, while many of those who were Evangelical were amillennial and not concerned with the Jews or Israel. Much of the Christian resistance to Hitler came from those who also hid Jews and they were often premillennial. Joop Westerville, a leader in the underground, was a Plymouth Brethren and has a prominent place in the Israeli memorial to the "Righteous of the Nations." Corrie Ten Boom's family in Holland were premillennial and are synonymous in the minds of American evangelicals with activism on behalf of the Jews in World War II. Rausch has noted, "Contrary to popular opinion, this prophetic viewpoint (premillennialism) combated anti-Semitism and sought to reinstate the biblical promises that God had made to the Jewish people through Abraham — biblical promises that postmillennial Christendom had determined were null and void."[50]

## Christian Palestinianism

Paul Wilkinson, a British Christian Zionist, a few years ago included a chapter in his book *For Zion's Sake*[51] about a movement that is the polar opposite of Christian Zionism he termed "Christian Palestinianism." He defines it as "a relatively new, largely intellectual, professedly Christian, anti-Zionist movement [that] has sprung up alongside [Christian Zionism], which I have classified as Christian Palestinianism."[52] "Naim Ateek essentially founded Christian Palestinianism in 1994 when he launched the Palestinian Ecumenical Liberation Theology Center known as Sabeel."[53]

Sabeel, at its Fifth International Conference in Jerusalem in 2004 entitled "Challenging Christian Zionism," advanced a leftist agenda against Christians who support the modern state of Israel. Some of those who claim to be evangelicals who attended and spoke at the conference include Stephen Sizer, Donald Wagner, Marc Ellis of Baylor University, and Gary Burge of Wheaton College. Demonstrating its alliance with Islam, the highlight of the conference for many was a meeting by the entire group with Yasser Arafat in his compound at Ramallah. The final statement issued at the conference included the following: "We warn that the theology of Christian Zionism is leading to the moral justification of empire, colonization, apartheid, and oppression."[54]

## What They Believe

Christian Palestinianism is basically a system of thought that opposes Christian Zionism. Philip Saa'd, a Palestinian Christian who lives in Haifa, Israel, says, "In recent years a phenomenon of palestinization has also occurred among the Christian Arabs who live in Israel." Saa'd describes these recent developments in the following way: "liberation theology," "amillennialism, Replacement theology and the Covenant of Grace theology." It also includes a "strong rejection of dispensationalism and of a literal interpretation of the Bible."[55] He notes that some Christian Palestinians "do not use the Old Testament as a source for their theology" and that "some writers still use the Old Testament but selectively," while he characterizes them as all using "a spiritual hermeneutic."[56]

Bat Ye'or, an Egyptian scholar, has an entire chapter in her recent book *Eurabia* about the Islamization of Christianity.[57] It is breathtaking to read her well-documented chapter in which she says, "Palestinian Marcionism

(Palestinianism) paves the way for the Islamization of the Church as it prepares mentalities for an Islamic replacement theology."[58] How do they attempt to reach this goal? Palestinianism "presses for the removal of the Gospels from their Judaic matrix and their grafting onto Arab Palestinianism, thus bringing them closer to Islam."[59] After citing some of the organizations advocating such things, she notes: "The process of Islamization of Christianity is rooted precisely in this separation from Judaism and the Arabization and Palestinization of the Jewish Jesus."[60] "Many Christian Palestinians, like Muslims, do not admit to any historical or theological link between the biblical Israel, the Jewish people, and the modern State of Israel."[61]

Melanie Phillips, a British Jew, has written a book entitled *Londonistan*,[62] warning England that Islam is taking over their country and culture, mainly because the Church has become pro-Islamic and against historic Christianity. She notes the rise of Christian Palestinianism as follows:

> So when Arab Christians reinterpreted Scripture in order to delegitimize the Jews' claim to the land of Israel, this kick-started replacement theology, which roared back into the imaginations, sermons, and thinking of the Anglican Church.
>
> This revisionism held that Palestinian Arabs were the original possessors of the land of Israel. The Anglican bishop of Jerusalem, Riah Abu el-Assal, claimed of Palestinian Christians: "We are the true Israel. . . ."[63]

This new breed of replacement theology or supersessionism not only replaces Israel with the Church, it goes a step further by moving the Church toward Islamic subjugation. Ye'or declares that the Palestinian Christian movement is guilty of "'de-biblicizing' the Bible," expelling "the Jews from their own Scriptures," and reinterpreting it "from the viewpoint of the Qur'an."[64]

Donald Wagner tries to argue that about half of the population in Israel at the time of Christ was not Jewish, so that he can bolster his pseudo-claim that Arab Christians are racially descended from the original Church in Acts 2 in Jerusalem.[65] There may have been a few Arab proselytes to Judaism at the birth of the Church, but the emphasis is clear that the earliest Church was primarily Jewish. In fact, Eusebius (about 263–339) tells us in his famous *Ecclesiastical History* "that up to the siege of the Jews by Hadrian

[A.D. 132–135] the successions of bishops were fifteen in number. He said that they were all Hebrews by origin. . . . For their whole church at that time consisted of Hebrews who had continued Christian from the Apostles down to the siege at the time when the Jews again rebelled from the Romans." Eusebius then lists their names starting with James, the half-brother of Jesus. He concludes his comments on this matter as follows: "Such were the bishops in the city of Jerusalem, from the Apostles down to the time mentioned, and they were all Jews."[66] Wagner's attempt to disestablish the role of Israel and to exalt Palestinians into their place is typical of the movement.

It is common for those involved with the Palestinian Christian movement to demonize their counterparts — Christian Zionists — as "racists,"[67] "a heretical interpretation of Scripture," a "deviant heresy,"[68] and a "heretical cult."[69] Palestinian Christians commonly believe that Christian Zionists are anxious for Armageddon,[70] when in reality we are anxiously waiting for Christ and His return for us at the rapture.

## Evangelicals

Such a movement would be somewhat easier to understand if it were composed of only liberals; however, many within the Palestinian Christian movement claim to be Evangelical in their theology. It is amazing to see someone like Gary DeMar of American Vision, who normally espouses a conservative theology and values, repeatedly give voice to those within the Christian Palestinian movement. DeMar has had Sizer on his radio program a number of times to discuss the evils of Christian Zionism, and recommends his books. He also promotes and sales the books of Colin Chapman.

Hank Hanegraaff of the Christian Research Institute has had on his daily national radio show, "The Bible Answer Man," most of the prominent spokesmen for the Palestinian Christian movement. Hanegraaff has had on his program Englishmen Sizer and Chapmen, as well as Burge and Brother Andrew. In his non-fiction book on eschatology *The Apocalypse Code*, when Hanegraaff deals with the issue of the current state of Israel, he primarily refers to Palestinian Christian advocates to make his case. It is because of his Palestinian Christian mindset that he labels Tim LaHaye and myself as racists because we believe the modern state of Israel has been brought into being by God.[71]

The Bible teaches Zionism (Psalm 132). It is becoming clear that when one rebels against God's Word on this point, it opens one to not only replacement theology, but to an increasing acceptance of Islamic viewpoints, which was founded upon an anti-Semitic foundation. As issues clarify, there is no place for neutrality where one can hide. Any Bible-believing Christian should repent of these views, if they have been influenced by them, and return to a true Bible faith.

In spite of our critics, who unjustly attempt to cast us in a bad light, dispensational premillennialism has always been the best friend the Jewish people have ever had within Christendom. For years many in Israel have recognized this. What is amazing is that in the last few years even the Orthodox community has come to realize that they have friends and supporters within the conservative Christian community. At the same time that we support Zion, dispensational premillennialists have been the leaders in evangelizing the Jewish community during the present Church Age. I believe that such support of Zion by Christians will continue to be the case from now throughout all eternity.

## Endnotes

1. *Encyclopaedia Judaica*, corrected edition, 17 vols. (Jerusalem: Keter Publishing House, n.d.), s.v. "Zionism," Vol. 16, p.1152.
2. Based upon a search of the New American Standard translation conducted by the computer program Accordance, version 11.2.1.
3. Walter Laqueur, *A History of Zionism: From the French Revolution to the Establishment of the State of Israel* (New York: Schochen Books, 2003), p. xxv.
4. Cited in *Encyclopaedia Judaica*, "Zionism," Vol. 16, p. 1032.
5. David W. Schmidt, *Partners Together in This Great Enterprise: The Role of Christian Zionism in the Foreign Policies of Britain and America in the Twentieth Century* (Meadville, PA: Xulon Press, 2011), p. xx.
6. Paul R. Wilkinson, *Understanding Christian Zionism: Israel's Place in the Purposes of God* (Bend, OR: The Berean Call, 2013), p. 12.
7. Shalom Goldman, *Zeal for Zion: Christians, Jews & the Idea of the Promised Land* (Chapel Hill, NC: The University of North Carolina Press, 2009), p. 7.
8. See chapter on the history of Christian Zionism.
9. Yaakov Ariel, *An Unusual Relationship: Evangelical Christians and Jews* (New York: New York University Press, 2013), p. 22.
10. Richard G. Kyle, *Apocalyptic Fever: End-Time prophecies in Modern America* (Eugene, OR: Cascade Books, 2012), p. 217.
11. Allen P. Ross, *Creation & Blessing: A Guide to the Study and Exposition of Genesis* (Grand Rapids, MI: Baker Book House, 1988), p. 264.
12. Wilkinson, *Understanding Christian Zionism*, p. 18.
13. Ibid.
14. "For the Love of Zion," *Christianity Today* (March 9, 1992), p. 46–50).

15. "Americans' Views Toward Israel Remain Firmly Positive," Gallup (Feb. 3–7, 2016), http://www.gallup.com/poll/189626/americans-views-toward-israel-remain-firmly-positive.aspx. The poll says 62% of Americans say their sympathies are toward Israel, while only 15% are with the Palestinians. This number has been fairly consistent for the last decade.

16. David Brog, "The End of Evangelical Support for Israel? The Jewish State's International Standing" *The Middle East Quarterly* (Spring 2014), http://www.meforum.org/3769/israel-evangelical-support. See also James Showers and Christopher J. Katulka, "The Eroding Evangelical Christian Support for Israel: The Cause and Cure," paper presented Dec. 7, 2015, at the Pre-Trib Study Group Conference, http://www.pre-trib.org/data/pdf/Showers-ErodingEvangelicalCh.pdf.

17. Timothy P. Weber, *On The Road to Armageddon: How Evangelical Became Israel's Best Friend* (Grand Rapids, MI: Baker Academic, 2004).

18. Dan O'Neill & Don Wagner, *Peace or Armageddon?: The Unfolding Drama of the Middle East Peace Accord* (Grand Rapids, MI: Zondervan, 1993).

19. Donald E. Wagner, *Anxious for Armageddon: A Call to Partnership for Middle Eastern and Western Christians* (Harrisonburg, VA: Herald Press, 1995).

20. Stephen Sizer, Christian Zionism: Road-map to Armageddon? (Downers Grove, IL: IVP Academic, 2006).

21. Victoria Clark, *Allies For Armageddon: The Rise of Christian Zionism* (New Haven, CT: Yale University Press, 2007).

22. Jon R. Stone, *Expecting Armageddon: Essential Readings in Failed Prophecy* (New York: Routledge, 2000).

23. Sigmund Brouwer with Hank Hanegraaff, *Fuse of Armageddon* (Carol Stream, IL: Tyndale House Publishers, 2000).

24. Craig Unger, *American Armageddon: How the Delusions of the Neoconservatives and the Christian Right Triggered the Descent of America — and Still Imperil Our Future* (New York: Free Press, 2008).

25. Dwight Wilson, *Armageddon Now! The Premillenarian Response to Russia and Israel Since 1917* (Grand Rapids, MI: Baker Book House, 1977).

26. Stafford North, *Armageddon Again? A Reply to Hal Lindsey* (Charleston, SC: Landmark Books, 1991).

27. Michael Standaert, *Skipping Towards Armageddon: The Politics and Propaganda of the Left Behind Novels and the LaHaye Empire* (Berkeley, CA: Soft Skull Press, 2006).

28. Michael Baigent, *Racing Toward Armageddon: The Three Great Religions and the Plot to End the World* (San Francisco, CA: HarperOne, 2009).

29. Richard Abanes, *End-Time Visions: The Road to Armageddon?* (New York: Four Walls Eight Windows, 1998).

30. Wagner, *Anxious for Armageddon*; Grace Halsell, *Forcing God's Hand: Why Millions Pray for a Quick Rapture — and Destruction of Planet Earth* (Washington, DC: Crossroads International Publishing, 1999); Stephen R. Sizer, "Dispensational Approaches to the Land," in *The Land of Promise: Biblical, Theological and Contemporary Perspectives*, ed. Philip Johnston & Peter Walker (Downers

Grove, IL: InterVarsity Press, 2000). Sizer, *Christian Zionists: On the Road to Armageddon* (Colorado Springs, CO: Presence Ministries International, 2004).

31. See chapter on the history of Christian Zionism.

32. "An Open Letter to Evangelicals and Other Interested Parties: The People of God, the Land of Israel, and the Impartiality of the Gospel," Knox Theological Seminary, 2002, http://www.ifamericansknew.org/cur_sit/wdoor.html.

33. Mike Stallard, "A Dispensational Response to the Knox Seminary Open Letter to Evangelicals," Irving, TX: The Pre-Trib Study Group, 2007.

34. Stephen Sizer, *Christian Zionism: Road-map to Armageddon?* (Downers Grove, IL: IVP Academic, 2006).

35. Stephen Sizer, *Zion's Christian Soldiers? The Bible, Israel and the Church* (Nottingham, England: Inter-Varsity Press, 2007).

36. No author cited, "Church of England Lowers the Boom on Stephen Sizer," CAMERA, Feb. 10, 2015, http://blog.camera.org/archives/2015/02/church_of_england_lowers_the_b.html.

37. Colin Chapman, *Whose Promised Land? The Continuing Crisis Over Israel and Palestine* (Grand Rapids, MI: Baker Books, 2002).

38. Ibid., p. 262.

39. Gary M. Burge, *Whose Land? Whose Promise? What Christians Are Not Being Told about Israel and the Palestinians* (Cleveland, OH: The Pilgrim Press, 2003).

40. Gary M. Burge, *Jesus and the Land: The New Testament Challenge to "Holy Land" Theology* (Grand Rapids, MI: Baker Academic, 2010).

41. Ibid., p. 129–30.

42. Gary DeMar, *Last Days Madness: Obsession of the Modern Church* (Power Springs, GA: American Vision, 1999), p. 407–23.

43. DeMar, *Last Days Madness*, p. 413.

44. David Rausch, *Zionism within Early American Fundamentalism, 1878–1918* (New York: The Edwin Mellen Press, 1979), p. 2.

45. Dwight Wilson, *Armageddon Now! The Premillenarian Response to Russia and Israel Since 1917* (Grand Rapids, MI: Baker, 1977), p. 96.

46. Noted by DeMar, *Last Days Madness*, p. 413.

47. Rausch, *Zionism*, p. 79–133.

48. Ibid., p. 243.

49. Ibid., p. 241.

50. David Rausch, *The Middle East Maze* (Chicago, IL: Moody Press, 1991), p. 64.

51. Paul Richard Wilkinson, *For Zion's Sake: Christian Zionism and the Role of John Nelson Darby* (Milton Keynes, England: Paternoster, 2007), xix.

52. Ibid., p. 48.

53. Ibid., p. 49.

54. Information about the conference taken from a non-published report by Paul Wilkinson who attended the conference.

55. Philip Saa'd, "How Shall We Interpret Scripture about the Land and Eschatology? Jewish and Arab Perspectives" in Wesley H. Brown and Peter F. Penner, editors, *Christian Perspectives on the Israeli-Palestinian Conflict* (Pasadena, CA: William Carey International University Press, 2008), p. 114.

56. Ibid. p. 115.

57. Bat Ye'or, *Eurabia: The Euro-Arab Axis* (Teaneck, NJ: Fairleigh Dickinson University Press, 2006), p. 211–24.
58. Ye'or, *Eurabia*, p. 213.
59. Ibid., p. 214.
60. Ibid., p. 214.
61. Ibid., p. 214.
62. Melanie Phillips, *Londonistan* (New York: Encounter Books, 2006), xxv, 237 pages.
63. Ibid., p. 152.
64. Ye'or, *Eurabia*, p. 215.
65. Donald E. Wagner, *Dying in The Land of Promise: Palestine and Palestinian Christianity from Pentecost to 2000* (London: Melisende, 2003), p. 41–50.
66. Eusebius, *Ecclesiastical History*, translated by Kirsopp Lake, *Loeb Classical Library* (Cambridge, MA: Harvard University Press, 1926), vol. I, p. 309–11.
67. Sizer, Christian *Zionism*, p. 205.
68. Ibid., p. 22, 259.
69. Donald E. Wagner, *Anxious for Armageddon: A Call to Partnership for Middle Eastern and Western Christians* (Scottdale, PA: Herald Press, 1995), p. 111.
70. Ibid.
71. Hank Hanegraaff, *The Apocalypse Code* (Nashville, TN: Thomas Nelson, 2007), p. xxii–xxiii.

## CHAPTER 2

# THE BIBLICAL CASE FOR ISRAEL

Then I will let you dwell in this place, in the land that I gave to your fathers forever and ever. — Jeremiah 7:7

"Turn now everyone from his evil way and from the evil of your deeds, and dwell on the land which the LORD has given to you and your forefathers forever and ever." — Jeremiah 25:5

I have on more than one occasion heard Bible teacher Chuck Missler say there is only one piece of real estate on planet Earth where God has specifically said it belongs to a specific people, and that is Israel. Yet that specified land is the most contested on the entire planet. This is true because God has spoken specifically on the matter. The fact that God's clear Word is contested by so many means Satan is behind such a consensus.

The dispersion of the Jewish people in A.D. 70, their preservation as an ethnically distinct people during the 1,900 years of their scattering, and their regathering to form the modern state of Israel is a miracle brought about by the hand of God. The arrival of the modern state of Israel on the world scene in 1948 was a big boon to the premillennial understanding of the Bible. This vindicates — in history — our biblical belief that God has a future plan for the land of Israel and the Jewish people. In spite of these developments, there is a group of evangelicals who think that the current state of Israel has nothing to do with God's biblical promises. How could anyone who claims to believe the Bible hold to such error? The current state of Israel is prophetically important because the Jewish people have been regathered in order to fulfill events during the coming seven-year Tribulation period, following the Rapture.

At least that's what those of us who hold to the biblical teaching of Zionism believe. It is not surprising to learn that critics of Zionism do not agree with us on this matter. Gary North has boasted that he has a book already in his computer for when "Israel gets pushed into the sea, or converted to Christ."[1] Lutheran Don Matzat has said,

> The present-day nation of Israel is no more involved in God's plans for the future than is France, England, Germany, the United States, etc. The teaching of the New Testament is very clear — Jesus fulfilled everything pertaining to Israel and formed the New Israel.[2]

Following the same train of thought as Matzat, perpetual critic Gary DeMar adds:

> Where is this "super sign" found in the Bible? Not in the New Testament. There is not a single verse in the entire New Testament that says anything about Israel becoming a nation again. Nothing prophetic in the New Testament

depends on Israel becoming a nation again. If Israel becoming a nation again is such "a significant sign," then why doesn't the New Testament specifically mention it?[3]

One of the most interesting books in my personal library is entitled *God and the Jew*,[4] by William Thomas Rouse. It is a whole book about why Israel would never become a nation again. It has chapters like: "God and the Rejection of the Jewish Nation," "Paul's Teaching Concerning God's Rejection of the Jews," and my favorite, "There Will Never Be a National Restoration of the Jews." When was this book written, you may ask? The copyright is 1946. Apparently Mr. Rouse died some time in 1946, since the title page refers to him as, "Late Professor of Bible. . . ." He did not live to see his book disproved by the events of history in 1948. The same will be true concerning many of the objections to Zionism that will be disproved by future events of history.

We do not have to wait on history to know what the Bible teaches concerning issues that it speaks to. Since Israel could be said to be one of the major subjects of the Bible then we can know what it says about the future of the nation of Israel. I want to, therefore, deal with major objections raised by non-Zionist Evangelical Christians to a future and permanent restoration of Israel to her land.

## Modern Israel IS a Work of God

First of all, Israel is not going to get pushed into the sea; God has other plans for her. That is not a scenario found in the Bible. Those who say that modern Israel has no more prophetic significance than France completely ignore a very significant fact. Israel is mentioned *thousands* of times throughout Scripture. And France? Not at all, of course. What's more, the Bible insists many times over that *Israel is not finished in history*. Paul said in Romans 11:1: "I say then, God has not rejected His people, has He? May it never be!" Paul continues in Romans 11 by saying: "From the standpoint of the gospel they [Israel] are enemies for your sake, but from the standpoint of God's choice they [Israel] are beloved for the sake of the fathers; for the gifts and the calling of God are irrevocable" (verses 28–29). The New Testament teaching is: God cannot, therefore will not, revoke His promises from the Old Testament to Israel.

Gary DeMar cannot find a New Testament promise of Israel's future restoration. Yet I have just cited a strong New Testament assertion — "May it never be!" — that God has not rejected Israel. Since we believe that all 66 books of the Bible are equally inspired and infallible, then Old Testament statements of Israel's national restoration will do just fine. What DeMar and any opponent of Zionism must come up with is any single passage that teaches that God is forever finished with His chosen people. In fact, Romans 11:1 says just the opposite.

## An Everlasting Promise

Zionists often point to the many times that the biblical text speaks of God's guarantee of the land of Israel to Abraham, Isaac, and Jacob and their descendants as an *everlasting* promise. For example, in Genesis 13:14–15 the Lord said to Abram: "Now lift up your eyes and look from the place where you are, northward and southward and eastward and westward; for all the land which you see, I will give it to you and to your descendants *forever*" (italics added.) Later in Genesis, when the Lord sealed His covenant promise to Abram by requiring circumcision, he said: "I will establish My covenant between Me and you and your descendants after you throughout their generations for an *everlasting* covenant, to be God to you and to your descendants after you. I will give to you and to your descendants after you, the land of your sojournings, all the land of Canaan, for an *everlasting* possession; and I will be their God" (Gen. 17:7–8, italics added). Similar *everlasting* promises are repeated many times throughout the Old Testament (Gen. 13:14–15, 17:7–8, 48:4; Exod. 32:13; Josh. 1:4, 9, 2:1; 2 Sam. 7:13, 16, 24–26, 29; 1 Kings 2:45, 8:15, 9:3, 5, 10:9; 2 Kings 21:7; 1 Chron. 16:17, 17:12, 14, 22–24, 27; 22:10, 23:25, 28:24; Isaiah 34:17, 55:3, 13, 59:21, 60:21, 61:8; Jer. 17:25, 25:5, 32:40, 50:5; Ezek. 16:60, 37:25, 26, 28, 43:7, 9; Joel 3:20; used dozens of times in the Psalms).

How can anyone who claims to be a Bible-believing individual not agree with the apparent meaning of God's everlasting promises to his people Israel? In fact, the same Hebrew word translated *everlasting* is used many times to describe God Himself. Anti-Zionist DeMar writes mockingly about the Zionist belief that God's promise to Abraham is an everlasting one.[5] DeMar never tells his readers what he believes *everlasting* means. Instead he lashes out at others by beating up a straw man of his own construction.

Some of the critics of Zionism argue that the word *everlasting* is used of many things in the Old Testament that have not and will not last forever. Examples they give include: many of the specific temple rituals the Levitical priests were to engage in were to be carried out forever, yet they have not been able to do them since the temple was destroyed in A.D. 70; ancient land boundaries were to remain in place forever; the Aaronic priesthood would last forever, yet it has been done away with according to Hebrews and replaced by Christ's Melchizedekian priesthood; the Mosaic covenant is said to be everlasting, but it has been replaced by the New covenant, etc. Therefore, in the same way *everlasting* is used of the things mentioned above and did not really mean everlasting, so also, the references to an everlasting land promise to Abraham, Isaac, Jacob, and their descendants does not mean forever.[6] So what does everlasting really mean in its original Hebrew?

The Hebrew (*'olam*) is the word often translated by the English word *everlasting* and occurs 439 times in the Hebrew Old Testament[7] and "20 times in the Aramaic parts of the Old Testament."[8] It is "probably derived from *'alam*, 'to hide,' thus pointing to what is hidden in the distant future or in the distant past."[9] Most scholars agree that "the basic meaning . . . is farthest time, distant time."[10] The precise nuance of the word "is a relative concept in the context of the given temporal horizon for *'olam* in reference both to the future and especially to the past."[11]

When I was a student at Dallas Theological Seminary I took a course entitled "Advanced Hebrew Word Studies" with Dr. Allen P. Ross, who is a renowned Hebrew scholar. Even though we were taught how to do Hebrew word studies in second-year Hebrew, this class trained us more deeply in the art and science of the craft. We examined many of the key Hebrew words found in the Old Testament. Toward the end of the course, Dr. Ross lectured on the meaning of *'olam*. He was passionate in his exhortation to us that even though it can mean "everlasting" in certain contexts, it was a word that is especially governed by the immediate context in order to discern the precise nuance of meaning. One scholar, while commenting on "eternal covenant" (Gen. 17:8, 48:4) and "eternal possession" of the land (Exod. 32:13) notes the importance of context:

> Here *'olam* signifies, then, "most remote time (in the future)"; the concept of an infinitely long time span results only from the combination of a governing noun, which already implies the notion of duration, with the governed noun, which, representing a preposition expression, extends this duration into infinity.[12]

Another scholar explains what Dr. Ross was telling us in class about *'olam*:

> The basic meaning of the nominative is farthest time, distant time. It does not seem to mean eternity in the philosophical sense of the word (i.e., neither unbounded time nor eternal timelessness), although there are a few verses where the meaning of the nominative is very much like the idea of eternity. In most cases, however, like other Hebrew terms for time, the meaning of *'olam* is closely linked to the occurrence of events. Thus, *'olam* is usually used to describe events extended into the distant past or future. Such distant time is clearly relative; it can be a time in one's own life (Ps. 77:5), a life span (Exod. 21:6), or the furthest conceivable time (15:18).[13]

Yet another scholar says of *'olam* in reference to Genesis 17:8, 48:4 and Leviticus 25:34: "With reference to the land itself, it speaks of 'perpetual holding.' "[14]

When we understand that there is no single English word that always translates accurately the Hebrew term *'olam*, and context is also important in selecting the best shade of meaning in various contexts, we are able to handle the supposed problem anti-Zionists sometimes say Zionists have in understanding the Land promises given by God to Israel. The supposed single use of *everlasting* for every use of *'olam* is invalid, and so is the sophistry that says Zionists cannot support their understanding of the Bible, which teaches that the land promises relating to Israel are still in force today. Robert Girdlestone explains how *'olam* relates to the land promises:

> Eternity is endless; and this idea is only qualified by the nature of the object to which it is applied, or by the direct word of God. When applied to things physical, it is used in accordance with the revealed truth that the heavens and earth shall pass away, and it is limited by this truth.[15]

When *'olam* is used of things relating to God, the word is used in its literal and absolute sense. Since God's promise of land to Israel is based upon His character and veracity, it follows that *'olam* is best translated, as most translations render it, with "everlasting" or "eternal." In no way could the land promise have been fulfilled in the past as anti-Zionists like DeMar contend. What do other passages say about the length of God's land promises to Israel?

### Length of God's Promises to Israel

In a number of places, the Old Testament spells out just how long God intends His promises to Israel to last. Almost as if God anticipates a debate on the meaning of *'olam*, and during Israel's greatest apostasy, the Lord says through Jeremiah:

> Thus says the LORD, who gives the sun for light by day and the fixed order of the moon and the stars for light by night, who stirs up the sea so that its waves roar; the LORD of hosts is His name: "If this fixed order departs from before Me," declares the LORD, "then the offspring of Israel also shall cease from being a nation before Me forever." Thus says the LORD, "If the heavens above can be measured, and the foundations of the earth searched out below, then I will also cast off all the offspring of Israel for all that they have done," declares the LORD (Jer. 31:35–37).

Based upon the above passage in Jeremiah we learn that *'olam*, in relation to God's promises to the nation of Israel, means until the present heavens and earth are destroyed. The last time I looked, the sun, moon, and stars were still in the sky, which means God's promises toward Israel are still in force and will be until the end of time. Just as the rainbow was installed as a sign God would keep an everlasting covenant, and rainbows still appear in our day, so also the fact that the sun, moon, and stars are still in the sky guarantees God's faithfulness to His promises to Israel. Thus, since the Lord has spelled out in a clear explanation as to how long He will keep His promise in these verses, it is reasonable to understand the biblical use of *'olam* in relation to God's promises to Israel, especially the land promise, means until the destruction of the heavens and the earth or until the end of the world. "When the additional phrases that are used in numerous contexts about the land being given in perpetuity to Israel and of the enduring nature of God's promises to Israel as a nation are all added up," contends Hebrew scholar Walter Kaiser, "the impression of all the contexts is overwhelmingly in favor of an oath delivered by God that is as enduring as the shining of the sun and moon (e.g., Jer. 33:17–22)."[16]

## Compound Intensifiers

In addition to the Lord spelling out just how long *everlasting* will be, the word *'olam* is sometimes used in conjunction with another word attached to it. In fact, the compound *'d-'olam* occurs 72 times in the Hebrew Old Testament.[17] When the participle *'d*, which means "until" or "as far as," is added to the front of *'olam* it intensifies or strengthens the basic meaning of *'olam*. Therefore, it is usually translated simply as "forever" or "everlasting." It is sometimes used to describe God's attribute of eternality: "Even from everlasting to everlasting, Thou art God" (Ps. 90:2).[18] Most uses of this compound word pair describe God's character or His dealings with mankind. "I will establish your seed forever, and build up your throne to all generations" (Ps. 89:4). It is often used when speaking of the Lord establishing David's kingdom, throne, house, and seed as eternal or everlasting in 2 Samuel (7:13, 16, 24–26).

The compound term *'d-'olam* is used concerning the Lord's gift of the land to Abram and his descendants. "The LORD said to Abram, after Lot had separated from him, 'Now lift up your eyes and look from the place where you are, northward and southward and eastward and westward; for all the land which you see, I will give it to you and to your descendants forever' " (Gen. 13:14–15). This intensified form is also used of the land in Exodus as Moses reminds God of His original promise. "Remember Abraham, Isaac, and Israel, Your servants to whom You swore by Yourself, and said to them, 'I will multiply your descendants as the stars of the heavens, and all this land of which I have spoken I will give to your descendants, and they shall inherit it forever'" (Exod. 32:13). In this passage, the Lord threatens to destroy the Jewish people because of disobedience. Moses reminded God, as if the God who knows everything needs to be reminded, of His original *eternal* promise to Abram. What was God's response to the point made by Moses? "So the LORD changed His mind about the harm which He said He would do to His people" (Exod. 32:14). Hey, if God Himself is persuaded by His own eternal promise about the land for Israel, should not anyone else who is seeking biblical truth on this matter? I think they should!

Now, to add even more support, there is another Hebrew phrase I believe seals the deal concerning the eternality of God's land promise to Israel. The

Hebrew phrase *min-'olam v'd-'olam* is usually translated "forever and ever" or "from everlasting to everlasting." Michael Rydelnik explains:

> As a general rule, the phrase is used of matters pertaining to God alone. For example, it is used to describe the eternal blessedness of God (e.g., 1 Chronicles 16:36: "Praise be to the LORD, the God of Israel, from everlasting to everlasting" NIV). The phrase declares the lovingkindness of God to be eternal (Psalm 103:17), and God's existence to be eternal (Psalm 90:2). Daniel uses the equivalent phrase in Aramaic to describe God's kingdom as existing "for all ages to come" (7:18). *"Min olam v'ad olam"* is the strongest expression in Hebrew to describe perpetuity and eternality. And, for the most part, it refers to God and His eternal nature.[19]

However, there are two exceptions to the use of this phrase as it otherwise always refers to God and they are found in Jeremiah in reference to God's eternal land promise to Israel. "Then I will let you dwell in this place, in the land that I gave to your fathers forever and ever" (7:7). "Turn now everyone from his evil way and from the evil of your deeds, and dwell on the land which the LORD has given to you and your forefathers forever and ever" (25:5). "Biblical Hebrew usage simply has no stronger way to indicate eternality. Thus, Jeremiah's words could not be any clearer. God has given the land of Israel to the people of Israel as a perpetual and eternal inheritance,"[20] notes Rydelnik.

There can be no doubt that the biblical text teaches that God has given the land to the Jews as a perpetual and eternal inheritance, at least until the end of the world. Later I will deal with those who attempt to say that the New Testament changes what the Old Testament clearly teaches is perpetual and unchangeable.

## Boundaries of the Land

Genesis 15:18 determined the boundaries of the land grant from God to Abram and his descendants. "On that day the LORD made a covenant with Abram, saying, 'To your descendants I have given this land, from the river of Egypt as far as the great river, the river Euphrates.' " The northern border is clear; it is a reference to the Euphrates River that runs through the heart of Babylon or modern-day Iraq. Students of the Bible, however, dispute over whether the southern border, "the river of Egypt," refers to the Nile River or the Wadi El-Arish, which is a little north of the Nile. Since there is no great difference between the two southern choices, I do not think it is worth debating. Charles Feinberg tells us, "The land grant of Genesis 15:18 calls for a stretch of land of 300,000 square miles or twelve and one-half times the size of Great Britain and Ireland."[21]

Have the Jews ever attained these boundaries? The short answer is no! This means that in order for Genesis 15:18 to be fulfilled it will have to take place future to our own day since it has never been realized in the past. Some, however, argue that the boundaries of Genesis 15:18 were fulfilled in the past for Israel. William Rouse contends:

> We know it is a historical fact that the boundaries of Israel were extended during the reigns of David and Solomon to their greatest extent. It is recorded concerning Solomon: "And Solomon reigned over all kingdoms, from the river (Euphrates) unto the land of the Philistines, and unto the border of Egypt." (1 Kings 4:21–24.) This corresponds exactly with the borders of the land as given by Moses and Joshua. (See 23:27–31.) Thus were fulfilled literally God's promises to the natural seed of Abraham.[22]

There is no doubt that Israel's borders reached their greatest extent under David and Solomon; however, did they reach the dimensions stated in Genesis 15:18? No, they did not! Notice that 1 Kings 4:21–24 says their reign did not include the land of the Philistines (an area a little larger than modern-day Gaza). This area should be included if there is to be a literal fulfillment of Genesis 15:18. Also, the 1 Kings 4 passage speaks of Solomon ruling over all kingdoms. For Genesis 15:18 to have been fulfilled, all of the various kingdoms that Solomon ruled over would have to be subsumed under the single kingdom of Israel. John Walvoord says:

> Even in Solomon's day at the height of his kingdom the land was not all possessed. At best it was placed under tribute as the very passage cited by amillennarians indicates (1 Kings 4:21). Certainly all must agree that possession was not permanent. Further at no time was all the land actually occupied by Israel.[23]

Regardless of whatever partial fulfillment of Genesis 15:18 occurred under the reign of Solomon, there was certainly no "literal" fulfillment as Rouse contends. This means that Genesis 15:18 has never been fulfilled and awaits a future fulfillment at Christ's return during His millennial kingdom.

## Is Israel Finished in History?

An increasing number of anti-Zionists, usually advocates of some kind of replacement theology, have been using a misinterpretation of Joshua 21:43–45, Nehemiah 9:7–8, and 1 Kings 4:21–24 as proof-texts, which they believe nullifies God's land promises to Israel. They present God as someone who is looking to discharge promises, in a legalistic way, by in essence saying, "I have fulfilled the letter of the law on that one, and now I can mark it off of my list of obligations." They claim that God has discharged all His promises to Israel regarding the land because of the statements in these passages as we have already touched upon.

In the process of making this claim, they either ignore or claim that God's eternal and perpetual promises to Israel about her land are no longer in force today. They want to do away with Israel, and they think they have found a biblical passage supporting their un-biblical notion. At least, that's what they think.

It is not surprising that DeMar is one who believes such things. He says concerning Israel's future: "The text says nothing about the restoration of Israel to her land as a fulfillment of some covenantal obligation. All the land promises that God made to Israel were fulfilled (Josh. 21:43–45)."[24] DeMar's perspective should not surprise us since he believes that virtually all prophecy has already been fulfilled. Based upon his reasoning, he believes the modern state of Israel has no legitimate biblical basis, since virtually all prophecy was fulfilled in the past. "When it is pointed out that there is a verse that emphatically states that the land promises made to Abraham have been fulfilled, dispensationalists will go to other verses in an attempt to disprove what Joshua 21:43–45 clearly teaches,"[25] declares DeMar.

> So the LORD gave Israel all the land which He had sworn to give to their fathers, and they possessed it and lived in it. And the LORD gave them rest on every side, according to all that He had sworn to their fathers, and no one of all their enemies stood before them; the LORD

> gave all their enemies into their hand. Not one of the good
> promises which the LORD had made to the house of Israel
> failed; all came to pass (Josh. 21:43–45).

For DeMar, apparently the canon of Scripture should have closed up with
Joshua 21, since he regularly quotes this verse and refuses to consider that
God had a few other things to say about the land of Israel after the Book of
Joshua. DeMar refuses to take into account the whole counsel of God on
the matter of Israel's land. He attempts to silence all further discussion by
autonomously insisting that we should not harmonize Joshua 21 with the
whole of God's Word by comparing Scripture with Scripture. Even most
who agree with DeMar on Joshua 21 would not put their foot down and
insist that the passage not be looked at in light of a broader biblical context.

Anti-Zionist Stephen Sizer also believes that the Joshua 21 passage
ends any future claims by the Jews to the land of Israel. Sizer says, "To the
claim that certain promises have yet to be fulfilled, Joshua is emphatic, *'Not
one of all the Lord's good promises to the house of Israel failed; every one was
fulfilled.'* "[26] Replacement theologian Keith Mathison agrees and declares,
"Joshua 21:43–45 explicitly declares that *all* the land that God promised
Israel was given to them."[27] "In putting the Israelites in possession of Canaan,
and in driving out their enemies, God did everything to them and for them
that He had promised," claims Rouse. "Joshua plainly says God had never
promised, up to that time, to restore the nation. The writer finds no such
promise after this time."[28] So have the land promises to Israel been totally
fulfilled as a result of Joshua 21 so that there is no hope at all for national
Israel? The answer is NO!

### What Does it Really Mean?

First of all, the passage does mean what it says, but what is it saying in
its context? A survey of commentaries reveals that virtually no one takes
such an understanding of this passage in the way outlined by the above
anti-Zionists.[29] That all of Israel's land promises have forever been fulfilled
in Joshua makes no sense in light of the whole counsel of God. Instead,
most commentators see the opposite problem, as noted by John Calvin,
who could hardly be considered a dispensationalist, when he says: "How
then can these two things be reconciled, that God, as he had promised, gave
possession of the land to the people, and yet they were excluded from some

portion by the power or obstinate resistance of the enemy?"[30] Calvin does not see this fulfilling God's land obligations to Israel; instead he sees the opposite problem. He offers the following solution:

> In order to remove this appearance of contradiction, it is necessary to distinguish between the certain, clear, and steadfast faithfulness of God in keeping his promises, and between the effeminacy and sluggishness of the people, in consequence of which the benefit of the divine goodness in a manner slipped through their hands. . . . The whole comes to this, that it was owing entirely to their own cowardice that they did not enjoy the divine goodness in all its fullness and integrity.[31]

Such a view is even supported by outspoken anti-Zionist Colin Chapman in a book recommended by DeMar, who says: "There are many indications in the text, however, that the conquest of the land was never complete (e.g. Joshua 13:1–32; Judges 1:1–36), and that many of the original inhabitants continued to live alongside the Israelites (e.g., Joshua 9:1–27)."[32]

The emphasis of this summary statement in the book of Joshua (21:43–45) must be seen against the backdrop of the Lord's overall charge and promise to give them the land in 1:2–11. Joshua is recording the historical fact that God was faithful, even when the tribes of Israel were only partially true to their word. In fact, we see here a major purpose found in all the historical books in the Old Testament[33] — to provide a record of performance of the parties of the Covenant made in Deuteronomy. The record tells us God is always faithful and gracious in dispensing His responsibilities in relation to the covenant. On the other hand, Israel is rarely faithful in performing her fiduciary responsibilities. The Joshua 21 passage, as with 1 Kings 4:21–24 and Nehemiah 9:7–8, is a performance report on God's faithfulness in discharging His fiduciary responsibilities in relation to the covenant. Keil and Delitzsch explain this aspect to us as follows:

> Notwithstanding the fact that many a tract of country still remained in the hands of the Canaanites, the promise that the land of Canaan should be given to the house of Israel for a possession had been fulfilled; for God had not promised the immediate and total destruction of the

Canaanites, but only their gradual extermination (Ex. xxiii. 29, 30; Deut. vii. 22). And even though the Israelites never came into undisputed possession of the whole of the promised land, to the full extent of the boundaries laid down in Num. xxxiv. 1–12, never conquering Tyre and Sidon for example, the promises of God were no more broken on that account than they were through the circumstance, that after the death of Joshua and the elder his contemporaries, Israel was sometimes hard pressed by the Canaanites; since the complete fulfillment of this promise was inseparably connected with the fidelity of Israel to the Lord.[34]

Joshua 21:43–45 must be understood within the overall context of the entire book, not simply trotted out as a proof text, which if not examined within the broader context of Joshua, appear to the ignorant as an argument of disinheritance of the land from Israel. Adrian Jeffers set the broader context of Joshua:

> The Book of Joshua clearly shows that Israel conquered the land in Canaan in two major campaigns (Joshua 10, 11). At the end of these campaigns a summary is given ("So Joshua took all that land, the hill-country . . ." 11:16-20) which indicates that his work was done, the Conquest was completed. That this also is somewhat ideal is seen in that chapter 13:1–6 says "there remaineth yet very much land to be possessed . . ." and describes the various areas remaining with a list of unconquered cities (cf. Judges 1:27ff.). A similar example is given near the end of the book (Joshua 21:43–35 — Israel possessed all the land, all their enemies were delivered, and all that Jehovah promised came to pass). Yet the Book of Judges makes it plain that this was not the case. Again the command to dispossess all the enemies in the land and to occupy their territory (Genesis 15:18; Exodus 23:23–31, Numbers 34:2, Deuteronomy 1:7, 8, etc.) has a similar implication. Ideally Israel was to dispossess all their enemies, but in actual fact many were left behind, and these became a snare to them. In fact it is

indicated that this was part of the will of God — in order to discipline them (Joshua 23:12, 13, Judges 3:1,2).[35]

Some anti-Zionists attempt to argue from Nehemiah 9 in a similar way that they have done with Joshua 21.

> You are the LORD God, who chose Abram and brought him out from Ur of the Chaldees, and gave him the name Abraham. You found his heart faithful before You, and made a covenant with him to give him the land of the Canaanite, of the Hittite and the Amorite, of the Perizzite, the Jebusite, and the Girgashite — to give it to his descendants. And You have fulfilled Your promise, for You are righteous" (Nehemiah 9:7–8).

George Murray declares: "Could any words be clearer than these? They are the words of one conversant with the history of his people. Whatever political movements we may witness now or in the future by way of a restoration of Hebrew economy in the land of Palestine, these will not come by way of fulfillment of God's promises to Abraham of possession of the land, for we have conclusive evidence that these promises have been fulfilled."[36] In this instance, Murray proves too much, since earlier he had argued that Joshua 21 and 1 Kings 4 were final fulfillments of the land promises to Israel. Now he presents his third final fulfillment in Nehemiah 9. The obvious leaps forth. If each of these are final fulfillments of the land promises to Israel, then why do the others appear later in history? I believe that Walvoord's explanation makes better sense of this passage:

> The priests in the Nehemiah reference do not claim complete fulfillment. They merely state that God had given the land to them — i.e., had done His part. The past occupancy of the land was a partial fulfillment but not a complete fulfillment of the promise. . . . It refers rather to the general faithfulness of God revealed in the following context (Neh. 9:9–38).[37]

Further, Gregory Harris summarizes the proper conclusion on the Joshua passage when studied in the context of Scripture:

Instead of all the land promises being fulfilled by Josh 21:41–43 and/or 1 Kings 4:20–21, the Bible clearly, repeatedly, and persistently presents just the opposite, and does so in a way that beautifully harmonizes with previous prophecies given by God, as in Lev 26:40–45 and Deut 30:1–10. In fact, *nothing* indicates that a fulfillment of these prophecies occurred by the time of Solomon's life or even up to our present time. Not only are these land boundary promises originally given in the Abrahamic covenant, reiterated in the Mosaic covenant as well as in opening of the book of Joshua, but also the Bible again presents the Euphrates River as the northern boundary for the nation of Israel long after 1 Kings 4. Yet even beyond this, as becomes more evident in the unfolding of God's revelation, twice the Euphrates River also specifically relates to the Messiah's reign, first in Ps 72:8, and then centuries afterward in the midst of "the times of the Gentiles" (Luke 21:24) came the second promise in Zech 9:10 that the Euphrates River will be the northern boundary of Israel for His worldwide rule.[38]

## God Is Faithful Even When Men Fail

"The theme here is the faithfulness of God in fulfilling his promises. God did his part," explains Trent Butler. "No matter what the political situation of Israel in a later generation, be it the division of the kingdom, the fall of the northern kingdom, or the destruction of Jerusalem and the Exile, Israel could not blame God. God had faithfully done for Israel what he promised. Blame belonged on Israel's shoulders, not God."[39] Walvoord echoes this understanding and says, "The Lord had not failed to keep His promise even though Israel had failed by faith to conquer all the land."[40] Donald Campbell speaks clearly to the issue in the following:

> Some theologians have insisted that the statement in Joshua 21:43 means that the land promise of the Abrahamic Covenant was fulfilled then. But this cannot be true because later the Bible gives additional predictions about Israel possessing the land after the time of Joshua (e.g., Amos 9:14–15). Joshua 21:43, therefore, refers to the

extent of the land as outlined in Numbers 34 and not to the ultimate extent as it will be in the messianic kingdom (Gen. 15:18–21). Also though Israel possessed the land at this time it was later dispossessed, whereas the Abrahamic Covenant promised Israel that she would possess the land forever (Gen. 17:8).[41]

When we read the passages that anti-Zionists bring up to say the land promises have already been fulfilled in history, we notice at least three things are missing from their arguments that were included in God's original promise to Abraham, Isaac, Jacob, and their descendants: First, Israel would possess the land; second, it would be a permanent possession; and third, the Jews would occupy the land.[42] None of these three things have occurred in any biblical passage in the past.

## Possession of the Land

The Bible makes a distinction between the fact that God has sovereignly given the land of Israel to the Jewish people as seen in the many repetitions of the Abrahamic covenant and the conditions required for them to possess that land. A major emphasis in Deuteronomy is a concern for Israel's possession of the land. The requirements for Israel's possession of the land are given in the Mosaic or Sinaitic covenant as noted in Deuteronomy 28–30.

Perhaps it would be helpful at this point to stop and contemplate the relationship of an unconditional covenant, such as the Abrahamic covenant, to a conditional covenant, such as the Mosaic covenant. Unconditional covenants provide humanity with God's *sovereign decrees* of where He is taking history, while conditional covenants provide us with the *means* He will use to get us there. God has said in the Abrahamic covenant He will do certain things for the descendants of Abraham, and the Mosaic covenant provides conditional stipulations that must be met before something will take place. God decreed Israel would receive certain blessings within the land of Israel, but they would only enjoy them if they were obedient. When the Israelites disobeyed, they would be cursed. Cursing would eventually lead to obedience and finally result in the ultimate blessing promised.

"The primary purpose of the Sinaitic covenant," explains George Harton, "was to instruct the newly redeemed nation how they were to live for YHWH."[43] Harton then concludes:

The covenant program revealed in the Pentateuch rests squarely on the twin pillars of the Abrahamic and Sinaitic covenants. This covenant program contains unconditional elements which reveal some things that God has bound himself to do for the nation Israel. It also contains some conditional elements which define the conditions upon which any individual Israelite may receive the benefits of the covenant. The Jews in Christ's day felt that the unconditional covenant guaranteed their participation in the promised kingdom. They had forgotten that an unconditional covenant may have conditional blessings. The Sinaitic covenant is essentially an amplification of these promises and covenant on which they rested.[44]

Blessings in the land, specifically in the case of possession of the land, are based upon the nation's obedience. They could not enjoy the prosperity, productivity, and peace in the land they were promised unless they obeyed the conditions spelled out in the blessing section of Deuteronomy (28:1–14). If they followed these stipulations faithfully, they could possess and prosper in the land. Yet, if they did not obey, then the Lord spells out the curses that will befall the nation (Deut. 28:15–68), including eventual expulsion from the land and scattering among the nations (Deut. 28:49–68).

There are similar warnings to the nation in Leviticus 26. If, over the years, the nation persists in disobedience to God's commands for dwelling and possessing the land, then "I will make the land desolate" (verse 32) and Israel "I will scatter among the nations" (verse 33). But this is not the end of the nation, as some anti-Zionists convey when they only quote the cursing passages, which, by the way, they take very literally. The Lord says, "'then I will remember My covenant with Jacob, and I will remember also My covenant with Isaac, and My covenant with Abraham as well, and I will remember the land'" (verse 42). In other words, the Lord will remember His sovereign decree that He made in the Abrahamic covenant and He will also equally employ a sovereign move to work in the lives of the Jewish remnant to enable them to obey the conditions necessary to possess the land.

True, Israel has been disobedient in history, just like all of humanity, but this does not mean that God has cast them away. It means that one day God will work in history to restore and complete His plan for His people. " 'Yet in spite of this, when they are in the land of their enemies, I will not reject them, nor will I so abhor them as to destroy them, breaking My covenant with them; for I am the LORD their God'" (verse 44). God is not finished in history with His elect nation and says, "'But I will remember for them the covenant with their ancestors, whom I brought out of the land of Egypt in the sight of the nations, that I might be their God. I am the LORD'" (verse 45).

Psalm 80 is a national lament psalm that speaks of Israel's conversion during the seven-year tribulation period. Asaph notes the fact when the time comes God will in essence enable Israel to believe in Him. "O God restore us and cause Your face to shine upon us, and we will be saved" (verse 3). Again, "O God of Hosts, restore us and cause Your face to shine upon us, and we will be saved" (verse 7). Finally, "Then we shall not turn back from You; revive us, and we will call upon Your name. O LORD God of hosts, restore us; cause Your face to shine upon us, and we will be saved" (verses 18 and 19). This is why we can be certain that Israel will be saved during the Tribulation because the Lord will enable them to believe. This same idea is seen in Zechariah "And I will pour out on the house of David and on the inhabitants of Jerusalem, *the Spirit of grace* and *supplication*, so that they will look upon Me whom they have pierced; and they will mourn for Him, as one mourns for an only son, and they will weep bitterly over Him, like the bitter weeping over a firstborn" (12:10, emphasis added). The Spirit of grace and supplication refers to God's provision of Divine enablement to Israel in order to believe. We see it leads to their salvation: "In that day a fountain will be opened for the house of David and for the inhabitants of Jerusalem, for sin and for impurity" (13:1).

Since the land of Canaan was given by the Lord to the Jews, it will surely come to pass one day in the future that they will possess the land. Walvoord provides the three essentials needed for Israel to possess her land:

> First, the land must be actually possessed, that is, occupied, not simply controlled. Second, the possession must continue as long as the earth lasts, i.e., forever. Third, the land during this period of possession must be under the rule of the Messiah in a time of peace, tranquility, and blessing. Nothing in history fulfills the many promises given to the prophets and, if it be judged that these promises must be fulfilled literally and surely, there remains only

one possible conclusion — that is, that Israel in some future time will possess their promised land, including the entire area described in Genesis 15.[45]

The nation in the land of Israel today does not meet these conditions and is why they are not yet fulfilling the final prophecies relating to the end-time possession of the land. However, one day they will! The modern nation of Israel has become a nation under God's sovereign oversight in preparation for fulfilling their prophetic destiny.

### Prophets Predict Israel's Return

There are many passages written after the time of Joshua and King Solomon that promise a future for Israel in relation to the land (Isa. 60:18, 21; Jer. 23:6–6, 24:5–6, 30:18, 31:31–34, 32:37–40, 33:6–9; Ezek. 28:25–26, 34:11–12, 36:24–26, 37:1–14, 21–25, 39:28; Hos. 3:4–5; Joel 2:18–29; Mic. 2:12, 4:6–7; Zeph. 3:19–20; Zech. 8:7–8, 10:6–12, 13:8–9, etc.). "If its promises regarding the land were fulfilled in Joshua's time or in Solomon's, why do the Scriptures which were written later still appeal to the hope of future possession of the land?" asks Walvoord. "Practically every one of the Major and Minor Prophets mention in some form the hope of future possession of the land. All of them were written after Solomon's day."[46] In addition, Deuteronomy 30:3–6 speaks of a still future restoration in belief. Walter Kaiser tells us:

> But despite this overwhelming array of texts to the contrary from almost every one of the prophets, many still insist on saying that this promise to restore Israel to her promised land was fulfilled when Zerubbabel, Ezra, and Nehemiah led their respective returns from Babylon back to the old land of Canaan. However, there is a serious deficiency to this line of reasoning. How then shall we explain the prophecy in Zechariah 10:8–12 that announces in 518 B.C. a still future return, which would not only emanate from Babylon, but from around the world?[47]

What does Zechariah 10 say?

> I will strengthen the house of Judah, and I will save the house of Joseph, and I will bring them back, because I

have had compassion on them; and they will be as though I had not rejected them, for I am the LORD their God and I will answer them. Ephraim will be like a mighty man, and their heart will be glad as if from wine; indeed, their children will see it and be glad, their heart will rejoice in the LORD. I will whistle for them to gather them together, for I have redeemed them; and they will be as numerous as they were before. When I scatter them among the peoples, they will remember Me in far countries, and they with their children will live and come back. I will bring them back from the land of Egypt and gather them from Assyria; and I will bring them into the land of Gilead and Lebanon, until no room can be found for them. And they will pass through the sea of distress and He will strike the waves in the sea, so that all the depths of the Nile will dry up; and the pride of Assyria will be brought down and the scepter of Egypt will depart. And I will strengthen them in the LORD, and in His name they will walk," declares the LORD (verses 6–12).

All these passages speak clearly of a future regathering that has not been fulfilled at any time in history, including our own day. Since Israel is back in the land it appears that God is setting the stage for these events to unfold in the near future. I believe these events will take place just before the Second Coming of Christ when the New Covenant will be implemented by God in the lives of the Jewish people. The classic statement of the New Covenant is found in Jeremiah 31.

"Behold, days are coming," declares the LORD, "when I will make a new covenant with the house of Israel and with the house of Judah, not like the covenant which I made with their fathers in the day I took them by the hand to bring them out of the land of Egypt, My covenant which they broke, although I was a husband to them, "declares the LORD. But this is the covenant which I will make with the house of Israel after those days," declares the LORD, "I will put My law within them, and on their heart I will write it; and I will be their God, and they shall be My people.

And they shall not teach again, each man his neighbor and each man his brother, saying, 'Know the LORD,' for they will all know Me, from the least of them to the greatest of them," declares the LORD, "for I will forgive their iniquity, and their sin I will remember no more" (verses 31–34).

The New Covenant (Deut. 29:4, 30:6; Isa. 59:20–21, 61:8–9; Jer. 31:31–40, 32:37–40, 50:4–5; Ezek. 11:19–20, 16:60–63, 34:25–26, 36:24–32; 37:21–28; Zech. 9:11, 12:10–14; Heb. 8:1-13, 10:15–18) provides for the yet future spiritual regeneration of Israel in preparation for the millennial kingdom. This is an unconditional covenant and is made between the Lord and the nation of Israel and has not yet been enacted for the nation of Israel. The New Covenant is predictive of Israel's new spiritual condition that begins at the end of the Tribulation and continues into and throughout the Millennial Kingdom. It is because of the prediction of the New Covenant we can know Israel will one day fulfill the conditions required to possess the land. Fruchtenbaum tells us the following about the New Covenant for Israel:

> The announcement of the New Covenant begins with a declaration that it will be a Jewish covenant, for it will be made with both houses of Israel (v. 31). It will be in sharp contradistinction with the older Mosaic Covenant (v. 32). Of the five Jewish covenants, the Mosaic was the only conditional one. Although God had been faithful in keeping His terms of the covenant, Israel had not been so faithful, resulting in the Mosaic Covenant's being broken. For while the Mosaic Covenant showed the standard of righteousness which the Law demanded, it could never impart to the Jew the power to keep it. But that problem will be rectified in the New Covenant (v. 33) through regeneration, which will provide the internal power necessary to meet and to keep the righteous standards of God. The result of the New Covenant will be a total national regeneration of Israel (v. 34). Jewish missions and Jewish evangelism will not be needed in the Messianic Kingdom because every Jew will know the Lord, from the least to the greatest. The sins of Israel will be

forgiven and forgotten. While there will be Gentile unbelievers in the Kingdom, there will not be Jewish unbelievers
in the Kingdom. To a man, all the Jews will believe. There
will be no need to tell a Jew to "know the Lord" because
they will all know Him.[48]

Within the prophetic framework of the Old Testament the Lord told the
Israelites even though they had agreed to keep covenant with the Lord they
would not be able to do it apart from Divine enablement. "Yet to this day
the Lord has not given you a heart to know, nor eyes to see, nor ears to
hear" (Deut. 29:4). (This is the condition of all humanity as well. Israel is no
different than the Gentiles in the area of their human nature after the Fall
into sin.) This shows even before they went into the Promised Land they
were lacking something as a human being, and it was the New Covenant
that would give them a new heart in order to enable them to obey the Lord
and then possess the Land in obedience.

The Bible is clear that Israel has a national future in which she will dwell
in blessing in her land. None of the supposed objections that critics have
raised will stand up to a proper examination of the whole counsel of God's
Word on the matter. This time will come after the entire nation of Israel
has been converted to Jesus as her Messiah. However, in the meantime, the
current regathering of Israel in unbelief is for the purpose of putting God's
covenant people through the fire of the Tribulation, which will result in
the salvation of the remnant. If one misses the clear message of this biblical
teaching it is only because they have a bias against this view, since Scripture
is clear. The bias explains why anti-Zionists evangelicals have abandoned the
normal, literal interpretative approach of Scripture and are guilty of reading
back into the text their *a priori* replacement theology. They have exchanged
proper exegesis of Holy Writ for a false theologizing. In the process of developing anti-Zionist doctrines, their rhetoric is increasingly sounding like
Muslim Arabs who call themselves Palestinians. I would like to ask them:
"What biblical texts speak specifically of this people?"

**Endnotes**
1. Personal letter from Gary North to Peter Lalonde, April 30, 1987, on file.
2. Don Matzat, "The Great Premillennial HOAX," *Issues, Etc. Journal*, Internet
   edition, www.issuesetc.com/resource/journals/v1.htm.

3. Gary DeMar, *End Times Fiction: A Biblical Consideration of the Left Behind Theology* (Nashville, TN: Thomas Nelson Publishers, 2001), p. 202–03.

4. William Thomas Rouse, *God and the Jew* (Dallas, TX: Helms Printing Co., 1946).

5. Gary DeMar, "The Abrahamic Covenant: Fulfilled or Postponed?" (Parts 1 and 2), located on the AmericanVision.org website. See at www.americanvision.org/articlearchive/08-22-05.asp.

6. In addition to those like Gary DeMar, some who have made similar arguments are: Roderick Campbell, *Israel and The New Covenant* (Philadelphia, PA: Presbyterian and Reformed Publishing Company, 1954), p. 199–205; George L. Murray, *Millennial Studies: A Search for Truth* (Swengel, PA: Bible Truth Depot, 1951), p. 26–30; William W. Baker, *Theft of a Nation* (Las Vegas, NV: Defender's Publications, 1982), p. 89–92.

7. Based upon the biblical computer search program of the NASB Accordance 11.2.1 for Macintosh computers from OakTree Software, Inc.

8. G. Johannes Botterweck, Helmer Ringgren, and Heinz-Josef Fabry, editors, *Theological Dictionary of The Old Testament, Vol. X* (Grand Rapids, MI: Eerdmans Publishing Co., 1999), p. 531.

9. R. Laird Harris, Gleason L. Archer Jr., Bruce K. Waltke, editors, 2 Vols., *Theological Wordbook of the Old Testament* (Chicago, IL: Moody Press, 1980), Vol. II, p. 672.

10. Willem A. VanGemeren, editor, *New International Dictionary of Old Testament Theology & Exegesis*, 5 Vols. (Grand Rapids, MI: Zondervan, 1997), Vol. 3, p. 346.

11. Ernst Jenni and Claus Westermann, *Theological Lexicon of the Old Testament*, 3 Vols. (Peabody, MA: Hendrickson Publications, 1997), vol. 2, p. 854.

12. Jenni and Westermann, *Theological Lexicon*, Vol. 2, p. 857.

13. VanGemeren, *Dictionary of Old Testament*, Vol. 3, p. 346.

14. Botterweck, Ringgren, and Fabry, *Theological Dictionary*, Vol. X, p. 539.

15. Robert Baker Girdlestone, Synonyms of the Old Testament (Grand Rapids, MI: Eerdmans Publishing Co., 1956), p. 317.

16. Walter C. Kaiser Jr., "An Assessment of 'Replacement Theology,' " *Mishkan*, no. 21; 1994, p. 17.

17. Based upon a search of the NASB from *Accordance* 11.2.1.

18. Other examples include 1 Chronicles 16:36, 29:10; Nehemiah 9:5; Psalm 89:53, 115:18, 106:48.

19. Michael Rydelnik, *Understanding the Arab-Israeli Conflict: What the Headlines Haven't Told You* (Chicago, IL: Moody Press, 2004), p. 141–42.

20. Rydelnik, Arab-Israeli Conflict, p. 142.

21. Charles L. Feinberg, *Israel at the Center of History & Revelation*, 3rd edition (Portland, OR: Multnomah Press, 1980), p. 168.

22. Rouse, *God and the Jew*, p. 89.

23. John F. Walvoord, *The Millennial Kingdom: A Basic Text in Premillennial Theology* (Grand Rapids, MI: Zondervan, 1959), p. 179.

24. Gary DeMar, *Last Days Madness: Obsession of the Modern Church* (Powder Springs, GA: American Vision, 1999), p. 332.

25. Gary DeMar, "Answering the 'Replacement Theology' Critics" (Part 2). Taken from the American Vision website at: www.americanvision.org/articlearchive/10-10-05.asp.

26. (Italics original) Stephen R. Sizer, "Whose Promised Land: Israel and Biblical ·Prophecy Debate between Neil Cornell (CMJ & ITAC) and Stephen Sizer," Guildford Diocesan Evangelical Fellowship St John's, Working. Surrey, March 18, 1997. Taken from the Internet at www.christchurch-virginiawater.co.uk/articles/debate.html, n. p.

27. Keith A. Mathison, *Dispensationalism: Rightly Dividing the People of God?* (Phillipsburg, PA: P & R Publishing, 1995), p. 27 (emphasis original).

28. Rouse, *God and the Jew*, p. 88–89.

29. See, for example, Reformed commentator M.H. Woudstra who would be expected to raise such an issue, but does not in *The Book of Joshua* (Grand Rapids, MI: Eerdmans, 1981), p. 314–15.

30. John Calvin, *Commentaries on The Book of Joshua* (Grand Rapids, MI: Baker, 1979), p. 248.

31. Ibid., p. 248.

32. Colin Chapman, *Whose Promised Land? The Continuing Crisis Over Israel and Palestine* (Grand Rapids, MI: Baker, 2002), p. 119.

33. The historical books of the Old Testament include the following: Joshua, Judges, Ruth, 1 and 2 Samuel, 1 and 2 Kings, 1 and 2 Chronicles, Ezra, Nehemiah, and Esther.

34. C.F. Keil and F. Delitzsch, *Commentary on the Old Testament, Joshua, Judges, Ruth, I & II Samuel*, 10 vols., (Grand Rapids, MI: William B. Eerdmans Publishing Company, 1975), Vol. II, p. 216.

35. Adrian Jeffers, "Ideal Versus Real History in the Book of Joshua," *Journal of the Evangelical Theological Society*, vol. 12, no. 3, Summer 1969, p. 183.

36. George L. Murray, *Millennial Studies: A Search for Truth*, 2nc edition, (Swengel, PA: Bible Truth Depot, 1951), p. 30.

37. Walvoord, *Millennial Kingdom*, p. 179.

38. Gregory Harris, "Did God Fulfill Every Good Promise? Toward a Biblical Understanding of Joshua 21:43–45 (Part 2)," *The Master's Seminary Journal* vol. 24, no. 1, Spring 2013, p. 95.

39. Trent C. Butler, *Word Biblical Commentary: Joshua*, Vol. 7 (Waco, TX: Word Books, 1983), p. 235.

40. John F. Walvoord, *The Prophecy Knowledge Handbook: All the Prophecies of Scripture Explained in One Volume* (Wheaton, IL: Victor Books, 1990), p. 44.

41. Donald K. Campbell, "Joshua," in John F. Walvoord and Roy B. Zuck, *The Bible Knowledge Commentary: Old Testament* (Wheaton, IL: Victor Books, 1985), p. 364–65.

42. Walvoord, *Millennial Kingdom*, p. 179.

43. George M. Harton, "Fulfillment of Deuteronomy 28–30 in History and in Eschatology," Th.D. Dissertation, Dallas Theological Seminary, August 1981, p. 16.

44. Harton, "Fulfillment," p. 17–18.

45. John J. Walvoord, *Israel in Prophecy* (Grand Rapids, MI: Zondervan, 1962), p. 76.

46. Walvoord, *Millennial Kingdom*, p. 178.

47. Walter C. Kaiser Jr. "The Land of Israel and the Future Return (Zechariah 10:6–12)," in H. Wayne House, editor, *Israel: The Land and the People: An Evangelical Affirmation of God's Promises* (Grand Rapids, MI: Kregel, 1998), p. 213.

48. Arnold Fruchtenbaum, *The Footsteps of the Messiah: A Study of the Sequence of Prophetic Events* (Tustin, CA: Ariel Ministries, 2003, [1982]), p. 410–11.

# CHAPTER 3

# MODERN ISRAEL'S RIGHT TO THE LAND

And I will make you exceedingly fruitful, and I will make nations of you, and kings shall come forth from you. I will establish My covenant between Me and you and your descendants after you throughout their generations for an everlasting covenant, to be God to you and to you descendants after you. I will give to you and to your descendants after you, the land of your sojournings, all the land of Canaan, for an everlasting possession; and I will be their God. — Genesis 17:6–8

If the grant of the Almighty Maker and Governor of the universe can constitute a legal title to an everlasting possession, the claim of the Jews to the land of Palestine will always be reasonable and just. — Charles Jerram, English Millennialist, 1796[1]

All throughout the Old Testament, God says that the land we know as Israel is for the descendants of Abraham, Isaac, and Jacob, or the Jews. Every Old Testament prophet except Jonah speaks of a permanent return to the land of Israel by the Jews.[2] Nowhere in the New Testament are these Old Testament promises ever changed or negated.[3] In fact, they are reinforced by some New Testament passages. Walter Kaiser notes that "the writer of Hebrews (6:13, 17–18) . . . swore by Himself when He made the promise: to show how immutable His purpose was."[4] Paul says of the promises to Israel: "for the gifts and the calling of God are irrevocable" (Rom. 11:29).

The only legitimate basis for the Jews to claim a right to the land of Israel comes from the Bible. In fact, if it were not for the biblical history of Israel, who would even know to associate the Jewish people with the land of Israel? It is precisely because God associates the Jewish people with the land that He gave them — located in today's Middle East — that we could even have a movement today known as Zionism. Detractors of Zionism must attempt to say that God's promise of the land of Israel to the Jews has somehow been invalidated. My, how many have tried down though the years to prove just that! But God's Word speaks louder than their shrill voices combined.

The case for Zionism rises or falls upon what the Bible teaches about Israel and the land of Israel. It is true that a just case for Israel can be presented upon many grounds, but ultimately it boils down to what God thinks about this matter as communicated through His inerrant and authoritative Word — the Bible.

## God's Promise of the Land

The Lord called Abram out of Ur of the Chaldeans and made an unconditional covenant, or contract, with him. This contract, known as the Abrahamic covenant, contained three major provisions: (1) a land to Abram and his descendants Israel, (2) a seed or physical descendants of Abraham, and (3) a worldwide blessing (Gen. 12:1–3).

In order to make His point clear, the Lord put Abram to sleep and made Himself the only signatory of the contract (Gen. 15:1–21). God told Abram, "To your descendants I have given this land" (verse 18). Even though the Lord was the only active signatory to the cutting of the covenant, as demonstrated in Genesis 15, nevertheless it is clear that Abraham obeyed the Lord during his lifetime: "Abraham obeyed Me and kept My charge, My commandments, My statutes and My laws" (Gen. 26:5). "It is significant that the promise is related to Abraham's obedience, not to Isaac's, as the promise now becomes immutable and certain of fulfillment,"[5] observes John F. Walvoord. This covenant is repeated to Abraham, Isaac, and Jacob, and their descendants a little over 20 times in the Book of Genesis.[6] God's promise to the patriarchs is said to be an everlasting covenant (Gen. 17:7, 13, 19).

The promise of the land covenant is passed from Abraham to Isaac, instead of Ishmael. The Lord told Isaac: "Sojourn in this land and I will be with you and bless you, for to you and to your descendants I will give all these lands, and I will establish the oath which I swore to your father Abraham. And I will multiply your descendants as the stars of heaven, and will give your descendants all these lands; and by your descendants all the nations of the earth shall be blessed" (Gen. 26:3–4). Here we see a duplication of God's promise to Isaac's father (cf. Gen. 12:3, 15:18).

Number three in the patriarchal descent is Jacob, rather than Esau. Jacob's name is later changed to Israel, which becomes the primary name of the new nation. In Jacob's famous dream of a stairway from heaven to earth, the Lord said, "'I am the LORD, the God of your father Abraham and the God of Isaac; the land on which you lie, I will give it to you and to your descendants. Your descendants will also be like the dust of the earth, and you shall spread out to the west and to the east and to the north and to the south; and in you and in your descendants shall all the families of the earth be blessed'" (Gen. 28:13–14). This statement also includes a repetition of the land promise made to Abraham and Isaac and would be passed on to Jacob's posterity, fulfilled in his 12 sons, the 12 tribes of Israel and their descendants. Walvoord notes:

> A careful study of these passages makes clear that the promise of the land was intrinsic to the whole covenant given to Abraham. Inasmuch as Abraham became a great man, had a great posterity, and brought blessing to the whole world through Christ, it is reasonable to assume that the rest of the Abrahamic covenant will be fulfilled just as literally as these provisions. The nonliteral or conditional interpretation of these promises is not supported in Scripture.[7]

Genesis closes with Jacob, his 12 sons, and their descendants sojourning in the land of Egypt. Exodus is the story of their deliverance from Egypt and preparation for entrance into the land of Canaan. Even though Israel wandered in the wilderness for 40 years because of unbelief, it was there that Moses received the Law that would become the new nation's constitution by which she would be governed in the land.

The Book of Deuteronomy says at least 25 times that the land is a gift to the people of Israel from the Lord (Deut. 1:20, 25, 2:29, 3:20, 4:40, 5:16, etc.). Old Testament scholar Walter Kaiser notes that, "sixty-nine times the writer of Deuteronomy repeated the pledge that Israel would one day 'possess' and 'inherit' the land promised to her."[8]

Deuteronomy 28–30 lays out the conditions for Israel to experience blessing within the land. We must remember that while the land was given unconditionally to the people of Israel, the Mosaic Law provides subconditions for the nation to enjoy God's blessings in the land. The Tribulation period will be a time of divine discipline on the nation, bringing about Israel's repentance obedience. And then, during those grand and golden days of the millennial kingdom, she will experience full occupation of her land, reaping the many blessings promised in the Old Testament.

The Psalms, Israel's handbook of praise to the Lord, often lead the worshiper in thanksgiving to the Lord for His covenant promises and faithfulness. For example, Psalm 105 says, "He has remembered His covenant forever, the word which He commanded to a thousand generations, the covenant which He made with Abraham, and His oath to Isaac. Then He confirmed it to Jacob for a statute, to Israel as an everlasting covenant, saying, 'To you I will give the land of Canaan as the portion of your inheritance' " (Ps. 105:8–11). Elsewhere in the Psalms the Lord declares: "For the LORD has chosen Zion; He has desired it for His habitation. 'This is My resting place forever; here I will dwell, for I have desired it' " (Ps. 132:13–14). God's choice of providing the land of Israel for the Jewish people has remained steadfast down through history.

Throughout the Old Testament the prophets convict Israel of her disobedience, but always with a view toward a future restoration, when ultimately Israel will dwell in peace and prosperity. Throughout the Old Testament the prophets provide promise after promise of this time of future restoration to the land (Isa. 11:1–9, 12:1–3, 27:12–13, 35:1–10, 43:1–8, 60:18–21, 66:20–22; Jer. 16:14–16, 30:10–18, 31:31–37, 32:37–40; Ezek. 11:17–21, 28:25–26, 34:11–16, 37:21–25, 39:25–29; Hos. 1:10–11, 3:4–5; Joel 3:17–21; Amos 9:11–15; Mic. 4:4–7; Zeph. 3: 14–20; Zech. 8:4–8, 10:11–15). A specific example of a restoration passage can be found at the end of Amos: " 'Also I will restore the captivity of My people Israel, and they will rebuild the ruined cities and live in them; they will also plant vineyards and drink their wine, and make gardens and eat their fruit. I will also plant them on their land, and they will not again be rooted out from their land which I have given them,' Says the LORD your God" (Amos 9:14–15).

It is important to note that Zechariah, following the return from the Babylonian captivity, speaks of a future restoration to the land, thus suggesting that Israel's past restorations did not ultimately fulfill the land promise given to Abraham, Isaac, and Jacob. Zechariah 9–14 lays out an end-time plan of restoration of the nation to Jerusalem and the land of Israel. Kaiser notes: "Repeatedly, the prophets of the Old Testament had depicted an Israelite remnant returning to the land (e.g., Isa. 10:20–30) and becoming prominent among the nations (Mic. 4:1) in the end day. In fact, Zechariah 10:8–12 is still repeating this same promise in 518 B.C., well after the days when many in Israel had returned from their last and final exile, the Babylonian Exile."[9] Further, Israel has a future in their land since nowhere in the Bible has the Lord revoked any of His promises to His people Israel: "for the gifts and the calling of God are irrevocable" (Rom. 11:29).

## Multiple End-Time Regatherings

To properly understand the end-time homecoming or regathering of the Jews to their promised land, we need to keep five major points in mind. Let's look briefly at each of these five points and see what the Bible says.

1. The Bible predicts that Israel will experience two worldwide, end-time regatherings to the promised land.

Dozens of biblical passages predict this global event. It is a common mistake, however, to lump all of these passages into one fulfillment time frame, especially in relation to the current state of Israel. Modern Israel is prophetically significant and is fulfilling Bible prophecy. But when we read God's Word, we need to be careful to distinguish which verses are being fulfilled in our day and which await future fulfillment.

In short, there will be two end-time regatherings: one before the Tribulation and one after the Tribulation. The first worldwide regathering will be a return in unbelief, in preparation for the judgment of the Tribulation. The second worldwide regathering will be a return in faith at the end of the Tribulation, in preparation for the blessing of the millennium, or thousand-year reign of Christ.[10]

One important passage that deals with Israel's two regatherings is Isaiah 11:11–12:

> Then it will happen on that day that the Lord will again recover *the second time* with His hand the remnant of His people, who will remain, from Assyria, Egypt, Pathros, Cush, Elam, Shinar, Hamath, and from the islands of the sea. And He will lift up a standard for the nations, and will assemble the banished ones of Israel, and will gather the dispersed of Judah from the four corners of the earth (italics added).

The return in Isaiah 11 clearly refers to the final worldwide regathering of Israel in faith, at the climax of the Tribulation, and in preparation for the millennial kingdom. Isaiah specifically says that this final regathering is the second one. That, of course, raises the obvious question: When did the first regathering occur?

Some maintain that the first return is the Babylonian return from the exile that began in about 536 B.C. But how could this return be described as *worldwide*, as set forth in Isaiah 11?[11]

Arnold Fruchtenbaum writes:

> The entire context is Isaiah 11:11–12:6. In this context, he is speaking of the final worldwide regathering in faith in preparation for blessing. Isaiah numbers the final worldwide regathering in faith in preparation of the Messianic Kingdom as the *second* one. In other words, the last one is only the second one. If the last one is the second one, how many can there be before that? Only one. The first one could not have been the return from Babylon since that was not an international regathering from the four corners of the world, only a migration from one country (Babylonia) to another (Judea). The Bible does not allow for several worldwide regatherings in unbelief; it allows for *one* worldwide regathering in unbelief; followed by the last one, the one in faith, which is the second one. This text only permits two worldwide regatherings from *the four corners of*

*the earth.* Therefore, the present Jewish State *is* very relevant to Bible prophecy.[12]

This chart provides a quick visual comparison and contrast between Israel's two great regatherings.[13]

| The Present (First) Regathering | The Permanent (Second) Regathering |
|---|---|
| Worldwide | Worldwide |
| Return to part of the land | Return to all the land |
| Return in unbelief | Return in faith |
| Restored to the land only | Restored to the land and the Lord |
| Man's work (secular) | God's work (spiritual) |
| Sets the stage for the Tribulation (discipline) | Sets the stage for the millennium (blessing) |

Here are some of the key Scripture verses related to each of these regatherings:

| Israel — Regathered Before the Tribulation in Unbelief (Current State of the Nation) | Israel — Regathered Before the Millennium in Belief (Future State) |
|---|---|
| Ezekiel 20:33–38, 22:17–22, 36:22–24<br>Isaiah 11:11–12<br>Zephaniah 2:1–2<br>Ezekiel 38–39 | Deuteronomy 4:29–31, 30:1–10<br>Isaiah 27:12–13, 43:5–7<br>Jeremiah 16:14–15, 31:7–10<br>Ezekiel 11:14–18<br>Amos 9:14–15<br>Zechariah 10:8–12<br>Matthew 24:31 |

### First Worldwide Gathering in Unbelief

2. The first worldwide regathering, in unbelief, will set the stage for the events of the Tribulation period.

When the modern state of Israel was born in 1948, it not only became an important stage-setting development, but also began an actual fulfillment of specific Bible prophecies about an international regathering of the

Jews in unbelief before the judgment of the Tribulation. The following Old Testament passages predict this development: Ezek. 20:33–38, 22:17–22, 36:22–24, 37:1–14; Isa. 11:11–12; Zeph. 2:1–2; and Ezek. 38–39 presupposes such a setting.

Zephaniah 1:14–18 is one of the most colorful descriptions of "The Day of the LORD," which we commonly call the Tribulation period. Zephaniah 2:1–2 says that there will be a worldwide regathering of Israel before the day of the LORD. "Gather yourselves together, yes, gather, O nation without shame, before the decree takes effect — the day passes like the chaff — before the burning anger of the LORD comes upon you, before the day of the LORD's anger comes upon you."

Ezekiel 20:33–38 sets forth a regathering that must take place before the Tribulation. The passage speaks of bringing the nation of Israel back "from the peoples and gather you from the lands where you are scattered, with a mighty hand and with an outstretched arm and with wrath poured out" (verse 34). "With wrath poured out" is a descriptive reference to the Tribulation. In order for this to occur in history, Israel must be back in the land before the Tribulation. This passage distinctly teaches that it is the Lord who is bringing them back, and the current nation of Israel is in the process of fulfilling this passage.

In a similar vein, two chapters later, Ezekiel receives yet another revelation about a future regathering of national Israel (Ezek. 22:17–22). This time, the Lord is "going to gather you into the midst of Jerusalem" (verse 19). Like a skilled metalworker, the Lord will use the fire of the Tribulation to purge out the unfaithful. The Lord is going to "gather you [Israel] and blow on you with the fire of My wrath, and you will be melted in the midst of it" (verse 21). Once again, "My wrath" depicts the time of the Tribulation. It also follows here that the nation must be regathered before that event can take place. The outcome of this event will be that the nation "will know that I, the LORD, have poured out My wrath on you" (verse 22).

Before these things can happen, Jews from all over the world must return to the land, just like we see happening with the modern state of Israel. This, of course, does not mean that *every* Jew in the world has to be back in the land. But it does clearly mean that many of the Jewish people must have returned to their ancient homeland. End-time prophecy in Scripture is built upon the assumption that Israel is both regathered to her land and is functioning as a nation.

The implications of Daniel 9:27 are unmistakable. "And he [Antichrist] will make a firm covenant with the many for one week [one week of years or seven years]." In other words, the seven-year Tribulation period will begin with the signing of a covenant between Antichrist and the leaders of Israel. Obviously, the signing of this treaty presupposes the presence of a Jewish leadership in a Jewish nation. This Jewish state must exist before a treaty can be signed.[14]

To summarize, then, the logic goes like this: The Tribulation cannot begin until the seven-year covenant is made. The covenant cannot be put in place until a Jewish state exists. Therefore, a Jewish state must exist before the Tribulation.

In view of all this, I believe that the main purpose for the regathering of Israel relates directly to the peace pact with Antichrist, as described in Daniel 9:24–27. For such a treaty to be viable, the Jews have to be present in the land and organized into a political state. And since 1948 *they have been.* It is this modern miracle — something unheard of in history — that we, our parents, and our grandparents have witnessed unfolding before our eyes. An ancient and scattered people have returned to their ancestral homeland after almost two millennia, making the peace covenant of Daniel 9:24–27 possible for the first time since A.D. 70.[15]

As a result, the stage is set for the very event that will trigger the Tribulation and usher in the final days of the world as we know it. Much to the disappointment of those who are opposed to Zionist theology, the modern state of Israel is in just such a position. This truly indicates that we are near the end of days.

## A Gathering in Stages

3. The Bible predicts that Israel's first regathering before the Tribulation will occur in phases or stages.

In A.D. 70, the land of Israel, the city of Jerusalem, and the Jewish temple were crushed under the heel of Roman domination. Since that time, the Jews have primarily been spread out all over the world, even though a remnant has always existed in the land.[16]

God's warning of worldwide exile in Deuteronomy 28:64–66 has been literally graphically fulfilled in the last 1,900 years:

> Moreover, the LORD will scatter you among all peoples, from one end of the earth to the other end of the earth; and there you shall serve other gods, wood and stone, which you or your fathers have not known. Among those nations you shall find no rest, and there shall be no resting place for the sole of your foot; but there the LORD will give you a trembling heart, failing of eyes, and despair of soul. So your life shall hang in doubt before you; and you shall be in dread night and day, and shall have no assurance of your life.

But as we have seen, the Bible predicts that Israel will return to the land in the end times. Scripture further indicates that this regathering will occur in stages.

In the famous "valley of dry bones" vision of Ezekiel 37:1–14, the bones symbolize the nation of Israel coming back together in the end times. In that passage, Ezekiel sees a graveyard vision illustrating the national return, restoration, and regeneration of "the whole house of Israel" (verse 11). Israel is first restored physically, and that restoration is pictured as bones, sinew, and skin coming together. The complete skeleton comes together bone by bone. Joint by joint. But it is still a lifeless corpse (verse 8). Ezekiel calls this a work of the Lord (verse 14). If, as we believe, this word picture portrays the modern state of Israel, then this regathering since 1948 has certainly been a work of God and is biblically significant.

Following this, Ezekiel witnesses Israel's spiritual regeneration, as the Spirit breathes spiritual life into the dead nation (verse 9). Of course, this spiritual regeneration will not occur until Messiah returns.

I believe that the process of physical regathering to the Land has begun. Preparations for the first worldwide regathering of Israel have been going on for about 130 years now. A pile of bones is beginning to come together and take shape. Let's consider what has happened so far.

The modern beginning of the return to the land goes back as early as 1871, when a few pioneering Jews began to trickle back. By 1881, about 25,000 Jews had settled there. At the first Zionist congress in 1897, led by founder Theodore Herzl, the goal of reclaiming the land for the Jewish people was officially adopted. The progress, however, was agonizingly slow. By 1914, only 80,000 Jews had moved into the land.

During World War I, the British sought support from the Jews for the war effort. On November 2, 1917, British Foreign Secretary Arthur

J. Balfour issued what has become known as the Balfour Declaration. The declaration was stated in a letter from Balfour to Lord Rothschild, a wealthy Jewish entrepreneur. In the letter, Secretary Balfour gave approval to the Jewish goal of reclamation: "His Majesty's Government views with favor the establishment in Palestine of a national home for the Jewish people. . . ."

In the face of persistent Arab pressure, however, and the desire of the British to maintain friendly relations with the Arabs, little was done in pursuit of the Balfour Declaration. Even so, it fanned into a flame Jewish hopes for the establishment of a homeland in the Holy Land — and encouraged more Jews to return. By 1939, when World War II broke out, about 450,000 Jews had managed to return to their homeland.

The Second World War and Nazi Germany's heinous, despicable treatment of the Jewish people created worldwide sympathy and a favorable environment for the Jewish people. Hitler's atrocities actually provided the greatest momentum for the establishment of a national homeland for the Jews. With United Nations approval, British control of the land ended on May 14, 1948 — and a nation was reborn. At that time, Israel was given 5,000 square miles of territory and had a population of 650,000 Jews and several hundred thousand Arabs.

Since that historic day, further waves of immigrants have poured into Israel from all over the world, most notably from Ethiopia and the Soviet Union. By 2002, 37 percent of the 12.2 million Jews in the world were back in the land of Israel. To put this in perspective, in 1948 only 6 percent of the Jews in the world were in Israel. It is estimated that by the year 2030, half of the Jews worldwide will be back in the land. And it is happening before our very eyes, even though many have their eyes closed tight.

## The Final Scattering

4. The Jewish people will be scattered for the final time during the persecution of the Antichrist.

During the Tribulation period, the Jewish people will be scattered over the face of the earth for the final time. With Antichrist in merciless pursuit, many will be killed, and many more will flee for their lives, becoming exiled and scattered across the globe (Dan. 7:25; Zech. 14:1–2; Matt. 24:15–21; Mark 13:14–20; Rev. 12).

## Second Worldwide Gathering in Belief

5. At the end of the Tribulation, Israel will be regathered in belief, in preparation for the reign of Jesus Christ on earth.

As the Tribulation grinds to its final, terrible moments, Jesus Christ will return from heaven to slay the Antichrist and his armies, assembled in Israel for the final showdown. Then the Jewish people will be regathered to the land of Israel from all over the world for the second and final time, to rule and reign with their Messiah for one thousand years.

Many passages in the Bible speak of this final regathering. What a moment in history it will be! God's people will acknowledge their Messiah at His coming, the Tribulation will be over, and the door to a glorious millennial kingdom will begin to swing open. Obviously, these references are not being fulfilled by the modern state of Israel today. Some of the citations include Deut. 4:29–31, 30:1–10; Isa. 27:12–13, 43:5–7; Jer. 16:14-15, 31:7-10; Ezek. 11:14–18; Amos 9:14–15; Zech. 10:8–12; Matt. 24:31 . . . and many more.

God will use the unparalleled horror of the seven-year Tribulation to bring many of the Jewish people to faith in the Lord Jesus as the Messiah of God, who died for their sins and rose again on the third day (Deut. 30:1–10; Jer. 31:27–34; Ezek. 36:22–32; Zech. 12:10–13:1)

I believe that this final return to the land will fulfill the prophetic aspects of the Feast of Trumpets (*Rosh Hashanah*) for the nation of Israel. This regathering requires a nation made up of those who are predominately believers in Jesus as their Messiah.

The reason the Jews must accept Jesus before He can return to earth is because of their rejection of Him at His first coming. According to Matthew 23:37, Christ will return to earth only when the nation of Israel, who spurned Him at His first coming, turns to Him in repentance and faith. In Matthew 23:37–39, He declared:

> "Jerusalem, Jerusalem, who kills the prophets and stones those who are sent to her! How often I wanted to gather your children together, the way a hen gathers her chicks under her wings, and you were unwilling. Behold, your house is being left to you desolate! For I say to you, from now on you shall not see Me until you say, 'Blessed is He who comes in the name of the LORD!' "

When Christ came to earth the first time, He offered the kingdom to the Jewish people, but they were "unwilling" to receive Him. Because of the nation's rejection of Jesus as their Messiah at His first coming, Christ now pronounces judgment upon them in verse 38 and says, "Behold, your house is being left to you desolate!" What does He mean by "house"? It is a reference to the Jewish temple. Jesus continues His prophecy in 23:39: "For I say to you, from now on you shall not see Me until you say, 'Blessed is He who comes in the name of the Lord!' "

We see three key points in our Lord's statement. First, when He says, "from now on you will not see Me," Jesus speaks of His *departure*. Second, with the word *until*, He speaks of delay and postponement. Third, He looks to a time of Israel's future *repentance*, when just as they rejected Christ in the past, they will one day change their minds and realize that indeed Jesus is the nation's promised Messiah and will say, "Blessed is He who comes in the name of the Lord" (verse 39). This is the condition for the Second Coming described in the next chapter, Matthew 24. Arnold Fruchtenbaum, further explains Matthew 23:39:

> But then He declares that they will not see Him again until they say, *Blessed is He that cometh in the name of the Lord*. This is a messianic greeting. It will mean their acceptance of the Messiahship of Jesus.
>
> So Jesus will not come back to the earth until the Jews and the Jewish leaders ask Him to come back. For just as the Jewish leaders lead the nation to the rejection of the Messiahship of Jesus, they must some day lead the nation to the acceptance of the Messiahship of Jesus.[17]

Matthew 24:31 records a future regathering of Israel, this time in belief: "And He will send forth His angels with a great trumpet and they will gather together His elect from the four winds, from one end of the sky to the other." This is said to take place after the tribulation, in conjunction with the Second Coming (verse 29).

The final regathering was mentioned by the Apostle Paul when he penned his section dealing with the nation of Israel (Rom. 9–11). Romans 10:13 declares concerning the Jewish people, "Whoever will call on the name of the LORD will be saved." Paul then poses the question in verse 14:

"How then will they call upon Him in whom they have not believed? How will they believe in Him whom they have not heard? And how will they hear without a preacher?" The point of Paul's reverse logic is that the Jews, within the context of the Tribulation, cannot call upon Jesus to come rescue them from great tribulation if they do not believe in Him. Thus, in this passage, calling upon the Lord is in relation to physical salvation or deliverance from the threat of extinction at the hands of the armies of the world at Armageddon. Believing relates to spiritual salvation or the forgiveness of their sins through faith in Jesus as their Messiah. Thus, the second regathering requires belief on behalf of the nation's part.

Finally, all the prophecies about Israel's total possession and blessing in the land — going all the way back to God's original covenant with Abraham — will be fulfilled. And then these words of hope from the prophet Amos will come to pass: "'I will also plant them on their land, and they will not again be rooted out from their land which I have given them,' says the LORD your God" (9:15).

This gathering will be final.

At last.

## Israel: God's Super Sign of the End Times

When we think about the unprecedented worldwide regathering and re-establishment of the nation of Israel, it prompts us to look more closely at *all* the international headlines. Now that Israel is poised in the very setting required for the revealing of Antichrist and the start of the Tribulation, we begin to realize that prophetically significant events are happening all over the world. Even the renowned liberal theologian Karl Barth is reported to have said when Israel recaptured Jerusalem in 1967, "The modern Christian must read with the Bible in one hand and the newspaper in the other."[18]

John F. Walvoord says:

> Of the many peculiar phenomena which characterize the present generation, few events can claim equal significance as far as biblical prophecy is concerned with that of the return of Israel to their land. It constitutes a preparation for the end of the age, the setting for the coming of the Lord for His church, and the fulfillment of Israel's prophetic destiny.[19]

God has not — *and will not* — cast away His people. Israel is indeed God's "super sign" of the end times. She is the powder keg fuse for the final world conflict. And for the first time in almost 2,000 years, the fuse is beginning to smolder. Zionism has been a tool used by God in history to get the snowball rolling downhill, and now it cannot be stopped.

Wonderful and terrible events lie just ahead.

## Endnotes

1. Charles Jerram, *An Essay Tending to Shew the Grounds Contained in Scripture for Expecting a Future Restoration of the Jews* (Cambridge, England: J. Burges Printer to the University, 1796), p. 9, spelling modernized.
2. Passages include: Gen. 12:7, 13:14–15, 15:18,31:2, 10, 23, 31–34, 33:4–16, 50:19; Ezek. 11:17, 20:33–37, 22:19–22, 28:25, 36:23–24, 38, 37:21–22, 39:28; Dan. 12:1; Hos, 3:4–5; Joel 3:20–21; Amos 9:9, 14–15; Mic, 2:12, 3:9–10, 4:7, 11–12; Zeph. 2:1–3; Zech. 7:7–8, 8:1–8, 10:6–12, 12:2–10, 13:8–9, 14:1, 5, 9; Mal. 3:6.
3. Passages include: Matt. 19:28, 23:37; Luke 21:24, 29–33, Acts 1:6–8, 3:18–21, 15:14–17; Rom. 11; Rev. 7:3–8, 11:1–2, 12:1–17, 14:1–5.
4. Walter C. Kaiser, Jr. "The Land of Israel and the Future Return (Zechariah 10:6–12)," in H. Wayne House, editor, *Israel: The Land and the People: An Evangelical Affirmation of God's Promises* (Grand Rapids, Kregel, 1998), p. 21.
5. John F. Walvoord, *Major Bible Prophecies: 37 Crucial Prophecies That Affect You Today* (Grand Rapids, MI: Zondervan, 1991), p. 77.
6. Note the following references in Genesis: 12:1–3, 7–9, 13:14–18, 15:1–18, 17:1–27, 22:15–19, 26:2–6, 24–25, 27:28–29, 38–40, 28:1–4, 10–22, 31:3, 11–13, 32:22–32, 35:9–15, 48:3–4, 10–20, 49:1–28, 50:23–25.
7. Walvoord, *Major Bible Prophecies*, p. 77–78.
8. Walter C. Kaiser Jr., *Toward an Old Testament Theology* (Grand Rapids, MI: Zondervan, 1978), p. 124-25.
9. Walter C. Kaiser Jr., "An Assessment of 'Replacement Theology,' " *Mishkan*, no. 21, 1994), p. 17.
10. Arnold Fruchtenbaum, *Footsteps of the Messiah: A Study of the Sequence of Prophetic Events* (Tustin, CA: Ariel Press, [1982] 2003), p. 99.
11. Fruchtenbaum, *Footsteps of the Messiah*, p. 102–03.
12. Ibid., p. 102–03.
13. Randall Price, *Jerusalem in Prophecy: God's Final Stage for the Final Drama* (Eugene, OR: Harvest House, 1998), p. 219.
14. Fruchtenbaum, *Footsteps of the Messiah*, p. 105.
15. John F. Walvoord, *Prophecy in the New Millennium: A Fresh Look at Future Events* (Grand Rapids, MI: Kregel, 2001), p. 61–62.
16. Benjamin Netanyahu, *A Place Among the Nations: Israel and the World* (New York: Bantam Books, 1993), p. 23–25.
17. Fruchtenbaum, *Footsteps of the Messiah*, p. 311.

18. Cited by R.C. Sproul, *The Last Days According to Jesus: When Did Jesus Say He Would Return?* (Grand Rapids, MI: Baker, 1998), p. 26.

19. John F. Walvoord, *Israel in Prophecy* (Grand Rapids, MI: Zondervan Publishing House, 1962), p. 26.

# CHAPTER 4

# MODERN ISRAEL'S
# LEGAL RIGHT TO
# THE LAND

It was not worth winning the Holy Land only to "hew it in pieces before the Lord. Palestine, if recaptured, must be one and indivisible to renew its greatness as a living entity."[1] — British Prime Minister, David Lloyd George

"The international legal basis for the establishment of the Jewish state in 1948 was the 1922 League of Nations Mandate for Palestine. That document gave the Jewish people the legal right to sovereignty over Judea, Samaria and Jerusalem, as well as all the land Israel took control over during the 1948–49 War of Independence."[2] — Caroline Glick

It is common to hear in the American media advocates who accuse the modern state of Israel of engaging in an occupation of land often stated to belong to Palestinian Arabs. Such rhetoric is factually wrong and has no basis of support in legal history. Often it is said Israel is violating various United Nations Resolutions like 242 and thus occupying Arab land illegally. I believe such is not the case since the Jews were awarded all of the land of what was called Palestine west of the Jordan River in the League of Nations mandate in 1922.

## The Balfour Declaration

About one hundred years ago, when the sun never set on the British Empire, Great Britain issued the Balfour Declaration, which was a statement of British foreign policy at the time when issued. David Lloyd George had ascended to Prime Minister on December 6, 1916, and appointed a former Prime Minister, Alfred Balfour, as foreign secretary. The idea for issuing the Balfour Declaration was clearly Lloyd George's idea, but Lord Balfour was in total agreement with him on the matter. The significant paragraph in the Declaration reads as follows:

> His Majesty's Government view with favour the establishment in Palestine of a national home for the Jewish people, and will use their best endeavors to facilitate the achievement of this object, it being clearly understood that nothing shall be done which may prejudice the civil and religious rights of existing non-Jewish communities in Palestine or the rights and political status enjoyed by Jews in any other country.[3]

The Balfour Declaration was issued on November 2, 1917, and addressed to Walter Rothchild, who was viewed as the titular head of the British Jewish community in his day.[4] Balfour's Declaration was adopted by Lloyd George's War Cabinet[5] after three presentations of evolving versions. George and Balfour sought and obtained American support before issuing the Declaration. "President Wilson, decisively influenced by Justice Brandeis via Colonel House, had telegraphed finally an unambiguous message of support for Zionism."[6] Had Lloyd George not had Wilson's full support, it is highly doubtful that the British would have put forward Balfour's Declaration. The Balfour Declaration was co-authored by Lord Balfour and Andrew Bonar

Law. The Balfour Declaration has rightly been viewed as a major break-through that launched the process resulting in the foundation of the modern state of Israel. However, in 1917 it was simply a statement concerning the official British foreign policy. It was destined to become more than just a statement of British foreign policy.

## The War Cabinet

It is important to take note of who composed the British war cabinet during the Great War in 1917 that approved the Balfour Declaration. The cabi-net was primarily made up of Zionists. "The one member who was firmly anti-Zionist was also the only Jewish cabinet member: Edwin Samuel Mon-tagu."[7] "Aside from Montagu, only one other member of the cabinet had been raised in England, and he was also the sole English-born Anglican in the war cabinet: Lord Curzon. . . . These two were the only English mem-bers of the war cabinet, and they were the two who were most opposed to Balfour's proposal."[8] Eventually, Montagu was called to India and was not at the meeting that voted on October 31, 1917. The rest of the war cabinet was non-English.

Prime minister Lloyd George was from Wales and adopted into a Bap-tist minister's home as a child. Lord Balfour was Scottish, along with three others: Arthur Henderson, George Barnes, and Andrew Bonar Law. Edward Carson was an Irish Protestant. Jan Christian Smuts was from Cape Town, South Africa, as was German-born Alfred Milner.[9]

I don't know if Lloyd George thought through the religious make-up of the war cabinet or it just worked out this way in the providence of God, but it would have been very difficult to have put together a more evangelical group of men at the highest level of British government in those days than the ones who made up that group. Donald Lewis describes them as follows:

> Seven of the nine Gentile members had been raised in evangelical homes or personally embraced evangelical-ism. More specifically, six of these seven had been raised in evangelical Calvinist homes: Balfour — Church of Scotland (Presbyterian); Lloyd George — Baptist; Lord Curzon — evangelical Anglican; Andrew Bonar Law — (Presbyterian) Free Church of Scotland; Jan Smuts — Dutch Calvinist; Edward Carson — Irish Presbyterian. Three of them were

sons of the manse (Curzon, Bonar Law, and effectively, Balfour). One was a Scottish Methodist — Arthur Henderson. Little is known of the religious backgrounds of Alfred Milner and George Barnes. But clearly the influence of Calvinist forms of evangelical Protestantism dominated the family backgrounds of the majority of the cabinet members.[10]

God certainly had His team in place when it came time to issue the Balfour Declaration. "Dominated by non-English members and by men with Calvinist evangelical upbringings," notes Lewis, "they did not reflect the British national makeup in either ethnicity or religion."[11]

## The Palestine Campaign

General Edmund Allenby conquered Jerusalem, and thus the region known as Palestine, on December 9, 1917, a little over a month after the issuance of the Balfour Declaration. The British were bogged down in the Middle East in their offensive against the Ottoman Turks. Lloyd George quietly moved his best general from the Western Front in Europe to take charge of the Palestine Campaign and Allenby did not disappoint. He also ordered an increase in the number of British troops to Palestine to make sure the British would capture Jerusalem before the French or the Germans. These moves were done quietly because the "capture of Jerusalem was seen as desirable and 'as a Christmas present for the British nation,' "[12] according to Lloyd George. In order to accomplish the capture of Palestine, Allenby "received extra aeroplanes, battalions and battleships, and also 10,000 cans of asphyxiating gas to knock out the Turks."[13]

Lloyd George had been a loyal Zionist for the last two decades before becoming prime minister in the middle of the war. It was clear that "he was brought up on the Bible. Repeatedly he remarked that the Biblical place names were better known to him than were those of the battles and the disputed frontiers that figured in the European war."[14] Lloyd George strongly wanted Britain to control what they called Palestine in those days, so they could help to reconstitute the nation of Israel. This was clearly his motive for opposing his entire general staff, who wanted all resources concentrated on the Western Front, while Lloyd George wanted to include a vigorous effort in the Middle East.[15] There is no doubt that his biblical convictions were the primary motive for pressing the Palestine Campaign so vigorously.

> Lloyd George was not, like Asquith or the other mem-
> bers of the Cabinet, educated at a public school on Greek
> and Latin classics; he was brought up on the Bible. . . . Unlike
> his colleagues, he was aware that there were age-old tenden-
> cies in British Evangelical and Nonconformist thought that
> favored the return of the Jews to Zion, and a line of Chris-
> tian Zionists which stretched back to the Puritans.[16]

There were soldiers from across the British Empire that fought in the Palestine Campaign. Countries where Christianity was the main religious orientation (England, Scotland, Wales, Ireland, Australia, and New Zealand) have
many accounts from the diaries of the soldiers expressing their excitement
about being in the Holy Land, which they had read so much about in their
Bibles. Many of the troops believed they were part of fulfilling Bible prophecy or on the verge of those events. General Allenby, who was a devout,
Bible-reading Anglican himself,[17] asked the men who were Christians not
to express their views so as not to cause conflicts in the ranks. Many of
the troops fighting with and for the British Empire were from Muslim and
Hindu cultures. "On 11 December 1917 General Sir Edmund Allenby and
his officers entered the Holy City of Jerusalem at the Jaffa Gate, on foot."[18]
"Directions were given to Allenby to dismount his horse before arriving
at the Jaffa Gate and humbly walk through on foot. . . . The War Cabinet wanted a simple, un-militaristic entrance, completely different from the
Kaiser's theatrical parade nineteen years earlier when, with much pomp, he
had ridden through the Jaffa Gate on a horse."[19]

## The San Remo Conference

A meeting to deal specifically with the unfinished business of Palestine,
which was to be an extension of the Paris Peace Conference, was commenced
on April 19, 1920, in San Remo, Italy. It was attended by the four principal
allied powers of World War I who were represented by the prime ministers of Britain (David Lloyd George), France (Alexandre Millerand), Italy
(Francesco Nitti), and Japan's Ambassador K. Matsui. (The United States
was not present, since it was not a member of the League of Nations.) The
San Remo Resolution adopted on April 25, 1920, incorporated the Balfour
Declaration into its final resolution. The San Remo resolution and Article
22 of the Covenant of the League of Nations, which was adopted at the Paris

Peace Conference on April 28, 1919, were the basic documents upon which the British Mandate for the stewardship of Palestine was constructed. It was at San Remo that the Balfour Declaration went from being just a statement of British foreign policy to international law under the jurisdiction of the League of Nations.

The British Mandate was fully implemented upon approval by the Council of the League of Nations on September 22, 1922. However, when the parties left San Remo in April 1919, the future state of Israel was to be made up of what now constitutes the Kingdom of Jordan, as well as all the land west of the Jordan River. After September 22, 1922, what is now the Kingdom of Jordan was taken away from Palestine and became another Arab nation known at the time as Trans-Jordan. This was the beginning of the trend still operative today that Israel needs to give up more land in order to achieve peace. The reality is that every time Israel gives up land, she experiences even less peace.

At San Remo, Israel was given the legal right, based on international law, to become a sovereign nation under the oversight of Great Britain and the mandate. The San Remo Resolution was later approved by the entire 52-member League of Nations in 1922, further entrenching it as settled international law. In addition, another instrument legally entrenched Palestine as a Jewish state at the 1924 Anglo-American Convention on Palestine. Howard Grief noted, "The U.S. thereby expressly recognized in a treaty the right of the Jewish People, in conjunction with the obligation of the British Government, to reconstitute their national home in all of Mandated Palestine and the Land of Israel."[20]

It is important that one understands international law is not made by United Nations resolutions voted on by the general assembly. International law can only be made by treaties or agreements between nations involved in a given matter. An armistice or agreement to stop a war does not qualify as international law. Thus, based upon international law, Israel is NOT occupying Arab land. Such a view is a myth constantly repeated in the media without rebuttal so that many think it is true.

## The British Mandate

On July 1, 1920, the British military administration, which had controlled Palestine since December 1917, was replaced by a British civil administration covering all of Palestine on both sides of the Jordan River, with its headquarters in Jerusalem. The Mandate instructed Great Britain to oversee Palestine with the goal of the establishment of a national home for the Jewish people in Palestine. At the time of the issuance of the Mandate, it was believed that there were not enough Jews in the land to establish a nation. Thus, Great Britain was to oversee the immigration of Jews to the land, and when there were enough, then Palestine would become the national homeland for the Jewish people. However, Britain ended up obstructing the goal of developing a Jewish homeland in Palestine.

A similar arrangement was made for Britain to oversee Mesopotamia (Iraq) and Trans-Jordan (Jordan); France was chosen as the mandatory authority for Syria.[21] Britain granted independence to Iraq in 1932 and to Trans-Jordan in 1946; France gave independence to Syria in 1936. But Israel never received a grant of independence from Britain, even though this was the specific goal of the British Mandate.

As the League of Nations was dissolved in 1946, the United Nations, which was founded in 1945, began to deal with the Palestine issue. The U.N. General Assembly passed a Partition Resolution (Resolution 181) on November 29, 1947. This U.N. resolution adopted the necessary legal status from the League of Nations needed for Israel to declare her independence on May 14, 1948. Under 181, the land of Palestine was partitioned and part of Palestine was given to the Arabs and the rest was given to Israel, except Jerusalem was to become an international city. Gauthier tells us, "The special international regime for the *corpus separatum* which was to be established on or prior to October 1, 1948, was to remain in force for a period of ten years. At the end of that period, 'the residents of the City shall be . . . free to express by means of a referendum their wishes as to possible modifications of the regime of the City.' "[22] The Arabs rejected resolution 181 and attacked the Jews, resulting in a larger land area for Israel when the fighting stopped in 1949. Israel's war for independence also prevented Jerusalem from becoming an international city as prescribed in resolution 181. The promised election by October 1959 to determine to whom Jerusalem belonged never took place. There is no doubt the city would have voted in favor of Israeli control if an election had taken place. Thus, all of the legal rights to the Old City of Jerusalem belong to Israel and the Jews under international law.

Under the legal status relating to Palestine from the League of Nations mandates in the early 1920s, the United Nations did not have jurisdictional authority to partition Palestine, since the San Remo Resolution and British

Mandate had given the land for the purpose of creating a Jewish national homeland. Grief explains:

> In dealing with the question of Palestine, the General Assembly was restricted by Article 80 of the Charter not to alter the terms of the existing Mandate instrument or the rights of the Jewish People set down in it. Despite the prohibition on the alteration of the Mandate, the General Assembly did exactly what it was not allowed to do, when it proposed a partition plan on November 29, 1947, to restrict Jewish national rights to only some regions of Palestine and called for an Arab state to be created alongside the Jewish State together with a plan to place the city of Jerusalem under trusteeship.[23]

### Britain Fails to Implement the Mandate

When people learn that Palestine was given to the Jewish people in the settlements after World War I they often ask: "Why then did the British not fulfill the Palestine Mandate, especially since they did complete their mandates to Arab nations?" The complicated and difficult 30-year period should have resulted in a peaceful recognition of what was legally established on April 24, 1920, at San Remo. But it did not.

First, the Treaty of Sevres (1920) was the legal document that governed the carving up of the remains of the Ottoman Empire. This Treaty recognized Palestine was for the Jewish people. Kemal Ataturk of Turkey overthrew the last Ottoman sultan, Muhammad VI, and created the modern state of Turkey. Later, the Treaty of Lausanne (1923) was negotiated and put in place as the formal treaty replacing the Treaty of Sevres. "Ataturk did not contest the provisions in the Treaty of Sevres relating to the disposition of Palestine" to the Jews.[24] Ataturk did object to the rest of the Treaty of Sevres because he thought it shortchanged Turkey, even though it "had already been signed by three representatives of the deposed Sultan's government."[25] The provisions relating to Palestine were not included in the later Treaty of Lausanne, which Ataturk did sign.

### Arab Opposition to Jewish Ownership

The second reason the British Mandate for Palestine was never fulfilled is because of the rise of Arab terrorism that paralleled the mandate era. Terrorism was developed and applied by Yasser Arafat's uncle, Haj Amin al Husseini (1893–1974), who became the Grand Mufti of Jerusalem. Opposition to the British Mandate for Palestine began in April 1920. Al Husseini is the father of Arab terrorism and a leading modern anti-Semite and anti-Israel protagonist. Even before the Muslim Brotherhood was formed (1928), al Husseini was doing all he could to make sure the modern state of Israel would be stillborn. While Islam has always had a terrorist streak, al Husseini is considered its modern architect, especially as it relates to early Zionism in the 1920s and 1930s.

Al Husseini was born in Jerusalem to a family originally from Yemen, whose grandfather had been appointed the mufti (expounder of Muslim law) of Jerusalem by the Turks, which was at that time largely a figurehead position with little authority.[26] After a childhood of average academic achievement, at 19 he was sent to Cairo to study Islamic philosophy. Without completing his studies, he collected enough money to make his pilgrimage to Mecca and Media in 1913. After his pilgrimage he returned to Jerusalem, foregoing further study in Cairo. Shortly after his return, World War I broke out and he served as a Turkish officer in Smyrna, Turkey. During the war he observed the massacre by the Turks of the Armenians. After the war he retuned to Jerusalem and became a tutor in a Moslem teacher's school. Starting in 1919, Haj Amin became active in Arab nationalism, and his writings and speaking struck a popular cord with many of the common Arabs as he made appeals in the name of the Koran. "He was passionate in his hatred of the British and the Jews."[27]

April 4, 1920, was a day that catapulted al Husseini into the public limelight of Jerusalem once and for all. This was the day that al Husseini incited Arab mobs into a four-day riot throughout Jerusalem against the Jews. The Arabs went through the Jewish quarter massacring, burning, and pillaging the defenseless Jews. The events in Jerusalem lead to similar activity in a number of towns throughout Palestine at that time. "A total of forty-seven Jews were killed and over 140 wounded in the first significant bloodshed in Palestine in hundreds of years."[28] Al Husseini, who had fled to Syria, was eventually convicted in absentia for "incitement to violence" by a British military court and sentenced to 10 years in prison. So it would be that the modern Arab terrorist movement was conceived and launched by al Husseini in the spring of 1920.

## Grand Mufti of Jerusalem

While al Husseini was in Syria, the first British High Commissioner for Palestine, Sir Herbert Samuel, was appointed to oversee the Mandate for Palestine. Since Samuel was a Jew, he appeared to bend over backward to appease the Arabs. Even though there were a number of Arab leaders who believed in cooperating with the Jews of Jerusalem, al Husseini was pardoned and brought back from Syria and on March 1921 named the Grand Mufti of Jerusalem. To add insult to injury, al Husseini was named president of the Supreme Muslim Council in May 1922, which meant that he became the virtual dictator of all things Arab and Muslim in Jerusalem. Later that year, al Husseini was "installed as virtual religious leader of the Muslim Arabs of Palestine."[29]

Things had been pretty quiet in Palestine until August of 1929, when al Husseini instigated a series of simultaneous attacks by Arabs against the Jews throughout Palestine. He used fabricated pictures showing the Dome of the Rock in Jerusalem supposedly vandalized by Jews who, it was said, were making plans to rebuild Israel's Temple. This pogrom against the Jews "resulted in the murders of one hundred and thirty-three Jews with over three hundred wounded."[30] This riot resulted in the murder of 67 Jews in Hebron and the Jewish abandonment of the ancient city until Jews returned in 1968.

"The election of Hitler as Chancellor of Germany, January 30, 1933, was an event that galvanized the entire Arab world and this would serve to further accelerate al Husseini's growing influence."[31] By April of 1936, in response to more propaganda from al Husseini, more Arab riots throughout Palestine broke out. In the Jewish quarter of Jerusalem, 16 Jews were murdered and 75 were seriously wounded. However, this time the Jewish communities had built up defense forces and were often able to fight back and defend themselves. Ongoing engagements by the Arabs against the Jews lead to near-warlike conditions throughout Palestine for the next three years. This time of "civil war" that al-Husseini led (1936–37) is called the "Arab revolt."

Finally, in 1937 the British decided to do something about the grand mufti of Jerusalem. Al Husseini not only killed Jews and the British, but would also kill fellow Arabs who opposed him. On October 1, 1937, the British began to round up al Husseini and his gang. Those who were captured were deported to the Seychelles Islands, east of Africa. However, the mufti hid in the Dome of the Rock, "confident that the British authorities would not dare to enter. A few days later, he slipped out of a side door and, dressed in the garb of an Arab peasant woman, was smuggled aboard a boat moored near Jaffa and escaped to Lebanon."[32] Some believe it was likely that the Nazis aided his escape to Lebanon.[33] On October 2, 1937, Nazi SS officers Adolf Eichmann and Herbert Hagen arrived in Haifa and had a meeting for 48 hours with al Husseini. Even while exiled in Beirut, al Husseini was able to direct many terrorist operations back in Palestine for another year and a half, ending in 1939. Al Husseini's "Arab revolt would result in the deaths of 2,652 Jews, 618 British, and 6,953 Arabs."[34] The mufti in effect had created a civil war in Palestine that greatly contributed to preventing the British Mandate for Palestine from being implemented.

Al Husseini never returned to Jerusalem after his 1937 departure and had very little influence. He lived within the Arab world until his death in 1974. The former grand mufti of Jerusalem left quite a legacy! As the father of Middle East Muslim terrorism, his place as leader of the radical, nationalist Palestinian Arabs was taken by his nephew Mohammed Abdel-Raouf Arafat As Qudwa al-Husseini, better known as Yasser Arafat. In August 2002, Arafat gave an interview in which he referred to "our hero al-Husseini"[35] as a symbol of Palestinian Arab resistance. Al-Husseini created an atmosphere within Palestine, from the perspective of the British, which disabled them from fulfilling the Mandate for Palestine. The British became weary of the conflict and developed the view that fulfilling their mandate of forming an autonomous Jewish state was impossible.

### Britain Undergoes a Change in Policy

After the Lloyd George government passed from the scene in October 1922, the new governments that followed were increasingly less supportive of the Jews. Additionally, Britain had made promises to the Arabs that sometimes conflicted with their mandate responsibilities, and too often they did not provide protection for the Jewish inhabitants in Palestine during the Arab revolt. In spite of these pressures, "it could not unilaterally modify the material terms and conditions of the Mandate for Palestine."[36] However, under the constant pressures coming from the Arabs, Britain began to change aspects of the how they went about implementing the mandate. Nevertheless, "the fulfillment of Great Britain's international obligations incurred under the Mandate for Palestine required the establishment of the

Jewish National Home in Palestine,"[37] which each new administration was eroding.

In the summer of 1937, the British formed a commission of investigation to see what Britain should do with the Palestine issue. The Peal Commission investigated the situation in Palestine over a six-month period and recommended a partition of Palestine. Within their recommendation, part of Palestine would go to the Arabs and the other part to the Jews, while Jerusalem would be an international city. The Peal Commission recommended cessation of the Mandate and partition of Palestine: "We feel justified in recommending that your Majesty's Government should take the appropriate steps for the termination of the present Mandate on the basis of Partition."[38] As has always been the case, the Arabs were totally against the recommendations of the Peal Commission, while the Jews responded with a resigned acceptance.[39]

Over time, Britain changed the San Remo Resolution and their Mandate over Palestine with the issuance of the White Paper in 1939, which recommended partitioning Palestine into Jewish and Arab sectors. However, the White Paper did not change the constraints of international law since it was merely a statement of British policy. Britain began putting quotas on how many Jews could immigrate to Palestine and spent most of their military resources stopping Jews from coming into Palestine; just the opposite of what their mandate stipulated. Thousands of Jews who were turned away from their homeland were sent back to Europe and died in Hitler's ovens. The British shift of policy had the effect of causing the international community and even most Jews in Israel itself to forget her legal rights as the great storm cloud of World War II and the Holocaust loomed on the horizon. Most of the Jews in Palestine during the Second World War were focused on surviving and providing a safe haven for their persecuted brethren, so they were willing to accept any offer that would further that goal.

### The United Nations Vote

On November 29, 1947, the United Nations meeting in San Francisco approved a partition resolution (Resolution 181) for Palestine, even though it had questionable authority to act on the Palestine question.[40] "Thirty-three Nations voted in favour of the Partition Resolution. Thirteen voted against and ten nations decided to abstain."[41] The resolution needed a two-thirds majority in order to pass, which it received by two votes. Great Britain famously abstained and promised to leave the country by May 14, 1948. Resolution 181 was not designed to create a Jewish state; its purpose was to partition or divide the land of Palestine into Arab and Jewish sections, with the Jerusalem area as an international zone. Chaim Weizmann, head of the Zionist Organization, later wrote in his autobiography his belief concerning Britain's neutrality:

> The British view [in 1947] seemed to be that Arabs and Jews should be left to themselves for an unavoidable period of blood-letting. The British clearly anticipated that the Arabs would make substantial inroads on the territory allotted to the Jews, and on the basis of the situation thus created a new solution would be reached, favorable, both politically and territorially, to the Arabs.[42]

The European nations that have a Christian heritage in their history and voted for 181, were thought to be "motivated by the need for a 'humanitarian solution' to the horrendous problems still facing the Jews of Europe who had survived the holocaust."[43] President Harry Truman led the United States to vote in favor of 181 and later the United States was the first nation to recognize Israel on May 14, 1948, because of Truman's belief in the Bible.[44] President Truman went against most of his advisors and certainly against the thought of the political elite in his own administration. Why did Truman go against almost all of his advisors and declare that the United States recognized Israel only 11 minutes after David Ben-Gurion made the announcement in Tel Aviv?

Melvin Leffler of the University of Virginia observed,

> Truman had a personal belief in the Bible. He believed that the land of Israel was the biblical home of the Jewish people. . . . He believed this was the land God promised to the Jews. His first reason was religious, based on his Evangelical beliefs. Secondly, he had significant Jewish friends and they were influential.[45]

"Eliahu Elath, speaking years later as the president of Hebrew University, told his audience that the Bible was Truman's 'main source of knowledge of the history of Palestine in ancient times.' "[46] In a speech that Senator Truman gave in 1943 he said concerning the Jews: "There must be a safe haven for these people."[47] Clearly, as a Bible reader he knew that place had to be Israel, so he did what he could to help bring it about. "It is fair to conclude as, David Niles did, that if FDR had lived and Truman not been president, there probably would not have been an Israel."[48]

In reality, Israel became a nation primarily because the provisional government headed by Ben-Gurion declared itself to be so and then backed up that claim by militarily defeating the Arabs in Palestine and the five other Arab nations that attacked her. However, the events leading up to 1948 positioned the Jewish people to be able to become an autonomous nation regardless of what many who opposed Israel thought. Since no nation rises without God's permission (cf. Acts 17:26), we have to assume that it was God's timing and design of the circumstances that led to the birth of the modern state of Israel.

## Conclusion

We have seen that a series of events took place in conjunction with the First World War that provided the international legal basis for the re-establishment of the modern state of Israel. "The establishment of a Jewish homeland meant eventual statehood and hence the transfer to the Jewish people of sovereignty to all parts of the homeland including Judea, Samaria, and Gaza,"[49] concluded Jewish legal expert Howard Grief. Canadian international lawyer Jacques Gauthier, who wrote a 1,143-page PhD Thesis at the University of Geneva in Switzerland on this topic concluded: "After our examination of the principles of international law pertaining to belligerent occupation, we have concluded that Israel has the right to occupy the territories under its control since 1967, including East Jerusalem and its Old City, until a peace treaty is concluded."[50]

In Israel during July 2012, a panel of judges headed by former Israeli Supreme Court Justice Edmond Levy issued a report. The Levy Report "did not present anything new in saying Judea and Samaria are not occupied territory according to international law."[51] The report recognized that Israel's right to its land was founded on the San Remo Resolution. Current Israeli Prime Minister Benjamin Netanyahu commissioned the panel "to investigate the international legal status of these towns and villages and to provide the government with guidance relating to future construction of Israeli communities beyond the armistice lines."[52]

God has clearly given His permission for the re-establishment of the modern state of Israel since He is the One who has ultimately brought it about through His sovereign oversight. God's Hand is seen in that He providentially oversaw a process whereby He provided a legal basis, based upon international law, in a hostile world for Israel's rebirth. It is like 50 things all had to go right for Israel to become a nation again, and sure enough, all 50 things have fallen into place. Israel has every right to be in their historic homeland, whether looked at through the eyes of Scripture or internal law.

## Endnotes

1. David Lloyd George, *Memoirs of the Peace Conference* (New Haven, CT: Yale University Press, 1939), Vol. 2, p. 721–22, cited in David Fromkin, *A Peace to End All Peace: The Fall of the Ottoman Empire and the Creation of the Modern Middle East* (New York: Henry Holt & Co., 1989), p. 268.
2. Caroline Glick, "Column One: Obama's Spectacular Failure" in *The Jerusalem Post*, July 7, 2012. <http://www.jpost.com/Opinion/Columnists/Column-One-Obamas-spectacular-failure>.
3. Jonathan Schneer, *The Balfour Declaration: The Origins of the Arab-Israeli Conflict* (New York: Random House, 2010), p. 341.
4. Schneer, *The Balfour Declaration*, p. xxi.
5. During wartime, parliamentary governments often select an inner circle of 9 to 12 representatives to pass legislation because the normal parliamentary process would be too slow and cumbersome to handle wartime decision-making.
6. Schneer, *The Balfour Declaration*, p. 341.
7. Donald M. Lewis, *The Origins of Christian Zionism: Lord Shaftsbury and Evangelical Support for a Jewish Homeland* (Cambridge, England: Cambridge University Press, 2010), p. 332–33.
8. Lewis, *Origins of Christian Zionism*, p. 333.
9. Ibid., p. 333.
10. Ibid., p. 333.
11. Ibid., p. 333.
12. Jill Hamilton, *God, Guns and Israel: Britain, The First World War and the Jews in the Holy City* (London: Sutton Publishing, 2004), p. 125.
13. Ibid., p. 125.
14. Fromkin, *A Peace to End All Peace*, p. 267–68.
15. Ibid., p. 264.
16. Robert Lloyd George, *David & Winston. How a Friendship Changed History* (London: John Murray, 2005), p. 176, cited in David W. Schmidt, *Partners Together in this Great Enterprise: The Role of Christian Zionism in the Foreign Policies of Britain and America in the Twentieth Century* (Xulon Press, 2011), p. 70.
17. Tom Segev, *One Palestine, Complete: Jews and Arabs under the British Mandate* (New York: Metropolitan Books, 2000), p. 22.
18. Fromkin, *A Peace to End All Peace*, p. 312.
19. Hamilton, God, Guns and Israel, p. 153.
20. Howard Grief, *The Legal Foundation and Borders of Israel under International Law: A Treatise on Jewish Sovereignty over the Land of Israel* (Jerusalem: Mazzo Publishers, 2008), p. 195.

21. Jacques Paul Gauthier, "Sovereignty Over the Old City of Jerusalem: A Study of the Historical, Religious, Political and Legal Aspects of the Question of the Old City," (PhD Thesis, University of Geneva International Law School, 2007), p. 369.

22. Gauthier, "Sovereignty Over Jerusalem," p. 599–600. Citation by Gauthier is from Article D, Part III of the Partition Resolution.

23. Grief, *Legal Foundation and Borders of Israel*, p. 227.

24. Ibid., p. 268.

25. Ibid., p. 269.

26. Information about al Husseini was condensed from the following resources: Moshe Perlman, *Mufti of Jerusalem: Haj Amin El Husseini, A Father of Jihad* (Philadelphia, PA: Pavilion Press, 2006); Chuck Morse, *The Nazi Connection to Islamic Terrorism: Adolf Hitler and Haj Amin al-Husseini* (New York: iUniverse, 2003); Klaus-Michael Mallmann and Martin Cuppers, *Nazi Palestine: The Plans for the Extermination of the Jews in Palestine*, translated by Krista Smith (New York: Enigma Books, [2005] 2010); *Encyclopaedia Judaica*, corrected edition 17 vols. (Jerusalem: Keter Publishing House, n.d.), s.v. Husseini, Hajj (Muhammad) Amin Al-, vol. 8, p. 1132; Zvi Elpeleg, *The Grand Mufti Haj Amin Al-Hussaini: Founder of the Palestinian National Movement* (Portland, OR: Frank Cass & Company, 1993).

27. Perlman, *Mufti of Jerusalem*, p. 15.

28. Morse, *The Nazi Connection*, p. 20.

29. Perlman, *Mufti of Jerusalem*, p. 18.

30. Morse, *The Nazi Connection*, p. 28.

31. Ibid., p. 31.

32. Perlman, *Mufti of Jerusalem*, p. 29.

33. Perlman, *Mufti of Jerusalem*, p. 30; Morse, *The Nazi Connection*, p. 45–47.

34. Morse, *The Nazi Connection*, p. 49.

35. Ibid., p. 91.

36. Gauthier, "Sovereignty Over Jerusalem," p. 498.

37. Ibid., p. 499.

38. Peel Report, Chapter XXII, Section 1. Cited in Gauthier, "Sovereignty Over Jerusalem," p. 502.

39. Gauthier, "Sovereignty Over Jerusalem," p. 506–13.

40. Grief, *Legal Foundation and Borders of Israel*, p. 225–66.

41. Gauthier, "Sovereignty Over Jerusalem," p. 577. Gauthier provides the national breakdown in footnote number 2313 as follows: *In favor* of Resolution 181: Australia, Belgium, Bolivia, Brazil, Belorussia, Canada, Costa Rica, Czechoslovakia, Denmark, Dominican Republic, Ecuador, France, Guatemala, Haiti, Iceland, Liberia, Luxembourg, Netherlands, New Zealand, Nicaragua, Norway, Paraguay, Peru, Philippines, Poland, Union of South Africa, Sweden, the Ukraine, the U.S.S.R., the United States, Uruguay and Venezuela. *Against:* Afghanistan, Cuba, Egypt, Greece, India, Iran, Iraq, Lebanon, Pakistan, Saudi Arabia, Syria, Turkey and Yemen. *Abstain:* Argentina, Chile, China, Columbia, El Salvador, Ethiopia, Honduras, Mexico, the United Kingdom and Yugoslavia. *Absent:* Siam.

42. Chaim Weizmann, *Trial and Error* (New York: Harper and Brothers, 1949) p. 475. Cited in Gauthier, "Sovereignty Over Jerusalem," p. 578.

43. Gauthier, "Sovereignty Over Jerusalem," p. 577.

44. For more information, see David W. Schmidt, *Partners Together in This Great Enterprise: The Role of Christian Zionism in the Foreign Policies of Britain and America in the Twentieth Century* (Meadville, PA: Xulon Press, 2011), p. 288–317.

45. Interview with Melvin Leffler, University of Virginia, Hebrew University, Jerusalem, May 29, 2008. Cited in Schmidt, *Partners Together*, p. 296.

46. Allis Radosh and Ronald Radosh, *A Safe Haven: Harry S. Truman and the Founding of Israel* (New York: Harper Collins Publishers, 2009), p.346.

47. Ibid., p. 332.

48. Ibid., p. 354.

49. Grief, *Legal Foundation and Borders of Israel*, p. 10.

50. Gauthier, "Sovereignty Over Jerusalem," p. 848.

51. Tzipi Hotovely, "Time to Apply Israeli Law Over Judea and Samaria," *The Jerusalem Post*, July 11, 2012, <jpost.com/Opinion:Op-EdContributors;Article.aspx?id=277141>.

52. Glick, "Obama's Spectacular Failure."

## CHAPTER 5

# WHAT IS REPLACEMENT THEOLOGY

"We believe that the international Church has superseded for all times *national* Israel as the *institution* for the administration of divine blessing to the world."[1] — Kenneth L. Gentry Jr., replacement theologian

"These three chapters [Romans 9—11] emphatically forbid us to speak of the Church as having once and for all taken the place of the Jewish people. . . . But the assumption that the Church has simply replaced Israel as the people of God is extremely common. . . . And I confess with shame to having also myself used in print on more than one occasion this language of the replacement of Israel by the Church."[2] — C.E.B. Cranfield, British commentator

Replacement theology, also known as supersessionism, "is the view that the NT Church is the new and/or true Israel that has forever superseded the nation Israel as the people of God."[3] Another term, often found in academic circles, for replacement theology is supersessionism. "The term *supersessionism* comes from two Latin words: *super* (on or upon) and *sedere* (to sit). It carries the idea of one person sitting on another's chair, displacing the latter."[4] Replacement theology has been the fuel that has energized Medieval anti-Semitism, Eastern European pogroms, the Holocaust, and contemporary disdain for the modern state of Israel. Mike Vlach notes: "The acceptance or rejection of supersessionism may also influence how one views the modern state of Israel and events in the Middle East."[5] Wherever replacement theology has flourished, the Jews have had to run for cover. Basically, Christian replacement theology says Israel has no national future and wherever such a view has gone it has always led to anti-Semitism.

## Definition and Description

Preterist and covenant theologian Kenneth Gentry defines replacement theology — to which he holds — as follows: "We believe that the international Church has superseded for all times *national* Israel as the *institution* for the administration of divine blessing to the world."[6] We dispensationalists believe that the Church is the current instrument through which God is working in this age, but God has a future time in which He will restore national Israel "as the institution for the administration of divine blessing to the world." Gentry adds to his initial statement the following embellishment:

> That is, we believe that in the unfolding of the plan of God in history, *the Christian Church is the very fruition of the redemptive purpose of God.* As such, the multiracial, international Church of Jesus Christ *supersedes* racial, national Israel as the focus of the kingdom of God. Indeed, we believe that the Church becomes "the Israel of God" (Gal. 6:16), the "seed of Abraham" (Gal. 3:29), "the circumcision" (Phil. 3:3), the "temple of God" (Eph. 2:19-22), and so forth. We believe that Jew and Gentile are eternally merged into a "new man" in the Church of Jesus Christ (Eph. 2:12–18). What God hath joined together let no man put asunder![7]

Pro-Israel scholar Walt Kaiser tells us that replacement theology "declared that the Church, Abraham's spiritual seed, had replaced national Israel in that it had transcended and fulfilled the terms of the covenant given to Israel, which covenant Israel had lost because of disobedience."[8] European scholar and a supporter of Israel, Ronald Diprose, defines replacement theology as follows: "The Church completely and permanently replaced ethnic Israel in the working out of God's plan and as recipient of Old Testament promises addressed to Israel." It appears that supersessionists believe Israel is a "has been" and has no future in the plan of God. The Church inherits all the blessings, while Israel is meant to endure only curses. If this is true, then why has God kept Jewish people around? Most ancient people have disappeared from history. I believe He has kept them around because He has a future for them as individuals and as a nation.

Randall Price provides an excellent and comprehensive definition:

> **Replacement Theology:** a theological perspective that teaches that the Jews have been rejected by God and are no longer God's Chosen People. Those who hold to this view disavow any ethnic future for the Jewish people in connection with the biblical covenants, believing that their spiritual destiny is either to perish or become a part of the new religion that superseded Judaism (whether Christianity or Islam).[9]

## The Rise of Replacement Theology

Replacement theology has been "the consensus of the church from the middle of the second century A.D. to the present day, with few exceptions."[10] Even though the ante-Nicene fathers were predominately premillennial in their understanding of future things, they laid a groundwork that would lead to the rise and development of replacement theology. Premillennialist Justin Martyr was the first to view "the Christian church as 'the true spiritual Israel' (*Dial. 11*)"[11] around A.D. 160. Justin's views laid the groundwork for the growing belief that the Church had superseded or replaced Israel. "Misunderstanding of it colours the Church's attitude to Judaism and contributes to anti-Semitism," notes Peter Richardson.[12] He adds, "In spite of the many attributes, characteristics, prerogatives of the latter which are applied to the former, the Church is not called Israel in the NT. The continuity between

Israel and the Church is partial; and the discontinuity between Israel B.C. and its continuation A.D. is partial."[13]

Further, by the time of Irenaeus (A.D. 165), it becomes entrenched in Christian theology that "the bulk of Israel's Scriptures [are] indecisive for the formation of Christian doctrine."[14] Soulen continues: "In addition to narrowing the thematic focus of the Hebrew Scriptures to the problem of sin and redemption, the standard model also foreshortens the Hebrew Scriptures into a temporal sense. As perceived through the lens of the standard model, the Hebrew Scriptures do not relate a story that extends indefinitely into the future."[15] Kaiser paints the following developmental picture in the early church:

> Replacement theology is not a new arrival in the theological arena, for it probably has its origins in an early political-ecclesiastical alliance forged between Eusebius Pamphilius and the Emperor Constantine. Constantine, regarding himself as God's representative in his role as emperor, gathered all the bishops together on the day of his tricennalia (30th anniversary of his reign), an event, incidentally, which he saw as the foreshadowing of the eschatological Messianic banquet. The results of that meeting, in Eusebius' mind, made it unnecessary to distinguish any longer between the Church and the Empire, for they appeared to merge into one fulfilled kingdom of God on earth in the present time. Such a maneuver, of course, nicely evacuated the role and the significance of the Jewish people in any kingdom considerations. Here began the long trail of replacement theology.[16]

The details about Israel's future, especially in the Old Testament, are simply missing as a part of the development of Christian theology. Siker cites this issue as the primary reason for the disinheriting of the Jews within the early Christian Church. "The first factor is the diminishing emphasis upon the eschatological dimensions of the Christian faith."[17]

### The Impact of Replacement Theology

"The doctrine of replacement theology reflects a wide range of Christian thinking," notes Menachem Benhayim. "From utterly malignant anti-Jewish hatred to simple misunderstanding and misapplication of biblical texts."[18] Since Israel is a subject found on just about every page of the Old and New Testaments, to get that subject wrong can only lead to a mega-distortion of Scripture. This has indeed been the case throughout the history of the Church.

Paul says in Romans 11:17–18, "But if some of the branches were broken off, and you, being a wild olive, were grafted in among them and became partaker with them of the rich root of the olive tree, do not be arrogant toward the branches; but if you are arrogant, remember that it is not you who supports the root, but the root supports you." Yet, this history of most during the Church Age has been an attitude of arrogance toward God's wayward, chosen people — Israel.

Such an attitude of arrogance has led to a distortion of so many biblical teachings. The Church often allegorizes many portions of the Bible, both Old and New Testaments, in order to teach that since the time of Christ, Israel has no claim to the land of Israel. Replacement theologian Colin Chapman obfuscates the issue as follows: "The coming of the kingdom of God through Jesus the Messiah has transformed and reinterpreted all the promises and prophecies in the Old Testament. . . . Jesus the Messiah, who lived, died and was raised from death *in the land*, has opened the kingdom of God to people of all races, making all who follow him into 'one new humanity' (Ephesians 2:15; NRSV)."[19] As Hebrew Christian Arnold Fruchtenbaum is fond of saying, "While the church is said to be a partaker in Israel's promises in the New Testament, nowhere is she said to be a taker over of Israel's promises." Fruchtenbaum has noted that Israelology it totally missing when it come to systematic theology, even though it is one of the most frequently mentioned subjects in the Bible. "Yet, while there are many Systematic Theologies today which have systematized all areas of biblical truth, none thus far have developed an Israelology as part of their system."[20]

"Replacement theology is just plain bad news for both the Church and Israel,"[21] declares Kaiser. Not only does the Bible distinguish between God's plan for Israel and His plan for the Church, but it also teaches a distinction between saved and lost Jewish individuals. This is one of the things denied by replacement theology. British commentator C.E.B. Canfield, who is by no means a Bible-thumping fundamentalist (a rare moment in academia), provides the following appropriate apology:

It is only where the Church persists in refusing to learn this message, where it secretly — perhaps quite unconsciously! — believes that its own existence is based on human achievement, and so fails to understand God's mercy to itself, that it is unable to believe in God's mercy for still unbelieving Israel, and so entertains the ugly and unscriptural notion that God has cast off His people Israel and simply replaced it by the Christian Church. These three chapters [Romans 9–11] emphatically forbid us to speak of the Church as having once and for all taken the place of the Jewish people. . . . But the assumption that the Church has simply replaced Israel as the people of God is extremely common. . . . And I confess with shame to having also myself used in print on more than one occasion this language of the replacement of Israel by the Church.[22]

Yet, today, many Evangelicals are attempting to develop new reasons to replace Israel with the Church. May God help us all to understand His Scripture more clearly!

## Galatians 6:16 and Replacement Theology

A couple of decades ago I was talking to a friend of mine about the modern state of Israel. This friend, born and raised in Damascus, Syria, is a Muslim. He is a well-educated man, who has lived in our country for over 40 years. As our conversation developed, I was taken back when he told me that the Jewish people of today had no claim to the land of Israel because the Church has replaced Israel. He then cited Galatians 6:16. I was amazed that a Muslim has such a grasp of the Christian false teaching called replacement theology. It is not surprising to hear this from certain segments of Christendom, but to realize that this errant viewpoint had penetrated into the American Muslim community was amazing to me.

Galatians 6:16 is often thought by many in the replacement theology camp to support their views. "And those who will walk by this rule, peace and mercy be upon them, and upon the Israel of God." Many Christians, and apparently some Muslims, believe Israel is permanently replaced by the Church and the Church is the new Israel of God from Galatians 6:16.

Gentry believes that Galatians 6:16 teaches that the Church has replaced or superseded Israel when he says, "If Abraham can have Gentiles as his 'spiritual seed,' why cannot there be a *spiritual Israel*? In fact, Christians are called by the name 'Israel': 'And as many as walk according to this rule, peace and mercy by upon them, and upon the Israel of God' (Gal. 6:16)."[23] Yes indeed! There is such a thing as "spiritual Israel." Spiritual Israel in Galatians 6:16 refers to Jewish people who have trusted Jesus as their Messiah; but the Church is never called "spiritual Israel," as Gentry claims. Let's look at Galatians 6:16 and see what it actually says.

The passage is simple and clear. The first part of verse 16, which says "those who walk by this rule," refers to the rule Paul had just stated in verse 15. "For neither is circumcision anything, nor uncircumcision, but a new creation." This is a spiritual category referring to all believers, to which Paul pronounces a blessing: "peace and mercy be upon them." This is followed by his copulative comment "and upon the Israel of God."

Greek scholar, S. Lewis Johnson surveys the different suggestions in Galatians 6:16 for translating the Greek word *kai*, which is normally translated "and." Johnson says, "In absence of compelling exegetical and theological considerations, we should avoid the rarer grammatical usages when the common ones make good sense."[24] He demonstrates there is no exegetical or theological reason to not take "and" in its normal sense in this passage. Johnson concludes:

> If it were Paul's intention to identify the "them" of the text as "the Israel of God," then why not simply eliminate the *kai* after "mercy?" The result would be far more to the point, if Paul were identifying the "them," that is, the Church, with the term "Israel." The verse would be rendered then, "And as many as shall walk by this rule, peace be upon them and mercy, upon the Israel of God." A case could be solidly made for the apposition of "the Israel of God" with "them," and the rendering of the NIV could stand. Paul, however, did not eliminate the *kai*.[25]

Johnson is saying that there is no textual or exegetical basis for Gentry's belief that Galatians 6:16 teaches the "Israel of God" includes the Church or Gentiles. Gentry's replacement theology or supersessionism — as he likes to call it — has no basis in the biblical text. It must be that he is so blinded by the demands of his false theology that he continues to insist upon such an interpretation of the Bible and his resulting errant theology. I wonder, along with Lewis Johnson, why? "In spite of overwhelming evidence to the contrary, there remains persistent support for the contention that the term *Israel* may refer properly to Gentile believers in the present age."[26]

E.D. Burton says, "In view of the apostle's previous strong anti-judaistic expressions, he feels impelled, by the insertion of and, to emphasize this expression of his true attitude towards his people."[27] Fruchtenbaum summarizes the passage as follows:

> Galatians is concerned with Gentiles who were attempting to attain salvation through the Law. The ones deceiving them were the Judaizers, who were Jews demanding adherence to the Law of Moses. To them, a Gentile first had to convert to Judaism before he was qualified for salvation through Christ. In verse fifteen Paul states that the important thing for salvation is faith, resulting in the new man. He then pronounces a blessing on two groups who would follow this rule of salvation by faith alone. The first group is the *them*, the Gentile Christians to and of whom he had devoted most of the epistle. The second group is the Israel of God. These are Hebrew Christians who, in contrast with the Judaizers, followed the rule of salvation by faith alone. Again a distinction between the two groups is seen, for the Hebrew Christians alone are the Israel of God. It is a matter of position which here acts out a definite function.[28]

### Israel Always Means Israel

A number of years ago, I was discussing biblical prophecy with a person who was writing articles in a magazine from a replacement theology perspective. I kept hammering away at him with the slogan "Israel always means Israel," as he would replace Israel with the Church in Old Testament passage after passage. Finally he complained to me something along the lines of "You keep bringing in your theological presupposition that 'Israel always means Israel.'" I replied this was not a theological *a priori*; instead it was an exegetical conclusion — and so it is.

In fact, there is not a single instance in the entire Bible where *Israel* refers to anything other than the Jewish people. Burton declares,

> There is, in fact, no instance of his [Paul] using Israel except of the Jewish nation or a part thereof. These facts favour the interpretation of the expression as applying not to the Christian community, but to Jews; yet, in view of "of God," not to the whole Jewish nation, but to the pious Israel, the remnant according to the election of grace (Rom. 11:5).[29]

Johnson is equally insistent when he says,

> There is no instance in biblical literature of the term *Israel* being used in the sense of the church, or the people of God composed of both believing ethnic Jews and Gentiles. Nor, on the other hand, as one might expect if there were such usage, does the phrase *ta ethnê* (KJV, "the Gentiles") ever mean the non-Christian world specifically, but only the non-Jewish peoples, although such are generally non-Christians.[30]

Fruchtenbaum summaries the distinction between Israel and the Church as follows:

> The first evidence is the fact that the church was born at Pentecost, whereas Israel had existed for many centuries. . . .
>
> The second evidence is that certain events in the ministry of the Messiah were essential to the establishment of the church — the church does not come into being until certain events have taken place. . . .
>
> The third evidence is the mystery character of the church. . . .
>
> The fourth evidence that the church is distinct from Israel is the unique relationship between Jews and the Gentiles, called one new man in Ephesians 2:15. . . .
>
> The fifth evidence for the distinction between Israel and the church is found in Galatians 6:16. . . .

Perhaps one more observation can be made. In the book of Acts, both Israel and the church exist simultaneously. The term *Israel* is used twenty times and *ekklesia* (church) nineteen times, yet the two groups are always kept distinct.[31]

It is not just a theological belief that "Israel always means Israel," and that Israel and the Church are distinct peoples of God. These things are specifically taught in the Bible. We are currently living in the Church Age, which will end with the any-moment Rapture when the last person is saved into the Body of Christ. Then, the history will complete the final week of Daniel's 70-week prophecy, which will end with Israel's conversion to Jesus as their Messiah. This will lead to the thousand-year kingdom in which Israel will be the head over all the nations. Not only does the Bible distinguish between God's plan for Israel and His plan for the Church, but it also teaches a distinction between saved and lost Jewish people in Galatians 6:16. This is one of the things denied by replacement theology.

## Fulfillment Theology?

Today there is a growing trend for some who teach replacement theology to deny that their views should legitimately be classified as supersessionism. Instead they say they believe in fulfillment theology and do not believe that anything has been replaced. Nevertheless, when one evaluates one's beliefs it becomes evident that they still believe that Israel has been disinherited and are no longer a chosen people. They do not believe that there is a future for national, ethnic Israel, nor do they think the modern state of Israel has anything to do with Bible prophecy.

We have a number of expressions within Americana that illustrate one who is not willing to exercise truth in labeling. For example we may say, "If it walks like a duck, quacks like a duck, and smells like a duck, then it must be a duck." Or, Shakespeare said it more eloquently: "A rose by any other name would smell as sweet." That dictum is true when it comes to some evangelicals who teach replacement theology, but then will not own up to what they actually advocate.

Amillennial and covenant theologian Samuel Waldron wrote a response to a lecture by John MacArthur in which he made a case for premillennialism. Waldron vigorously denied that he was a replacement theologian, even though he holds the classic beliefs of replacement theology. He says, "The Church *is* Israel in a newly reformed and expanded phase of existence. . . . the Church is really the *continuation* of Israel."[32] How can someone with a PhD in theology, as Waldron has, not realize that the statement noted above and the rest of his book demonstrates that he advocates a form of replacement theology? The fact is, he states that the Church represents a new "phase of existence" and then defines the New Testament "phase" of Israel as including Gentiles.[33] This is classic replacement theology since the outcome and logic of his position is that ethnic and national Israel have been replaced by the Church. Such a view teaches that Israel has been disinherited and does not have a future that includes a national future for a redeemed Israel. Waldron displays a blindness that does not allow him to see that two plus two equals four.

Hank Hanegraaff is another neo-supersessionist who said, "I have never argued for Replacement Theology."[34] This is a surprising statement since his book *The Apocalypse Code* is filled with replacement theological statements and arguments.[35] He gives the following reason for denying that he holds supersessionist views:

> God has only ever had one chosen people who form one covenant community, beautifully symbolized in Scripture by one cultivated olive tree. Indeed, the precise terminology used to describe the children of Israel in the Old Testament is ascribed to the church in the New Testament. . . . As such, the true church is true Israel, and true Israel is truly the church — one cannot replace what it already is. Rather than reason together in collegial debate, dispensationalists have coined the phrase "Replacement theologian" as the ultimate silencer.[36]

For some reason, a new trend by some today is to reject the label but teach the historic viewpoint of replacement theology.

## Replacement Reasons

Hanegraaff errs in thinking that replacement theology is something invented by dispensationalists by which they might name-call those who disagree with them. "While it is true that Israel occupies an important place in dispensational theology, it is also true that reflection concerning the place of

Israel in God's plan predates this school of thought by many centuries,"[37] notes Ronald Diprose. While noting that an early form of replacement theology began in the second century with Justin Martyr, Diprose describes it as consisting of the belief that "Israel has been repudiated by God and has been replaced by the Church in the working out of his plan. A variation of this idea is that true Israel always has been the Church,"[38] which is the view expressed by Waldron and Hanegraaff throughout *The Apocalypse Code* (*AC*).[39]

Mike Vlach, in his Ph.D. dissertation on the subject, describes both the method of replacement theology and the theology or outcome it produces. "In the realm of hermeneutics, supersessionists argue that: (1) the New Testament has interpretive priority over the Old Testament; (2) national Israel functioned as a type of the New Testament church; and (3) the New Testament indicates that Old Testament prophecies regarding national Israel are being fulfilled with the church."[40] It is obvious that Hanegraaff has adopted the hermeneutics or method, and then the conclusions of replacement theology, and believes that the Jews have been disinherited.

That the New Testament has interpretive priority over the Old is seen throughout *AC* as Hanegraaff dismisses Old Testament prophecy that has never been fulfilled for Israel by subsuming it into a supposed New Testament fulfillment. For example, by characterizing Israel in the Old Testament as "the prostituted bride" who is replaced in the New Testament by "the purified bride," which is the Church, Hanegraaff reinterprets the Old in light of the New.[41] After comparing a number of Old Testament characters with Jesus of the New Testament (for example, Joshua and Jesus), Hanegraaff says, "In each case, the lesser is fulfilled and rendered obsolete by the greater."[42] I agree that the New Testament often notes God's progress in revelation by noting Christ's fulfillment of the Old, but nowhere does the New indicate that Old Testament promises to ethnic Israel are superseded by Christ's work. Instead, Christ is the basis for the fulfillment of Old Testament promises. Hanegraaff says, the "old covenant shadows find their final consummation in the person and work of Jesus Christ."[43] This is clearly true about many of the prophecies Christ fulfilled at His first advent, but there is still more to come. It is not an either/or situation; it is best to see the relationship between the testaments as a both/and.

Vlach's second methodological point is that advocates of replacement theology see national Israel as a type of the New Testament church.

"Jerusalem symbolized all that Israel was to be. . . . Jerusalem is typological of the greater purposes of God,"[44] declares Hanegraaff. He speaks of Paul illustrating a "typologically heightened fulfillment . . . that all who fixate on an earthly Jerusalem with a rebuilt temple and reinstituted temple sacrifices are in slavery to types and shadows."[45] Hanegraaff speaks of "the typological fulfillment of the temple and the rest of the old covenant."[46] His views are summarized as follows: "The New Testament's typological interpretation of the Old Testament thus stands as the ultimate corrective to Zionist zeal."[47]

The third point, that the Old Testament promises to Israel are fulfilled with the Church, is also evident in Hanegraaff. He says, "The land promises are fully and finally fulfilled in the final future through Jesus. . . . the promise is typologically fulfilled in the Lord."[48] Again he says, "Peter uses the very language once reserved for national Israel and applies it to spiritual Israel."[49] "Furthermore, the land promises are fulfilled in the far future through Jesus who provides true Israel with permanent rest from their wanderings in sin."[50] Hanegraaff uses the term "true Israel" as a reference to the Church, classic replacement theology terminology.

Vlach also describes the theological arguments that supersessionists construct as follows: "(1) the New Testament teaches the permanent rejection of national Israel as the people of God; (2) application of 'Israel' language to the church shows that the church is now the true Israel; (3) salvific unity between Jews and Gentiles rules out a restoration of national Israel; and (4) fulfillment of the new covenant with the church shows that the church is now the true Israel."[51] Clearly, Hanegraaff and Waldron hold to these theological beliefs.

Hanegraaff even uses the term "superseded" in the following statement: "History, like the New Testament, reveals that the Holy City — turned harlot city — is superseded by the holy Christ. Jesus is the antitype who fulfills all of the typology vested in Jerusalem."[52] Hanegraaff says that Genesis 12:3, which I take to include ethnic Israel, refers instead "to true Israel, which consists of every person who through faith has been adopted into the family of God."[53] When speaking of the land promises which have never yet been completely fulfilled, he insists that they are "fulfilled and rendered obsolete by the greater."[54] Such are classic replacement theology statements.

It is safe to conclude that in spite of their denials, Hanegraaff and Waldron are clearly advocates of replacement theology. Norm Geisler also understands that Hanegraaff's *AC* teaches replacement theology when he notes the following: "In general *The Code* repeatedly takes the Old Testament promises to Jews out of their original context by replacing Israel with the New Testament church. The 'Replacement Theology' is a classic example of taking texts out of their context."[55] Even though they vigorously reject the label, both Hanegraaff, Waldron and others today have some form of replacement theology, whether they will admit it or not.

## 1 Peter 2 and Replacement Theology

A major passage often put forward by replacement theologians in an effort to teach that the Church has replaced Israel by becoming the "New Israel" or the "True Israel" is found in 1 Peter 2. For example, commentator Peter Davids says, "This position is described by transferring to the church the titles of Israel in the OT (for the church is the true remnant of Israel, as the use of Israel's titles from 1:1 on indicates)."[56] Another says, "God's chosen people are no longer said to be those physically descended from Abraham, for Christians are now the true 'chosen race.' . . . What more could be needed in order to say with assurance that the church has now become the true Israel of God."[57] Yet another tells us the following: "Peter proceeds to apply title after title conferred on the old Israel to the church as the new Israel of God. . . . Nothing could show more clearly than these two verses the claim of the early Christian church to be the true people of God, heir to all the promises made to the old Israel."[58] I believe such interpretations of this passage are wrong and there are no New Testament passages teaching that the Church has replaced Israel. Certainly not 1 Peter 2! The debate revolves around the following two verses: "But you are a chosen race, a royal priesthood, a holy nation, a people for God's own possession, that you may proclaim the excellencies of Him who has called you out of darkness into His marvelous light; for you once were not a people, but now you are the people of God; you had not received mercy, but now you have received mercy" (1 Pet. 2:9–10).

## To Whom Did Peter Write?

One's interpretation of Peter's epistle is determined (assuming one is consistent with the application of their starting point), by those to whom he is writing. Peter says, "Peter, an apostle of Jesus Christ, to those who reside as aliens, scattered throughout Pontus, Galatia, Cappadocia, Asia, and Bithynia, who are chosen" (1 Pet. 1:1). The Apostle Paul tells us that Peter was the Apostle to the Jewish people. "But on the contrary, seeing that I had been entrusted with the gospel to the uncircumcised, just as Peter had been to the circumcised (for He who effectually worked for Peter in his apostleship to the circumcised effectually worked for me also to the Gentiles)" (Gal. 2:7–8). Peter describes those to whom he is writing as "aliens" and "scattered" throughout the region we know today as Turkey. An alien is someone who is not originally from the location of his residence. One Greek lexicon says it refers "to staying for a while in a strange or foreign place, *sojourning, residing temporarily*."[59] The next word translated "scattered" is the Greek word from which we get the well-known English word "diaspora," which speaks of Jews living outside the land of Israel in Gentile nations. The Greek lexicon defines this word as the "state or condition of being scattered, dispersion, diaspora."[60] The only other time it is used in the Greek New Testament is in James 1:1: "James, a bond-servant of God and of the Lord Jesus Christ, to the twelve tribes who are dispersed abroad: Greetings." James was clearly writing to Jewish believers.

It seems clear from Peter's opening statement that he is writing this letter to Jewish believers, just as James also did. Arnold Fruchtenbaum correctly notes:

> Of the twenty-one epistles in the New Testament, five were written to Jewish believers dealing with the needs of Jewish believers and specific issues that Jewish believers faced. There are things in these epistles applicable to all believers, but some are true only of Jewish believers. These five epistles are Hebrews, James, I & II Peter, and Jude.[61]

Interestingly, most of the post-apostolic early Church fathers also agreed that 1 Peter was written to Jewish believers scattered throughout the stated regions of modern-day Turkey.

> With few exceptions, the Fathers believed that this letter was written by the apostle Peter and sent to Jewish Christians in the Diaspora (Eusebius of Caesarea, Didymus, Andreas, Oecumenius). They recognized that the letter has close resemblances to James, and they accounted for this by saying that both men were apostles to the Jews, though Peter seems to have concentrated more on those who lived outside Palestine (Andreas).[62]

It is clear that Peter, an Apostle who was specifically called to minister to the Jews, is writing a letter to encourage Jewish believers who are in the diaspora. It makes no sense to speak of Gentile Christians as aliens living in Gentile nations. It makes good sense to speak of Jewish believers as aliens living in Gentile lands, who had likely been there since their dispersion by the Assyrians and Babylonians. Fruchtenbaum explains:

> It should be kept in mind that Peter is writing to Jewish believers. Throughout Scripture, there are always two Israels: Israel the whole that comprises all Jews; and, Israel the Remnant that comprises only believing Jews. Here, Peter distinguishes between the Remnant and the non-Remnant. Replacement Theology, however, relies on this passage as proof that the true Israel is the church.[63]

If one sees that this epistle was written to Jewish Christians then this will be a key issue for how one understands the disputed statements in chapter two. If one believes, in spite of the evidence, that it is a general epistle written to the Church at large this will also color how they understand chapter two differently.

## The Israel of God

In the course of writing to Jewish believers and informing them of the fact that because they have accepted Jesus as their Messiah they have received the full blessing intended by the Lord for a member of God's elect nation — Israel. However, replacement theologians attempt to use 1 Peter 2:9–10 as a proof the Church has forever replaced Israel. While many examples of replacement interpretations of this passage could be cited, I will only mention one example. Paul Achtemeier says, "The twofold description of the new community (2:5; 2:9–10) shows by its language that the church has now taken over the role of Israel."[64]

Replacement theology teaches that since clear terms used for Israel in the Old Testament are cited in this New Testament epistle, then if follows that they are applied to the Church, thus, the Church has replaced Israel. There is no doubt that clear Old Testament language used in the first testament in relation to Israel is used in 1 Peter 2. These terms include: "a chosen race," "a royal priesthood," "a holy nation," "a people for God's own possession"

(1 Pet. 2:9). However, since Peter is writing to "the Israel of God" or Jewish believers, he is listing these Old Testament descriptions of Israel to let them know that everything promised them in the Old Testament is being fulfilled through their faith in Jesus as their Messiah. This is juxtaposed by a comparison with unbelieving Jews who have not trusted Jesus as the Messiah of Israel in verses 7–8. Peter speaks of "the stone which the builders rejected" (2:7) as a likely reference to Jewish leadership that lead the nation to reject Jesus as the Messiah. Peter further describes Jewish unbelievers as ones who view Jesus as "a stone of stumbling and a rock of offense." He notes that these Jewish unbelievers "stumble because they are disobedient to the word, and to this doom they were also appointed" (2:8). Clearly, Peter is contrasting Jewish unbelievers and Jewish believers.

A clear contrast is noted as verse 9 begins with "But you. . . ." In contrast to Jewish unbelievers, believing Jews will actually be benefactors of the Old Testament blessings decreed for the nation of Israel through faith in Jesus. Thus, these four descriptives in verse 9 are not being transposed upon the Church; instead, they are reiterated to Jewish believers within the Church by the Apostle to the circumcised. Fruchtenbaum expounds:

> It is important to recognize that the contrast Peter makes here is not between the Church and Israel, or between believers and non-believers, or between unbelieving Jews and believing Gentiles. Rather, the contrast here is between the Remnant and the Non-Remnant of Israel. Peter's point is that while Israel the whole failed to fulfill its calling, the Remnant of Israel has not failed to fulfill its calling.[65]

Peter further explains his point as he moves to verse 10 where he refers to the Old Testament prophet Hosea. One of Gomer's illegitimate children was named "Lo-ammi" (Hos. 1:9) which means in Hebrew "not My people." The child was so named since he was the offspring, not of Hosea, Gomer's husband, but from her harlotry. Since Hosea is a type of God in that book, the Lord is saying that not all of the children of Israel are His offspring. (I take it this is the Lord's way of saying many within national Israel were unbelievers in relation to their individual salvation while still a part of national Israel.) However, the very next verse says, "Yet the number of the sons of Israel will be like the sand of the sea, which cannot be measured or numbered; and in the place where it is said to them, 'You are not My people,' it will be said to them, 'You are the sons of the living God' " (Hos. 1:10). This sounds like what Peter is saying in 2:10 of Jewish believers of his day. Again, Fruchtenbaum notes:

> The Hosea context deals with Israel: that for a period of time Israel, experientially at least, was not to be God's people. However, in the future, when Israel undergoes a national salvation, they will again experientially become *my people*. What will be true of Israel as a nation in the future is true of the Remnant of Israel in the present: they have experientially become God's people again because they are members of the believing Remnant.[66]

While much more could be said about 1 Peter 2, it is abundantly clear that the passage does not support any form of replacement theology. Instead, it speaks of a fulfillment of God's Old Testament promises to the Israel of God through Christ, not a replacement of Israel by the Church. God will indeed keep all His promises to Israel even though during the Church Age He is combining elect Jews and Gentiles into a single co-equal body (Eph. 2:11–22).

If the New Testament actually taught supersessionism or replacement theology there would need to be a clear statement of just such a doctrine. However, no clear teaching of this nature appears, in spite of the many inferences by interpreters. In addition, the Apostle Paul teaches just the opposite in Romans 9–11. Even a liberal scholar such as Peter Richardson is able to recognize this truth when he says: "There is also discontinuity between the Church and Israel A.D. In spite of the many attributes, characteristics, privileges, and prerogatives of the latter which are applied to the former, the Church is not called Israel in the NT."[67]

### Endnotes

1. Kenneth L. Gentry Jr., "Supersessional Orthodoxy; Zionistic Sadism," *Dispensationalism in Transition*, vol. VI, no. 2; Feb. 1993, p. 1 (emphasis original).
2. C.E.B. Cranfield, *A Critical and Exegetical Commentary on the Epistle to the Romans*, 2 vols. (Edinburgh, Scotland: T & T Clark, 1979), Vol. 2, p. 448.
3. Michael J. Vlach, *Has the Church Replaced Israel: A Theological Evaluation* (Nashville, TN: B & H Academic, 2010), p. 12.
4. Ibid., p. 9 (italics original).

5. Michael J. Vlach, "The Church as a Replacement of Israel: An Analysis of Supersessionism," Ph.D. diss. (Wake Forest, NC: Southeastern Baptist Theological Seminary, 2004), p. 10.

6. Gentry, "Supersessional Orthodoxy," p. 1 (emphasis original).

7. Kenneth L. Gentry Jr., "The Iceman Cometh! Moronism Reigneth!" *Dispensationalism in Transition*, vol. VI, no. 1, Jan. 1993, p. 1.

8. Walter C. Kaiser Jr., "An Assessment of 'Replacement Theology,'" *Mishkan*, no. 21; 1994, p. 9.

9. Randall Price, *Unholy War: America, Israel and Radical Islam* (Eugene, OR: Harvest House, 2001), p. 412.

10. H. Wayne House, "The Church's Appropriation of Israel's Blessings" in H. Wayne House, editor, *Israel: The Land and the People* (Grand Rapids, MI: Kregel, 1998), p. 77.

11. R. Kendall Soulen, *The God of Israel and Christian Theology* (Minneapolis, MN: Fortress Press, 1996), p. 35.

12. Peter Richardson, *Israel in the Apostolic Church* (Cambridge: At The University Press, 1969), p. 2.

13. Richardson, *Israel*, p. 7.

14. Soulen, *God of Israel*, p. 50

15. Ibid., p. 53

16. Kaiser, "Replacement Theology," p. 9.

17. Jeffrey S. Siker, *Disinheriting The Jews: Abraham in Early Christian Controversy* (Louisville, KY: Westminster/John Knox Press, 1991), p. 194.

18. Menachem Benhayim, "The Church Has Replaced the Jewish People — A Response," *Mishkan*, no. 21, 1994, p. 31.

19. Colin Chapman, *Whose Promised Land? The Continuing Crisis Over Israel and Palestine* (Grand Rapids, MI: Baker, 2002), p. 285.

20. Arnold G. Fruchtenbaum, *Israelology: The Missing Link in Systematic Theology* (Tustin, CA: Ariel Ministries Press, 1993), p. 1.

21. Kaiser, "Replacement Theology," p. 20.

22. Cranfield, *Epistle to the Romans*, Vol. 2, p. 448.

23. Kenneth L. Gentry Jr., *He Shall Have Dominion: A Postmillennial Eschatology* (Tyler, TX: Institute for Christian Economics, 1992), p. 167, (emphasis original).

24. S. Lewis Johnson Jr., "Paul and 'The Israel of God': An Exegetical and Eschatological Case-Study," in Stanley D. Toussaint and Charles H. Dyer, *Essays in Honor of J. Dwight Pentecost* (Chicago, IL: Moody Press, 1986), p. 187.

25. Johnson, "The Israel of God," p. 188.

26. Ibid., p. 181.

27. Ernest De Witt Burton, *A Critical and Exegetical Commentary on the Epistle to the Galatians* (Edinburgh, Scotland: T & T Clark, 1920), p. 358.

28. Arnold G. Fruchtenbaum, *Hebrew Christianity: Its Theology, History, and Philosophy* (Washington, DC: Canon Press, 1974), p. 33 (emphasis original).

29. Burton, *Galatians*, p. 358.

30. Johnson, "The Israel of God," p. 189.

31. Arnold G. Fruchtenbaum, "Israel and the Church," in Wesley R. Willis and John R. Master, gen. editors, *Issues in Dispensationalism* (Chicago, IL: Moody Press, 1994), p. 116–118.

32. Samuel E. Waldron, *MacArthur's Millennial Manifesto: A Friendly Response* (Owensboro, KY: Reformed Baptist Academic Press, 2008), p. 7 (emphasis original).

33. Waldron, *Manifesto*, p. 35–55.

34. Hank Hanegraaff, "Response to *National Liberty Journal* article on *The Apocalypse Code*," www.equip.org/site/apps/nl/content2.asp?c=muI1L-aMNJrE&b=2616123&ct=3839317.

35. Hank Hanegraaff, *The Apocalypse Code: Find Out What the Bible Really Says About the End Times and Why It Matters Today* (Nashville, TN: Thomas Nelson, 2007). For a book-length rebuttal of Hanegraaff's book see Mark Hitchcock and Thomas Ice, *Breaking The Apocalypse Code: Setting The Record Straight About the End Times* (Costa Mesa, CA: The Word For Today, 2007).

36. Hanegraaff, "Response."

37. Ronald E. Diprose, *Israel in the Development of Christian Thought* (Rome: Instituto Biblico Evangelico Italiano, 2000), p. 3.

38. Diprose, Israel, p. 31 (emphasis original).

39. Hanegraaff calls the church the "true Israel" (p. 116, 124, 127, 180, 199, 200) or "spiritual Israel" (p. 221) a number of times in *AC*.

40. Vlach, "Replacement of Israel," p. xvii.

41. Hanegraaff, *Code*, p. 124.

42. Ibid., p. 201.

43. Ibid., p. 174.

44. Ibid., p. 190.

45. Ibid., p. 202–03.

46. Ibid., p. 223.

47. Ibid., p. 223.

48. Ibid., p. 182.

49. Ibid., p. 221.

50. Ibid., p. 180.

51. Vlach, "Replacement of Israel," p. xvii.

52. Hanegraaff, *Code*, p. 197.

53. Ibid., p. 200.

54. Ibid., p. 201.

55. Norman L. Geisler, "Review of Hank Hanegraaff's *The Apocalypse Code*," www.ses.edu/NormGeisler/ReviewApocalypseCode.html.

56. Peter H. Davids, *The First Epistle of Peter* (Grand Rapids, MI: Eerdmans, 1990), p. 93.

57. Wayne Grudem, *1 Peter, Tyndale New Testament Commentary* (Grand Rapids, MI: Eerdmans, 1988), p. 113.

58. Archibald M. Hunter, "The First Epistle of Peter," *The Interpreter's Bible in Twelve Volumes* (Nashville, TN: Abingdon Press, 1957), Vol. 12, p.110–11.

59. Frederick W. Danker, *A Greek-English Lexicon of the New Testament and Other Early Christian Literature*, 3rd. ed. (Chicago, IL: The University of Chicago Press, 2000), p. 775.

60. Ibid., p. 236.

61. Arnold G. Fruchtenbaum, *The Messianic Jewish Epistles: Hebrews, James, First Peter, Second Peter, Jude* (Tustin, CA: Ariel Ministries, 2005), p. xvii.

62. Gerald Bray, ed., "James, 1–2 Peter, 1–3 John, Jude," *Ancient Christian Commentary on Scripture: New Testament* (Downers Grove, IL: InterVarsity, 2000), p. 65. In fact, D.E. Hiebert lists others who think 1 Peter was written to Jewish Christians as Calvin, Bengel, Weiss, Alford, English, and Wuest. D.E. Hiebert, *1 Peter* (Chicago, IL: Moody, 1992), p. 24 as cited in Vlach, *Has the Church Replaced Israel?* p. 148.

63. Fruchtenbaum, *Messianic Jewish Epistles*, p. 336.

64. Paul J. Achtemeier, *1 Peter: A Commentary on First Peter* (Minneapolis, MN: Augsburg Fortress, 1996), p. 152.

65. Fruchtenbaum, *Messianic Jewish Epistles*, p. 344.

66. Ibid., p. 344.

67. Richardson, *Israel*, p. 7.

## CHAPTER 6

# ARE MODERN JEWS DESCENDANTS OF ABRAHAM, ISAAC, AND JACOB?

"Modern Jews are a separate nation of people with a self-identity, spread out among many other nations. The closest analogy to them are the Gypsies. The only difference between Modern Jews and Gypsies is that the Modern Jews claim to have a relation to the Bible Jews, a claim I maintain is false. . . . Modern Jews think of themselves as Jews, but they are not Jews. They are counterfeits of Biblical Jews. I say this not to disparage them, but to be accurate."[1] — James Jordan, Replacement Theology Theologian

"In summary . . . the largest, and most influential, proportion of Eastern European Jews came from Central Europe. By this analysis we can show that the dominate ethnic element among Eastern European Jews is Judean — the ancient Jewish people of Judea in the Middle East."[2] — Kevin Alan Brook, Jewish Researcher

Some people contend that modern Jews do not have the blood of Abraham, Isaac, and Jacob in their veins. They contend that modern Jews, whether in or out of the land of Israel, have no genetic basis from which to claim that they are Jews, let alone the chosen descendants of Abraham, Isaac, and Jacob. Some say that since they are not true Jews then they are not descendants of those who were scattered across the globe in A.D. 70, and they cannot return to what they never really left, which is the land of Israel. Is this true or just another effort to disinherit God's ancient chosen people?

## Are Modern Jews Frauds?

The conviction that modern Jews are fraudulent has been clearly expressed by Presbyterian replacement theologian James B. Jordan.[3] "With the passing away of the Old Covenant, there is no longer any such a thing as a Jew in the Biblical sense," declares Jordan. I wonder, "Is there any other sense in which one could be a Jew except for the biblical sense?" "Unless by 'True Jews' we mean Christians. There is no covenant, and therefore there is no nation, no 'race.' "[4] Nowhere does the New Testament call Gentile Christians "True Jews," "Jews," "Israel," or any such term. New Testament believers are called the seed of Abraham because he was the father of those who believe. Abraham was the only Gentile in the history of the world who became a Jew or Israelite, since the Jewish race descended from him, Isaac, and Jacob. Thus, all Christian believers in the current Church Age, whether Jew or Gentile, are offspring of the spiritual seed of Abraham (Rom. 4:1–5; Gal. 3:6–7, 14, 16–18). Abraham is both the father of physical Israel, known as the Jews, and father of spiritual descendants, that is, everyone who believes in Jesus as the Messiah, whether Jew or Gentile (Gen. 15:6).

Jordan makes one of the most outlandish statements possible on this topic when he declares: "It is entirely possible that there is not one drop of Abraham's blood in any modern Jew."[5] One might think that only a radical Islamic terrorist would publicly write such things, but Jordan is an Evangelical Christian. He does not stop with the preceding comment, he continues with the following pontification:

> Modern Jews are a separate nation of people with a
> self-identity, spread out among many other nations. The
> closest analogy to them are the Gypsies. The only difference
> between Modern Jews and Gypsies is that the Modern Jews

claim to have a relation to the Bible Jews, a claim I maintain is false. . . . Modern Jews think of themselves as Jews, but they are not Jews. They are counterfeits of Biblical Jews. I say this not to disparage them, but to be accurate.[6]

Jordan's "scholarship" leads him to believe that today's Jews (he even coins a special term for the Jews of today — "modern Jews") are fraudulent, merely posing as Jews. History would be totally different if Hitler had thought this way, or if the Muslims of today would come to learn of Jordan's discovery. "Modern Jews are people who choose to think of themselves as descendants of Israel," insists Jordan. "Most modern Jews are not semites, but are descended from Eastern European tribes converted to Judaism in the middle ages."[7] So Jordan believes that the true Jews of the Bible and history lost their identity in the Middle Ages in relation to a nation called Khazaria.

## The Khazar Theory

One of the tactics used by some anti-Zionists is to say that most modern Jews are not true descendants of Abraham, Isaac, and Jacob. This errant theory is based upon wrong conclusions they have drawn from the history of a medieval nation named Khazaria in which some of the Gentiles converted to Judaism. This is alleged to have diluted the stock of Jewish progeny through a great influx of Gentiles into Judaism. Through racial inflation, the Jews are said to have lost their genetic descent from Abraham, Isaac, and Jacob, resulting in the loss of genuine Jewish DNA in those who call themselves Jews today.

The Khazar theory was introduced to the broader public in 1976 by Arthur Koestler, a Jewish communist and novelist in his book entitled *The Thirteenth Tribe*.[8] The theory had been floating around various Arab and anti-Semitic groups for a number of years before Koestler's book.[9] It is not surprising to learn that his theory has been very attractive to Arabs, Muslims, Holocaust deniers, skinheads, Nazis, Christian Identity, some within Evangelical Christian circles who hold to replacement theology, and even a number of leftist Jews. The Khazar theory is a convenient way for some to simply dismiss the modern state of Israel, since according to this view the Jewish people in the land are not really descendants of Abraham, Isaac, and Jacob. Therefore, the so-called "Jews" do not have legitimate claim to the land of Israel. Robert B. Thieme Jr. outlines the implications of the Khazar theory:

If the Khazars, not the biblical Israelites, are indeed the ancestors of European Jews, then European Jews have no connection with God's people of the Old Testament, and do not fall under the protective auspices of Genesis 12:1–3. Since European Jews constitute the largest group of immigrants in present day Israel and in the United States, how much easier for anti-Semites to discredit and persecute those whom they consider to be impostors, disconnected with the elect, Old Testament race of people. Anti-Semites sometimes cite this "loophole" to justify their hatred and persecution of Jews. Also, Middle Eastern Arabs can reject the Semitic background of Jewish immigrants to Palestine and thereby preserve the concocted view that gives sanction for conquest of the Land.[10]

Since the Khazar theory teaches that the Jews are largely a people who are now extinct as an ethic people, therefore, it renders mute, in their minds, the issue of the land of Israel as a future promise that will be fulfilled by God to the descendants of Abraham, Isaac, and Jacob. When people, especially those within Christendom, start thinking this way, it usually does not take long for anti-Semitic pogroms to arise. Today, with the re-established state of Israel, the Jew-hatred will increasingly be directed toward the national collective — the nation of Israel, which constitutes the new anti-Semitism.

## Growth of the Khazar Theory

Many who traffic in Jew-hatred or anti-Zionism have taken Koestler's thesis and run with it. They have developed a whole school of thought revolving around the notion that "Jews are such imposters to begin with and I can prove that they are not even really Jews at all." Thus, many influenced by the Khazar theory expand its horizons far beyond Koestler's intentions, as misguided as they were to begin with. In fact, Koestler concludes, "The problem of the Khazar infusion a thousand years ago, however fascinating, is irrelevant to modern Israel." Again he declares, "I am aware of the danger that it may be maliciously misinterpreted as a denial of the State of Israel's right to exist."[11] This is exactly what is now taking place! Israel's opponents use these claims in an attempt to justify their enmity to individual Jews and especially against the modern state of Israel, especially in the Muslim world. Princeton scholar Bernard Lewis tells us, "This theory, first put forward by an Austrian anthropologist in the early years of this century [20th], is supported by no evidence whatsoever. It has long since been abandoned by all serious scholars in the field, including those in Arab countries, where the Khazar theory is little used except in occasional political polemics."[12]

Just as Hitler's *Mein Kampf* and *The Protocols of The Learned Elders of Zion* have become popular reading in much of the radical Muslim world, so too has the Khazar theory made significant inroads onto the radical Muslim must-read list. One Muslim writer in an article on Aljazeera.com said,

> The irony of "the law of return" is that many of today's jews have no direct ancestral link to the jews of the Old Testament. Many, perhaps even most jewish people are descended from the Khazars, a people whose rulers converted to Judaism sometime during the 800's A.D. The Khazars never even set foot in Palestine![13]

James Jordan spews forth an invective when he speaks of "the heresy of Christian Zionism."[14] He then concludes "that most modern Jews are not Jews at all: They are Khazars."[15] Jordan continues as follows:

> The Khazari race seems to lie behind the Ashkenazik Jews of Eastern Europe. This kind of assertion can, of course, be debated. The real problem in the discussion is the notion that Jewishness is a blood or racial phenomenon. It is not.
>
> Biblically speaking, a Jew is someone who is covenanted into the people of Jews by circumcision. . . .
>
> All these people were Jew, but only a small fraction actually had any of Abraham's blood in them. . . . What this demonstrates is that covenant, not race, has always been the defining mark of a Jew.[16]

Following Jordan's lead, another replacement theologian, Southern Baptist John L. Bray, asserts that "the pure fact is that many of the Jews of the world are not only not pure Jews, but not even Jews at all."[17] "In addition to findings about the Khazar Jewish beginnings, we need to consider also that because of intermarriage, cross-breeding, etc.," declares Bray, "there is very little that can be called 'Jewish race' today."[18]

Evangelical Theodore Winston Pike, another militant anti-Zionist, also is attracted to the Khazar theory in his polemics against the legitimacy of the modern state of Israel. Pike tells us:

> The truth is, the majority of Jews living in Palestine highhandedly expelling Arabs from their homes are no more the descendants of Abraham than such Jewish converts as Sammy Davis Jr., Marilyn Monroe, or for that matter, the rest of us.
>
> The Jewish encyclopedias admit, of course, that the kingdom of Khazaria was converted to Judaism, but they do not pursue the implications of that fact as does the Jewish author, Koestler. It was Nesta Webster in the 1920s who first perceived the Khazar origins of most Eastern European Jews. Her deduction, however, was dismissed as "anti-Semitic" until Koestler, a liberal Jew of equal scholarship, has made the same claim with even greater insistence.[19]

Application of the Khazar theory can lead to a significant distortion of a Christian understanding of God's Word. Jordon wonders: "Are Bible-believing Christians supposed to support a Jewish State, for theological reasons? Such is the assertion of Jerry Falwell, and of the heresy of Christian Zionism."[20] I will now examine the veracity of such claims.

## The Khazar Theory Explained and Examined

No informed person on these issues questions the existence of a country in the Middle Ages composed largely of Turkish stock, between the Black and Caspian Seas during the seventh to tenth centuries named Khazaria, where the royal family only converted to Judaism. Khazaria was an actual nation in history.[21] However, it is still an unproved theory, as attractive as it may appear to some, lacking any scientific evidence that Ashkenazi Jews (about 85 percent of world Jewry) are primarily descended from the Khazars.

In 1976, when Koestler, a non-specialist in this field, put forth this theory, it was never taken seriously by linguists and most other scientists. This explains why the most vigorous promotion of his views are usually found within the circles of propagandists who have an ideological axe to grind and not by the scientific community. Like the *Protocols of the Learned Elders of Zion*, the forged document supporting a supposed Jewish world conspiracy, they so much want their theories to be real history, when they are not. Thieme provides an overview of the Khazars as follows:

> Who were the Khazars? They were semi-nomadic, Tataric in origin, a Turkic-speaking people who first appeared north of the Caucuses in the late second century A.D. In the fifth century they were subjugated by the Huns but rose to power two centuries later. Charging across the Russian steppes, these legendary warriors conquered the Crimea and extended their empire from the western shores of the Caspian Sea to the River Don, from the southern Ukraine to the region north of the Black Sea and as far as Kiev. They fought the Persians and Armenians; they battled Arab expansion, which was inspired by the advent of Islam after the death of Mohammed in 632. In addition, they fought the Byzantine Empire, which forcibly tried to make them Christian.
>
> The "khakan" or ruler was also the religious head of state of the Khazars. Tolerant of other religions, the khakan welcomed thousands of Jews from Asia Minor and the Byzantine Empire as well as Mohammedans and Christians. These three religious groups vied to convert the Khazars who practiced a primitive idolatrous religion.
>
> In A.D. 740 after considering the various religious viewpoints among these groups, the khakan embraced Judaism for himself and his people. His conversion was a compromise between Christianity and the religion of Islam. While Judaism was accepted as the official religion of the empire, the Khazar state still maintained tolerance toward other religious groups. The empire continued until A.D. 965 when it was overthrown by a coalition of Christian Russians and the Byzantines.[22]

Why did the khakan convert to Judaism and not Christianity or Islam? It is commonly thought that had the Khazars converted to Islam then they would have been swallowed up into the growing Islamic empire and lost their national identity and their autonomous authority as rulers. The same would have been true had they converted to Christianity. Khazaria would have been likely become part of the Byzantine Empire as well. By converting to Judaism, the khakan was able to maintain complete independence for the territory that he ruled. "But it could only maintain its independence by accepting neither Christianity nor Islam," notes Koestler of the Khazarian rulers, "for either choice would have automatically subordinated it to the authority of the Roman Emperor or the Caliph of Baghdad."[23]

Some scholars in this field of study think that it was primarily the elite of the Khazars that converted to Judaism[24] since "Khazar Judaism was never very strong."[25] Some think a primary reason for the national conversion is because some of the advisors were already Jewish, having immigrated there years earlier and worked their way up into governmental positions. Steven Collins, quoting from *The Universal Jewish Encyclopedia,* tells us, "It was chiefly due to the cultural superiority of the Daghestan Jews that the 'Kahan' (king) of the mighty state of Khazars was converted to Judaism together with his court and part of the Khazar population between the 8th and 9th centuries."[26] Besides the rulers, only a part of the Gentile Khazar population adopted Judaism over the next century, which means the Khazars were not a majority Jewish state. Other than the Jewish leadership, only a sizeable minority of Jews resided within Khazaria. "A total of only 4,000 new conversions to Judaism in a large nation was actually a small number of converts. The requirement of circumcision was likely a disincentive for most Khazar men to convert to Judaism."[27]

It is clear that there were already a great number of Jews who lived in Khazaria in the 8th century. "Large numbers of Jewish refugees had settled in what became Khazaria long before the Khazars were even a recognizable people," notes Collins. "The Jews had seen the Caucasus region as a hospitable refuge for centuries, and they went there in large numbers."[28]

When word began to circulate that the nation of Khazaria had converted to Judaism we learn that many Jews, especially from the Byzantine Empire and the Muslim world, immigrated to Khazaria since Jews were commonly persecuted in those Empires. They migrated to Khazaria for sanctuary and religious freedom. "Khazaria itself was full of Jewish immigrants from Constantinople . . . and these immigrants actually outnumbered the converts according to some sources,"[29] says Cameron Sawyer. This immigration greatly increased the number of Jews in the nation, and it was known to have a very large population of Jews migrating in from many other counties in those days. Sawyer makes the following point:

> Also, if the Ashkenazis are supposed to be Khazars, what happened to all the "real" Jews of Europe? The Khazars were only converted to Judaism in the 8th century. Jews — descendants of Jews from biblical Israel — have been living on the Black Sea coast, Southern Russia, and the Caucasus since before the birth of Christ . . . not to mention Germany, France, Italy, and Spain. So all these people just disappeared one day, to be suddenly replaced by Khazar converts?[30]

Since Khazaria was one of the few nations on earth at that time practicing religious freedom, this explains why the nation also had large populations of Christians, Muslims, and pagans who never converted to Judaism. The notion that multitudes of Gentiles simply overwhelmed Jewish bloodlines is simply not the case. The Jews of Khazaria appear to have had Jewish bloodlines just as strong as other Jews of their day.

When the nation was conquered, the Jews fled to other countries, and most of the population of Khazaria that were not Jewish were killed in these battles, immigrated elsewhere, or joined up with the Muslims and Christians. We are told, "The Jews of Khazaria migrated to Kiev and parts of Russia, while the remaining Khazars joined the Magyars and migrated to modern Hungary, becoming Christians."[31] Those converting to Christianity would not come into play when analyzing the modern Jewish gene pool. Here is a summary of what happened after the breakup of Khazaria:

> Most of the East European Jews migrated from the west to the east of the continent, and were not descended from the inhabitants of the Khazar Empire. They are actually a fusion of Balkan-Greek Jews from the Byzantine Empire, Babylonian Jews from the Abbasid Caliphate, Yiddish-speaking Jews from Germany, Sephardic Jews fleeing the Spanish inquisition, and Khazars. All these groups intermarried over the centuries, so that the Khazar converts disappeared as a distinguishable ethnical entity and their descendants became fully Jewish with Israelite ancestry. . . .
>
> If Khazarian ethnicity may be considered in any way of relevant influence among Russian Jews, the same is not valid for those of Poland; which is confirmed also by the following facts:

Polish life is completely extraneous to the Khazars.

The majority of Polish Jews came from the west, not the east.

There are no places in Poland that may recall Khazar origin.

Most Ashkenazi Jews have Germanic, not Khazar, surnames and customs.

There's not any relevant trace of the Khazarian language among Jews; on the contrary, the Ashkenazim's tongue, Yiddisch, is evidently of German origin.[32]

It seems clear, based upon the historical records of the matter, that the Khazar aspect of Ashkenazi Jewish history provided a very small contribution to the makeup of their gene pool. Based upon the historical records alone, there is precious little support to actually think that about 85 percent of Jews in the world today are not descendants of Abraham, Isaac, and Jacob. The Khazar theory falls to the ground due to lack of evidence to support its conclusions based upon sifting the historical evidence.

## DNA and the Khazars

The opinion previously reached by historians and ethnologists concerning the Khazars is now confirmed with the development of the modern science of DNA analysis as a reliable way to discover one's genealogical heritage. Kevin Alan Brook[33] is a leading researcher on the Khazars and tells us the following:

> We no longer need to rely on speculation. It is now a known FACT that German Jews mingled with other Jews when they came east. It is also clear that the ancient Israelites possessed those Y-DNA patterns that are found in common among Sephardic Jews, Ashkenazic Jews, Kurdish Jews, and Indian Jews, despite the fact that ultimately those patterns may have earlier stemmed, in part, from somewhere in Kurdistan or Armenia or Iraq. The Middle Eastern Y-DNA patterns in the J and E haplogroups cannot be explained by Khazars.[34]

Brook's overall conclusion of Khazar origins is as follows:

In summary, Eastern European Jews are descended from a mixture of German and Austrian Jews, Czech Jews, and East Slavic Jews. The East Slavic Jews may have roots in both the Khazar and Byzantine empires, hence necessitating our further study of Jewish life in those lands. But the largest and most influential proportion of Eastern European Jews came from Central Europe. By this analysis we can show that the dominant ethnic element among Eastern European Jews is Judean — the ancient Jewish people of Judea in the Middle East.[35]

Cameron Sawyer, based upon examination of DNA analysis, comes to a similar conclusion about the authenticity of the ethnic descent of the Jewish group under investigation.

In any case, modern genetic analysis now gives us very precise information about bloodlines, migrations, and the genetic relationships between peoples, and has settled the matter once and for all. Ashkenazi Jews are, in fact, close relatives of Sephardic and other Jews (except, apparently, the Ethiopian Jews), somewhat less close but still very close relatives of the Arabs and other Eastern Mediterranean peoples, and are predominantly descended from the Hebrews who lived in Israel 2,000 years ago, with a notably small admixture of European, Slavic, and other blood. Tracing direct paternal lines of descent (based on analysis of the "Y" chromosome), researchers found that the most common direct paternal ancestors of modern Ashkenazi Jews are the Judeans of ancient Israel, with more than 50% of modern Ashkenazi Jews being so descended. 12.7% of modern Ashkenazi Jews have direct paternal lines of descent from either Eastern Europeans (including Slavs) or Khazars.[36]

DNA analysis is able to establish with certainty what history has already demonstrated: the Jews of modern Israel really are descendants of Abraham, Isaac, and Jacob as concluded by Rabbi Yaakov Kleiman:

The genetic studies of Jewish men from all of the major communities of the Jewish Diaspora confirm that the original Jewish population originated in the Middle East, and from there, spread throughout the world. As the Bible predicted, the Hebrews who lived in the Land of Israel for over one thousand years were dispersed and scattered literally to the four corners of the earth. . . .

Also predicted and prophesized was that, despite worldwide dispersal, the Jewish nation would not become lost among the nations. Scriptures prophesized and promised that the Jewish People would retain their unique identity, and eventually be restored to their ancient homeland. The genetics studies have shown that this most unlikely scenario has in fact come true as well.[37]

## Khazar Conclusions

The Khazar theory has been completely refuted by both scholarly research into the history of the Khazars and, more recently, by ethnologist evidence showing that Jews from all parts of the world are genetically closely related to Middle Eastern Jews and not so closely related to non-Jewish Russians, Eastern Europeans, or others from that region. "Dr. Michael Hammer showed that based exclusively on the Y-chromosome (parental) shows that Ashkenazi Jews are more closely related to Yemenite Jews, Iraqi Jews, Sephardic Jews, Kurdish Jews, and Arabs than they are to European Christian populations,"[38] notes Joel Bainerman. True research on the matter reveals that only a small percentage of Jews have any descent through the Khazars. So it appears that the Khazar theory is just that, a theory, and not a very good one.

The Khazar theory canard was developed last century by individuals and groups that were already predisposed toward anti-Semitism. When the self-hating Jew, Arthur Koestler, penned his book in the 1970s, these groups were attracted to his work like a bee to honey. Driven by anti-Zionist impulses, many of these biased "researchers" exaggerated Koestler's claims. Even Koestler did not claim that Ashkenazi or Khazar Jews have no Middle Eastern ancestry. Koestler did not want his research, flawed as it may have been, taken to extreme conclusions.

> In the first place, I am aware of the danger that it may be maliciously misinterpreted as a denial of the State of Israel's right to exist. But that right is not based on the

hypothetical origins of the Jewish people, nor on the myth-
ological covenant of Abraham with God; it is based on
international law — i.e., on the United Nations' decision in
1947 to partition Palestine, once Turkish province, then a
British Mandated Territory, into an Arab and a Jewish State.
Whatever the Israeli citizens' racial origins, and whatever
illusions they entertain about them, their State exists *de jure*
and *de facto*, and cannot be undone, except by genocide.
Without entering into controversial issues, one may add, as
a matter of historical fact, that the partition of Palestine was
the result of a century of peaceful Jewish immigration and
pioneering effort, which provide the ethical justification
for the State's legal existence. Whether the chromosomes
of its people contain genes of Khazar or Semitic, Roman or
Spanish origin, is irrelevant, and cannot affect Israel's right
to exist — nor the moral obligation of any civilized person,
Gentile or Jew, to defend that right. Even the geographical
origin of the native Israeli's parents or grandparents tends to
be forgotten in the bubbling racial melting pot. The problem of the Khazar infusion a thousand years ago, however
fascinating, is irrelevant to modern Israel.[39]

"The results support the hypothesis that the paternal gene pools of Jewish
communities from Europe, North Africa, and the Middle East descended
from a common Middle Eastern ancestral population," concludes Sawyer,
"and suggests that most Jewish communities have remained relatively iso-
lated from neighboring non-Jewish communities during and after the Diaspora."[40] It is safe to conclude that most of the Jews living today in Israel and
still in the Diaspora are clear descendants of Abraham, Isaac, and Jacob.

## Are Modern Jews Really of Jewish Descent?

In addition to advocating the Khazar theory, James Jordan tells us: "The
real problem in the discussion is the notion that Jewishness is a blood or
racial phenomenon. It is not." Jordan continues, "Biblically speaking, a Jew
is someone who is covenanted into the people of the Jews by circumcision.
. . . What this demonstrates is that covenant, not race, has always been the
defining mark of a Jew."[41] Jordan does not stop with these remarks; he was

just warming up. He states further, "Modern apostate Jews have absolutely no theological, and therefore no historical and legal right to the land of Palestine."[42] "Christian Zionism is blasphemy. It is heresy. Christians have no theological stake whatsoever in the modern State of Israel. It is an anti-God, anti-Christ nation."[43] So those who think like Jordan believe that Israel either never had a Jewish racial identity or lost it over time.

It is the Bible that divides mankind into Jew and Gentile, denoting one's descent by birth. One may repudiate the religious aspects of Judaism, but one cannot escape the genealogical fact that he or she was born within the Jewish race. The same is true of a Gentile. One may be born of Chinese descent, but there is nothing that can be said or done to change the fact that he or she is Chinese. The Nazis during the Holocaust made little distinction between deeply religious Jews and secular Jews. They killed them all when they had the opportunity. The same is true today. The Muslims kill Jews today whether they are religious or secular. It does not matter to them.

## The Biblical Definition of Jewishness

Since the Bible is God's inerrant revelation, it is the supreme authority on which to settle any matter to which it speaks. God's viewpoint on any issue is how we know ultimately what is true or false. The Bible speaks clearly and loudly concerning the issue of Jewishness. Scripture teaches that those who are descendants of Abraham, Isaac, and Jacob make up the people or nation we call Israel (Gen. 12:1–3, 13:15–16, 15:4–5, 26:2–5, 24, 28:13–15). Jewishness is a nationality based upon descent, whether one obeys God or not. Hebrew Christian Arnold Fruchtenbaum correctly summaries Israel as "all descendants of Abraham, Isaac, and Jacob, also known as the Jews, the Jewish people, Israelites, Hebrews, etc. The term is not limited to the present political and national state in the Middle East, which is merely a part of the whole; nor is it limited to those who adhere to the religion of Judaism only."[44] British postmillennialist Erroll Hulse provides an excellent overview of the biblical use of the word *Jew*.

> Most references to the Jews (Yehudiim) made in the Old Testament are to be found in the book of Esther, but frequently also in Jeremiah, Nehemiah, and Ezra. In Babylon, the word Jew in the strict sense signified someone of Judah. Almost every reference (and there are about two

hundred) in the New Testament refer to the Jews in a general sense whether they lived in the South, the North or abroad. The terms "children of Israel" and "sons of Jacob" are often used in the Old Testament to describe the Jews.[45]

The broader term *Israel* "appears over two thousand times in the Old Testament and seventy times in the New Testament. This term refers to a specific ethnic group. . . . The name *Yisra'el* was conferred on Jacob (Ge 32:28), Abraham's grandson, and means 'solider of God' or 'God persists.' "[46] Israel began as a patriarchal clan when Abraham came out of Babylon, went to Egypt, and 400 years later returned to the Promised Land as a true nation of two or three million. Yet Jordan imagines a problem in that Israel did indeed incorporate into the nation many non-Jews down through her history.

> When Abraham was commanded to circumcise, he was told to circumcise his entire household, including his 318 fighting men and his other domestic servants (Gen. 14:14, 17:10–14). Competent scholars imagine that Sheik Abraham's household probably included at the very least 3,000 persons. These servants multiplied as the years went by, and Jacob inherited them all (Gen. 27:37). Although only 70 from the loins of Jacob went down into Egypt, so many servants went along that they had to be given the whole land of Goshen in which to live.[47]

Is this supposed to be a problem? Over time it appears that the Gentiles who became part of Abraham's clan integrated with his descendants so that by the time of the Exodus that nation was indeed Jewish — descendants of Abraham, Isaac, and Jacob. At least this is the view that the Bible takes toward this matter. The Lord promised Abraham: "To your descendants I will give this land" (Gen. 12:7). "I will make your descendants as the dust of the earth, so that if anyone can number the dust of the earth, then your descendants can also be numbered" (Gen. 13:16). "And He took him outside and said, 'Now look toward the heavens, and count the stars, if you are able to count them.' And He said to him, 'So shall your descendants be' " (Gen. 15:5). "God said to Abram, 'Know for certain that your descendants will be strangers in a land that is not theirs, where they will be enslaved and oppressed four hundred years' " (Gen. 15:13). "Moreover, the angel of the LORD said to her, 'I will greatly multiply your descendants so that they will be too many to count' " (Gen. 16:10). "I will establish My covenant between Me and you and your descendants after you throughout their generations for an everlasting covenant, to be God to you and to your descendants after you" (Gen. 17:7). I could go on with many more similar passages that indicate that God thought of all of those in the line of descent as the offspring of Abraham, Isaac, and Jacob.

Even though the Jews surely have intermarried with Gentiles, that does not invalidate their Jewishness any more than intermarriage that was practiced in the Old Testament did not invalidate their Jewishness. Jesus Himself had a number of Gentiles within His genealogical line, yet He was certainly Jewish. In the time of the New Testament these people were still known as Jews — the descendants of Abraham, Isaac, and Jacob. Jesus referred to the residents of Israel in His day as *Jews*. When reading the New Testament, there does not appear to be a problem identifying who the Jews were in Christ's day. The notion that Jews cannot have the blood of Abraham, Isaac, and Jacob flowing through their veins is purely one manufactured by those with an anti-Semitic bias.

Since there was about a 2,000-year period from the call of Abraham until the time of Christ, and Jesus referred to the residents of Israel as Jews, then we have a precedent to do so today. It has been about another 2,000 years since the time of Christ until our present day. If the descendants of Abraham, Isaac, and Jacob were considered Jews after 2,000 years by Jesus in His day, then why should they not be considered descendants of Abraham, Isaac, and Jacob today, after another 2,000 years have passed? In fact, the last 2,000 years have seen some Gentile intermarriage, but for the most part, the nations have shut up the Jewish people into their own ghettos and not allowed them to intermingle with Gentiles. Even though an unintended result by perpetrators, anti-Semitism has helped to keep the blood of Abraham, Isaac, and Jacob flowing through the veins of modern Jewry. Also, those Jews that have repeatedly married Gentiles have lost their Jewish identity and are no longer part of the Jewish race and indeed are not considered Jews after a while.

### Future Biblical References to Jews

Since the Bible is the ultimate authority on any matter, it is significant to realize that both the Old and New Testaments speak of a specific destiny for Israel or the Jewish people in a day future to our own time. Since God's Word tells us that there will be Jewish people in the world even beyond our own day, then Divine viewpoint should trump the imaginations of human viewpoint any day. This means that there has to be Jewish people who have the blood of Abraham, Isaac, and Jacob flowing through their veins for these prophecies to occur. When has God ever failed to bring to pass what He has decreed? Never! What are some of these passages?

About 3,400 years ago Moses predicted a future time when the nation of Israel "will seek the LORD . . . with all your heart and all your soul. When you are in distress . . . in the latter days, you will return to the LORD your God and listen to His voice" (Deut. 4:29–30). No biblically literate person would say that the nation of Israel has ever fulfilled this passage at any time in their past, and thus, it is still a future event. So there must me a nation of Israel in the future, which would mean that the Jews of today would have to be actual Jews in order to provide a bridge to this future time.

God spoke through Jeremiah about 2,600 years ago and said, " 'For, behold, days are coming,' declares the LORD, 'when I will restore the fortunes of My people Israel and Judah.' The LORD says, 'I will also bring them back to the land that I gave to their forefathers, and they shall possess it' " (Jer. 30:3). " 'Alas! for that day is great, there is none like it; and it is the time of Jacob's distress, but he will be saved from it' " (Jer. 30:7). " 'Fear not, O Jacob My servant,' declares the LORD, 'and do not be dismayed, O Israel; for behold, I will save you from afar and your offspring from the land of their captivity. And Jacob will return,and will be quiet and at ease, and no one will make him afraid. For I am with you,' declares the LORD, 'to save you; for I will destroy completely all the nations where I have scattered you, only I will not destroy you completely. But I will chasten you justly and will by no means leave you unpunished' " (Jer. 30:10–11). " 'You shall be My people, and I will be your God' " (Jer. 30:22). "In the latter days you will understand this." (Jer. 30:24). When has this ever occurred in the past? Like the passage in Deuteronomy, we see that Israel will go through a time of tribulation or distress, which will be in the *latter days*, leading to the spiritual restoration of the nation. Once again, no one would say that national Israel has ever in history arisen to such a spiritual level. It can only be in the future, which means the Jews have to exist as Jews future to our own day in order for this to occur.

Many other Old Testament passages could be cited that speak of Jewish existence beyond our current day, but one final example from Daniel will be noted. "Now at that time Michael, the great prince who stands guard over the sons of your people, will arise. And there will be a time of distress such as never occurred since there was a nation until that time; and at that time your people, everyone who is found written in the book, will be rescued" (Dan. 12:1). "He said, 'Go your way, Daniel, for these words are concealed and sealed up until the end time.' " (Dan. 12:9). As in the two previous passages, we see that same pattern in Daniel. There will be a time of tribulation or distress for "your people," which are Daniel's people (i.e., the Jewish people). This will take place in the end time and Israel will come into a new spiritual relationship with the Lord.

The Bible anticipates a future time in which God will interact with His people Israel. Such a future period is also expected in the New Testament. Paul speaks of future plans for Israel in Romans when he says,

> For I do not want you, brethren, to be uninformed of this mystery — so that you will not be wise in your own estimation — that a partial hardening has happened to Israel until the fullness of the Gentiles has come in; and so all Israel will be saved; just as it is written, "The Deliverer will come from Zion, He will remove ungodliness from Jacob. This is My covenant with them, when I take away their sins." From the standpoint of the gospel they are enemies for your sake, but from the standpoint of God's choice they are beloved for the sake of the fathers; for the gifts and the calling of God are irrevocable (Rom. 11:25–29).

We see in this passage that current Jewish rejection of the gospel by most, not all, is temporary and will come to an end when the full number of elect Gentiles are added to the Church through faith in Christ. It will be after that time that every Jewish person alive, when the Deliverer will come from Zion, will come to faith in the Messiahship of Jesus. No one would say that this has yet to occur in history. Thus, Jews must exist as descendants of Abraham, Isaac, and Jacob in the future for this to occur. This means that there has to be Jewish people alive and well on planet Earth today.

The Apostle John, in his well-known and final book of the New Testament canon, speaks of future events in Revelation 4 through 22. It is clear that the Jewish people will be around when these events unfold since they are referenced throughout the book. Revelation 12 is an entire chapter that speaks of their persecution during the second half of that seven-year period. However, Revelation 7 not only speaks of a multitude of the bond-servants of God, but that they are said to be "one hundred and forty-four thousand sealed from every tribe of the sons of Israel" (Rev. 7:4). If that is not clear enough, the biblical text tells us the specific tribes of Israel from which 12,000 males are taken from as follows: "from the tribe of Judah, twelve thousand were sealed, from the tribe of Reuben twelve thousand, from the tribe of Gad twelve thousand, from the tribe of Asher twelve thousand, from the tribe of Naphtali twelve thousand, from the tribe of Manasseh twelve thousand, from the tribe of Simeon twelve thousand, from the tribe of Levi twelve thousand, from the tribe of Issachar twelve thousand, from the tribe of Zebulun twelve thousand, from the tribe of Joseph twelve thousand, from the tribe of Benjamin, twelve thousand were sealed" (Rev. 7:5–8). Even if Israel's tribal records were lost to human beings 2,000 years ago, it does not mean that God cannot keep track of one's nationality. After all, He is the one who will seal the 144,000 Jewish servants via a supernatural act.

Revelation 7 not only demonstrates that Jewish men will exist in the future, but that God Himself can identify who they are. Such implications mean that not only are Jews viewed by the Bible as a distinct race in contrast to Gentiles, but they will remain so throughout history. Not only does the Bible teach that Jewish descendants of Abraham, Isaac, and Jacob can be identified as a distinct race after almost 4,000 years, but that God will even be able to distinguish their tribal identity into the future. This can only mean that there is a distinct Jewish race today.

## Conclusion

Israel, during her 4,000 years of existence, has been by far the most literate people in the history of the world. Rabbi Kleman's DNA studies demonstrate that, "Genetics research as described has clearly shown that the Jewish people today are the descendants of the ancient biblical Hebrews."[48] In addition, no nation has kept better records of her own history, whether through divinely inspired Scripture or mere human writings than the Jewish people. These records provide ample evidence that the Jews of today have had continual existence, even though they were often scattered around the world for much of their existence. We see that not only do recent DNA studies provide a scientific basis for verifying that modern Jewry really are descendants of Abraham, Isaac, and Jacob, this view is also supported by biblical logic and the testimony of history. Jews are a racial class that stands in contrast with Gentiles, according to the Bible. Only bias or prejudice would lead one to a contrary opinion when examined in the light of Scripture. Therefore, it is with utmost certainty that anyone examining the record should conclude that those who are Jews today, whether in or out of the land of Israel, have the blood of Abraham, Isaac, and Jacob flowing through their veins. This fact provides a basis for their Zionistic claim that the land of Israel belongs to the Jews because God gave it to them.

## Endnotes

1. James B. Jordan, "The Future of Israel Reexamined" (Part 1), *Biblical Horizons*, no. 27, July 1991, p. 4.
2. Kevin Alan Brook, "From the East, West, and South: Documenting the Foundation of Jewish Communities in Eastern Europe" in *Roots-Key*, Newsletter of the Jewish Genealogical Society of Los Angeles, vol. 24: no. 1, Spring 2004, p. 6.
3. James B. Jordan is a Presbyterian replacement theologian coming from the preterist, postmillennial, and covenant theology orientation.
4. Jordan, "Future of Israel" (Part 1), p. 4.
5. Ibid., p. 4.
6. Ibid., p. 4.
7. Ibid., p. 4.
8. Arthur Koestler, *The Thirteenth Tribe* (New York: Random House, 1976).
9. For a history of the rise of the Khazar theory see Robert Singerman, "Contemporary Racist and Judeophobic Ideology Discovers the Khazars, or, Who Really Are the Jews?" on the website of the National Foundation for Jewish Culture located at the following: www2.jewishculture.org/jewish_scholarship/feinstein/singerman.html.
10. Robert B. Thieme Jr., *Anti-Semitism* (Houston, TX: Robert B. Thieme, Jr., Bible Ministries, 1991), p. 77.
11. Koestler, *Thirteenth Tribe*, p. 223.
12. Bernard Lewis, *Semites and Anti-Semites: An Inquiry into Conflict and Prejudice* (New York: W.W. Norton and Company, 1999), p. 48.
13. Albert D. Pastore, "The Dancing Israelis: An Unprecedented Honest Analysis of 9/11 and Bush's War on Terror" from the website Aljazeera.com; www.aljazeera.com/cgi-bin/conspiracy_theory/fullstory.asp?id=303.
14. James B. Jordan, "Christian Zionism and Messianic Judaism," in *The Sociology of the Church: Essays in Reconstruction* (Tyler, TX: Geneva Ministries, 1986), p. 176.
15. Jordan, "Christian Zionism," p. 176–77.
16. Ibid., p. 177.

17. John L. Bray, *Israel in Bible Prophecy* (Lakeland, FL: John L. Bray Ministry, 1983), p. 44.
18. Ibid., p. 44.
19. Theodore Winston Pike, *Israel: Our Duty . . . Our Dilemma* (Oregon City, OR: Big Sky Press, 1984), p. 328.
20. Jordan, "Christian Zionism," p. 178.
21. *Encyclopaedia Judaica*, Vol. 10, reference to "Khazars," p. 944–54.
22. Thieme, *Anti-Semitism*, p. 76–77.
23. Koestler, *Thirteenth Tribe*, p. 58.
24. Kevin Alan Brook, *The Jews of Khazaria* (Lanham, MD: Rowman & Littlefield Publishers, 2002), p. 136–39.
25. *Encyclopaedia Judaica*, Vol. 10, reference to "Khazars," p. 949.
26. Steven M. Collins, "The Khazars and The Modern Jews," posted at www.britam.org/steven-collins-khazars.html.
27. Collins, "The Khazars."
28. Ibid.
29. Sawyer, "Zionism and the Talmud," World Association of International Studies, Blog Archive at cgi. stanford.edu/group/wais/cgi-bin/index.php?p=108.
30. Ibid.
31. Collins, "The Khazars."
32. Anonymous, "The Khazars: Who Were the Khazars, and With Whom Should They Be Identified Today?" http://www.imninalu.net/Khazars.htm.
33. Brook, *The Jews of Khazaria*.
34. Kevin Alan Brook, "Re: Jews and the Khazars," on the Jewish Genealogy Forum, www.genealogy.com, posted on Aug. 4, 2004.
35. Brook, "From the East, West, and South," p. 6.
36. Sawyer, "Zionism and the Talmud."
37. Rabbi Yaakov Kleiman, DNA & Tradition: The Genetic Link to the Ancient Hebrews (Jerusalem: Devora Publishing Co., 2004), p. 169.
38. Joel Bainerman, "So What If a Small Portion of World Jewry Are Descendants Of Khazars!" Jan. 3, 2003, www.rense.com/general33/sowhat.htm.
39. Koestler, *Thirteenth Tribe*, p.223.
40. Sawyer, "Zionism and the Talmud."
41. Jordan, "Christian Zionism," p. 177.
42. Ibid. p. 183.
43. Ibid. p. 184.
44. Arnold Fruchtenbaum, *Israelology: The Missing Link in Systematic Theology*, rev. ed. (Tustin, CA: Ariel Ministries Press, 1992), p. 2
45. Erroll Hulse, *The Restoration of Israel* (Worthing, England: Henry E. Walter, Ltd., 1982), p. 175.
46. Ronald E. Diprose, *Israel in the Development of Christian Thought* (Rome: Istitutio Biblico Evangelico Italiano, 2000), p. 7.
47. Jordan, "Christian Zionism," p. 177.
48. Kleiman, *DNA & Tradition*, p. 173.

CHAPTER 7

# WHAT IS
# ANTI-SEMITISM?

**anti-Semitism**, n. — Theory, action, or practice directed against the Jews. Hence anti-Semite, one who is hostile or opposed to the Jews; anti-Semitic.[1] — Oxford English Dictionary

**anti-Christian Zionism** — Stephen Sizer "claimed his fellow Christians who support Israel — Christian Zionists, are really no different from ISIS or Al Qaeda."[2]

Traditional anti-Semitism relates to the hatred and persecution of the Jews during the last two millennia. Such anti-Semitism was all too common before the rebirth in 1948 of the modern state of Israel. Since Israel's founding, a second form of anti-Semitism has developed, which involves hostility toward this new national entity. Thus, the "new anti-Semitism" is primarily a hatred of the current state of Israel.

The new anti-Semitism began to develop shortly after the establishment of the modern state. By 1974, Arnold Forster and Benjamin Epstein wrote a book entitled *The New Anti-Semitism*[3] to call attention to this development. Forster and Epstein say that their book "exposes, in all its complexity, a new anti-Semitism that is based on the old but emanates from different and surprisingly respectable sources."[4] "While the memory of the Nazi Holocaust was fresh in mind, anti-Semitism was silenced," note Foster and Epstein. "As that memory fades, however . . . there are new growths of anti-Semitism."[5]

Fast forward to our present time and we find that there are a number of new books calling our attention to the new anti-Semitism, which revolves around the world's hatred of national Israel. In August 2003, Harvard Law professor Alan Dershowitz released *The Case For Israel*;[6] joined by Phyllis Chesler's *The New Anti-Semitism: The Current Crisis and What We Must Do About It*.[7] Both books recognize that many hide their anti-Semitism in the guise of being anti-Israel or anti-Zionist. Such anti-Zionism has been on open public display since the attack on the World Trade Center and the Pentagon on 9/11. Today it is common to hear many blame American support for Israel as the root cause of Arab and Islamic terror against us. Just like a battered wife, if the USA would just develop a more "balanced" foreign policy then she would not have provoked these supposedly deserved attacks. This kind of rhetoric is bad enough coming from the Arab and Islamic world, but we are now starting to hear this mantra echoed within the evangelical Christian world.

## Evangelical Opposition to Israel

There have always been evangelicals opposed to the modern state of Israel. In the past, however, they were usually content to simply state their views and not really exhibit much public opposition to modern Israel. Things have changed since 9/11. In parallel to Arab and secular criticism to national Israel, we have seen a number of books,[8] articles,[9] and even an "Open

Letter,"[10] warning of evangelical support of Israel. This is sad in light of the fact that God has brought them back to His land in preparation for the fulfillment of future prophetic events. The current state of Israel is the beginning phase of great things that the God of the Bible has in store for His elect nation. So why would any Bible-believing Christian oppose what God is doing in Israel today?

Basically, at the core of almost all evangelical opposition to Israel is the belief that the Church has replaced Israel forever. The historic theological terms for this view are "replacement theology" or "supersessionism." For Colin Chapman, his replacement theology means that "because the coming of the kingdom of God through Jesus the Messiah has transformed and reinterpreted all the promises and prophecies in the Old Testament."[11] Such views are usually, though not always, related to a system of belief known as "covenant theology." Why is this important?

These views are important because down through Church history when the Church becomes dominated by such thought, it usually gives rise to theological anti-Semitism. Theological anti-Semitism is based upon the belief that national Israel is finished in history, forever replaced by the Church. I believe that evangelicals who hold such a view are susceptible to some degree of anti-Semitism, even though many of them would scoff at such a notion. I believe history supports my opinion.

## The Road to Holocaust

Historian Raul Hilberg has summarized this historical tendency[12] with the following insightful statement, as noted by Hal Lindsey:

> Throughout Western history, three consecutive policies have been applied against Jewry in its dispersion.
>
> To summarize: Since the fourth century after Christ there have been three anti-Jewish policies: *conversion, expulsion,* and *annihilation.* The second [*expulsion*] appeared as an alternative to the first, and the third [*annihilation*] as an alternative to the second.
>
> The Nazi destruction process did not come out of a void; it was the culmination of a cyclical trend. We have observed the trend in three successive goals of anti-Jewish administrators. (1) The missionaries of Christianity has said

in effect: YOU HAVE NO RIGHT TO LIVE AMONG US AS JEWS. (2) The secular rulers who followed had proclaimed: YOU HAVE NO RIGHT TO LIVE AMONG US. (3) The German Nazis at last decreed: YOU HAVE NO RIGHT TO LIVE.

These progressively more drastic goals brought in their wake a slow and steady growth of anti-Jewish actions and anti-Jewish thinking. The process began with the attempt to drive the Jews into Christianity. The development was continued in order to force the victims into exile. It was finished when the Jews were driven to their deaths.[13]

In a rare moment of candor, Reformed theologian Steve Schlissel seems to share Lindsey's and my basic view on the rise and development of anti-Semitism within the history of the Church. After citing an overview of the history of anti-Semitism through Origen, Augustine, Chrysostom, Ambrose, and Jerome, Schlissel (himself of Jewish descent) then quotes approvingly Hilberg's famous quote from Lindsey.

> Viewing the plight of the Jews in Christian lands from the fourth century to the recent holocaust, one Jew observed, "First we were told 'You're not good enough to live among us as Jews.' Then we were told, 'You're not good enough to live among us.' Finally we were told, 'You're not good enough to live.' "[14]

Schlissel then comments upon Hilberg's assessment by declaring something Hal Lindsey and I could have said:

> This devastatingly accurate historical analysis was the fruit of an error, a building of prejudice and hate erected upon a false theological foundation. The blindness of the church regarding the place of the Jew in redemptive history is, I believe, directly responsible for the wicked sins and attitudes described above. What the church believes about the Jews has *always* made a difference. But the church has not *always* believed a lie.[15]

Only when the Church believes God has a future for national Israel does she believe what the Bible teaches (both Old and New Testaments), and this view vaccinates her from any susceptibility to theological anti-Semitism.

## Anti-Zionism and Anti-Semitism

Some evangelicals say that anti-Zionism is not the same as anti-Semitism.[16] This is true. But in our day, it is almost the same because of the close identity of the Jewish race with Israel. David Rausch points out that many evangelicals "believe that some of their colleagues who oppose the premillennial view can go too far in their hostility toward Israel. In other words, anti-Zionism could become anti-Semitism."[17] Rausch expresses further concern when he calls our attention to an interview conducted with G. Douglas Young[18] in Israel: "Dr. Young expressed deep concern about the ugliness of the anti-Israel teaching that was being spread through evangelical liberal arts colleges and seminaries by an ever-growing, hostile force of academicians."[19] Catholic scholar Father Edward Flannery, who has written much on the subject of anti-Semitism, has said, "To the question, Is anti-Zionism in its various degrees and forms anti-Semitic? . . . Not necessarily, but almost always."[20]

However, many evangelicals seem unwilling to admit that one's view of eschatology makes a difference on this matter, as noted above. Rausch points out:

> Contrary to popular opinion, this prophetic viewpoint [dispensationalism] combated anti-Semitism and sought to reinstate the biblical promises that God had made to the Jewish people through Abraham — biblical promises that postmillennial Christendom had determined were null and void.[21]

One's view of eschatology makes a difference! July 18, 1290, was the day in which Jews were expelled from England because they were viewed as dangerous people who were considered a threat to "Christian" England. Once again, theological anti-Semitism within the Church resulted in persecution of the Jews. In 1655, the Jews were readmitted to England under Oliver Cromwell, a premillennialist.[22] Why? It was because of eschatology. Due to Puritan influence, many English Christians began to see a future for the Jews and national Israel.[23] It was as the "Hebraic and Judicial tendencies in England thought and theology reached their zenith by 1650 and it is in this 'prophetical' context,"[24] notes Peter Toon, that led to the readmission of the Jews. Some Puritans even "believed that the tribulations that had come upon England in the Civil War were, in part God's judgment upon the nation for its maltreatment of Jews in the past."[25] The arguments that won the day, according to Toon, were eschatological. He summarizes, "The more common ground of advocating readmission, amongst theologians and preachers, seems to have been based on eschatological considerations."[26]

More recently, Hal Lindsey revealed that a classmate of his in seminary (early 1960s) was from Germany. The student's father was "head of the German army officer's union, which in English is called The Steel Helmet."[27] Before Hitler rose to power in Germany, the seminary student remembered many meetings that took place between his father and Hitler and his friends, trying to win his favor in order to help them rise to power. "But when he began to grasp Hitler's 'Final Solution' plan for the Jews, he flatly disagreed. He was an evangelical Christian, a Plymouth Brethren who believed in a literal interpretation of prophecy and the covenants God made with the Israelites. In other words, he was a true Premillennialist."[28] "At considerable personal risk and financial loss," notes Lindsey, "he packed up the family, sneaked out what money he could, and came to the USA. He left Hitler's Germany for one fundamental reason — he believed God's Word, what it said concerning Israel."[29]

The Bible indicates that even greater days of anti-Semitism and persecution are yet future for the Jewish people in and out of the land of Israel. (See Ezek. 20, 22; Zech. 12–14; Matt. 24:4–31; Rev. 12, etc.) Yet Genesis 12:3, which says, "I will bless those who bless you, and the one who curses you I will curse," has not expired and is still in force. This is true in spite of the multitude of theological systems men devise in their attempts to deny God's clear Word on this matter.

## Are Christian Zionists Dangerous?

There is a wide-ranging group of people in society who are voicing their opinion that Christian Zionists are a dangerous group of people. Many from liberal leftist to right wing conservatives warn their constituency about the supposed real dangers our message possesses. Frankly, such scare tactics are nothing more than an attempt to demonize those within our camp as a tactic to smear us in the eyes of the general public. Other than some political power that we are capable of exerting at the polls occasionally, Christian Zionists in no way pose a threat to anyone.

The late Grace Halsell, a secular, non-Christian, wrote in 1986 concerning a feared "Israeli-U.S. fundamentalist alliance," and concluded the following:

> . . . it can last long enough to cause a catastrophe of far-reaching consequences. If we do not recognize the danger they pose, the extremists will have time enough in their unsacred alliance to trigger a war that would not end until we have destroyed Planet Earth through self-fulfilling prophecy.[30]

We are dangerous because we are said to pursue a self-fulfilling prophecy. That our prophecy views could be the catalyst for nuclear war is such an extreme stretch that even anti-Christian Zionist Gary DeMar cannot buy it and says of Halsell: "This is not an accurate picture of the Armageddon scenario."[31] Halsell came out with another book, entitled *Forcing God's Hand: Why Millions Pray for a Quick Rapture — And Destruction of Planet Earth.*[32]

Jane Lampman of the *Christian Science Monitor* has written an article on the supposed dangers of Evangelicals who support Israel in an article entitled "Mixing Prophecy and Politics."[33] She says some Christians and Jews are speaking out against our prophetic views, "which they see as a dangerous mix of religion and politics that is harmful to Israel and endangers prospects for peace with the Palestinians."[34] Lampman quotes Timothy Weber saying, "The danger is that, when people believe they 'know' how things are going to turn out and then act on those convictions, they can make these prophecies self-fulfilling, and bring on some of the things they predict."[35] Preterists, especially full-preterists,[36] often teach that Christian support for Israel is such a dangerous viewpoint that they fear it will lead to a self-fulfilling prophecy of World War III.[37]

A number of anti-Christian Zionists are painting the following scenario concerning the implications of our pro-Israel stance: The United States is the only significant country that regularly supports Israel, thus enabling the Jewish state to be a strong military force in the Middle East. If it were not for American support, it is likely Israel would not be the supposed bully they are to the poor, oppressed Arabs in Israel. The United States is Israel's enabler.

Support within the United States is because of the influence of pro-Israel, Christian Zionists that are a swing influence politically. If American foreign policy were left to the normal geo-political factors and not the result of religious influence, then we would have a more balanced policy toward the Middle East; one that would be more cordial to the Arab world. Since so many American Evangelicals are pro-Israel, this has provoked the Arab and Muslim world to attack us. If it were not for Christian Zionism, they say, we would not have had the first Gulf War, the war in Iraq or Afghanistan, 9/11 would have never happened, oil would be in much greater supply and cheaper, and the economy would be much better. It almost sounds as if there would be no real problems in the world if it were not for Israel and their prime enablers, Christian Zionists, to hear them talk. If this is true, then the Gentiles were able to have a couple of pretty big wars on their own in the first two world wars.

Pro-Palestinian evangelicals like Don Wagner imply the same kind of criticism in *Anxious for Armageddon* and *Dying in the Land of Promise*.[38] Wagner says, "The Christian Right pose[es] a risk for the future of a peace settlement."[39] British anti-Christian Zionist Stephen Sizer makes the self-fulfilling prophecy claim in a series of video lectures against Christian Zionism.[40] The liberal Presbyterian Church, USA, passed a resolution in the summer of 2004 in which they "officially disavow Christian Zionism as a legitimate theological stance."[41] Christian Zionism is increasingly being declared a dangerous theology by various voices from all walks of society. These people are out to demonize us through distorting our views and declaring us to be more extreme than we really are. This is an unethical approach.

### Self-Fulfilling Prophecy?

When one thinks through the idea, in terms of what Christian Zionists actually believe and teach, the notion that we are so dangerous that we could provoke a self-fulfilling prophecy is ridiculous. How could we provoke a self-fulfillment of the Rapture? Perhaps someone could identify all born-again Christians and send a global e-mail suggesting that on a given day we all go hide. How do you fake the Rapture? How does one set off a chain of natural events culminating in the Rapture? Perhaps some New Ager could suggest a scenario. Let's face it, those of us who believe in the *Left Behind* theology genuinely believe that the Rapture will be a supernatural event and such an event cannot be staged or provoked by human action in any way. If God does not do it, then it will not happen. If God does it, then there is nothing anyone will be able to do about it. So where is a genuine basis for concern over such an event as the Rapture being a self-fulfilled prophecy?

Some say Christian Zionists are dangerous because we believe the Temple must be rebuilt in Jerusalem by the middle of the Tribulation. Liberal Jewish commentator Gershom Gorenberg says, "Millennial movements have resorted to terror ever since the Jewish Zealots who rebelled against Rome nearly two thousand years ago." Gorenberg concludes that "believers must expect that redemption is very near, and that it depends on human action."[42] The problem with Gorenberg's analysis is that the Christian Zionist prophetic viewpoint sees these events as things that will be brought about after the Rapture by the Jewish people and are genuinely supernatural. Our prophetic beliefs are something only God can bring to pass. Thus, there is no compulsion within our mindset that "depends on human action." Such reality renders his theories about us being a dangerous group of people who believe the Bible. The only human action some Christian Zionists might see impacting prophetic fulfillment would be our responsibility to live a holy life unto the Lord and engage in tireless evangelism. These are things said to be valued by all true Evangelicals and not thought to be dangerous activities, except by the world.

For the last 45 years or so I have attempted to keep up on news relating to prophecy beliefs. There have been a number of events by religiously motivated groups or individuals that have caught the public's attention. None of the people involved in trying to advance their prophetic belief through human action have held to the same prophetic ideas dispensational Christian Zionists advocate. We are waiting on God's decision, which He will implement on the day He has already chosen from eternity past (Acts 1:7).

Even though there are currently millions of Christians around the world who hold to a Christian Zionist view of the prophetic future (perhaps 100 million), I do not think they will become frustrated at some point in the future and take matters into their own hands, because it is impossible for us to bring these supernatural events to pass through human action. Only God can do these things! I think this is the case, because we also believe we do not know when these events are destined to take place. Although many of us do believe we are likely near the time of the Rapture and the subsequent Tribulation period, we never know when they will actually occur. Thus, there is no pressure to act upon most Christian Zionists, as critics contend. Instead, we believe we should be busy about the Lord's business, while waiting eagerly for His any-moment return to Rapture His church into the clouds and take her to heaven. We do not believe the fictional speculation will ever develop that is being espoused by opponents.

## Rewriting History

Hank Hanegraaff displays a Palestinian Christian mentality when he accuses Israel of "the ethnic cleansing of Palestinians."[43] He cites as his authority discredited and revisionist Israeli historian Benny Morris, who said, " 'We must expel the Arabs and take their places' said David Ben-Gurion."[44] Hanegraaff is most likely unaware that Morris' statement about Ben-Gurion is a total fabrication. It is hard to learn this kind of information when surrounded by Palestinian Christian advocates. Nevertheless, such is the case.

Efraim Karsh, in the introduction of his book *Fabricating Israeli History*, tells us about how he first suspected Morris's fabrications: "The text in question was a book on the birth of the Palestinian refugee problem by Israeli academic Benny Morris. . . . While leafing through the book's English-language version, I came across a quote from a letter written by David Ben-Gurion to his son Amos in 1937, stating 'we must expel Arabs and take their places.' This rang a distant bell. Having read the book's Hebrew edition several years earlier, I recalled the letter as saying something quite different. Indeed, an examination of the Hebrew text confirmed my recollection. It read as follows: 'We do not wish, we do not need to expel Arabs and take their place. . . . All our aspiration is built on the assumption . . . that there is enough room in the country for ourselves and the Arabs.' "[45] Karsh goes on to examine Morris's overall body of research and concludes: "To my bewilderment I discovered that there was scarcely a single document quoted by Morris which had not been rewritten in a way that distorted its original meaning altogether."[46]

The Bible teaches Zionism (Psalm 132). It is becoming clear that when one rebels against God's Word on this point, it opens them to not only replacement theology, but to an increasing acceptance of Islamic viewpoints. As issues clarify, there is no place for neutrality where one can hide.

## Endnotes

1. *The Compact Edition of the Oxford English Dictionary*, Vol. III (Oxford: Oxford at the Claredon Press, 1987), p. 105. OED cites the first use of this word in English as occurring in 1881.

2. Oliver Melnick, "Rev. Stephen Sizer Claims Christian Zionists Are the Same as ISIS and Al-Qaeda," Israel, Islam, & End Times website, Nov. 7, 2014, http://www.israelislamandendtimes.com/rev-stephen-sizer-claims-christian-zionists-isis-al-qaeda/.

3. Arnold Forster and Benjamin R. Epstein, *The New Anti-Semitism* (New York: McGraw-Hill, 1974).

4. Ibid., p. xi.

5. Ibid., p. xii.

6. Alan Dershowitz, *The Case for Israel* (San Francisco, CA: Jossey-Bass, 2003).

7. Phyllis Chesler, *The New Anti-Semitism: The Current Crisis and What We Must Do About It* (San Francisco: Jossey-Bass, 2003).

8. For example, Colin Chapman, *Whose Promised Land? The Continuing Crisis over Israel and Palestine* (Grand Rapids, MI: Baker, 2002); Michael Prior, *Zionism and The State of Israel: A Moral Inquiry* (London: Routledge, 1999); Stephen Sizer, *Christian Zionism: Road-map to Armageddon?* (Downers Grove, IL: Intervarsity Press, 2004).

9. To name a couple: Stephen Sizer, "Countering Armageddon Theology," April 2003, Presence Ministries International, www. presence.tv/cms/journal.shtml. Although not recent, one of the most famous articles is by Timothy P. Weber, "How Evangelicals Became Israel's Best Friend," *Christianity Today*, Oct. 5, 1998; vol. 42, no. 11), p. 38.

10. Knox Theological Seminary, "An Open Letter to Evangelical and Other Interested Parties: The People of God, the Land of Israel, and the Impartiality of the Gospel," www.knoxseminary.org/Prospective/Faculty/WittenbergDoor/index.html. For a response see Mike Stallard, "A Dispensational Response to the Knox Seminary Open Letter to Evangelicals," August 2003, www. faculty.bbc.edu/mstallard/Biblical_Studies/Eschatology/eschatology_dr.htm.

11. Chapman, *Whose Promised Land?* p. 285.

12. For an overview of the history of anti-Semitism in the Church see David Rausch, *Building Bridges: Understanding Jews and Judaism* (Chicago, IL: Moody, 1988), p. 87–171.

13. Raul Hilberg, *The Destruction of the European Jews* (New York: Harper Colophon Books, 1961), p. 1–4 as cited in Hal Lindsey, *The Road to Holocaust* (New York: Bantam, 1989), p. 6–7 (emphasis original).

14. Steve Schlissel and David Brown, *Hal Lindsey & The Restoration of the Jews* (Edmonton, Canada: Still Waters Revival Books, 1990), p. 47.

15. Schlissel, *Restoration of the Jews*, p. 47–48 (emphasis original).

16. Ibid., p. 29–30.

17. David Rausch, *The Middle East Maze: Israel and Her Neighbors* (Chicago, IL: Moody Press, 1991), p. 85.

18. Douglas Young was the founder of the American Institute of Holy Land Studies, now Jerusalem University.

19. Rausch, *Middle East Maze*, p. 85.

20. Edward Flannery, "Israel, Jerusalem and the Middle East," in Twenty Years of Jewish-Catholic Relations, edited by Eugene J. Fisher, A. James Rudin, and Marc H. Tanenbaum, (Mawhaw, NJ: Paulist Press, 1986), cited in Rausch, *Middle East Maze*, p. 88.

21. Rausch, *Middle East Maze*, p. 64.

22. See Robert O. Smith, *More Desired Than Our Owne Salvation: The Roots of Christian Zionism* (New York: Oxford University Press, 2013), p. 95–115.

23. For an excellent account of the history leading up to the readmission of the Jews to England, see Douglas J. Culver, *Albion and Ariel: British Puritanism and the Birth of Political Zionism* (New York: Peter Lang, 1995). Interestingly, Dr. Culver was on the faculty at Knox Theological Seminary when this book was first released. Apparently he was not consulted concerning their "Open Letter."

24. Peter Toon, "The Question of Jewish Immigration" in Peter Toon, editor, *Puritans, the Millennium and the Future of Israel: Puritan Eschatology 1600–1660* (UK: James Clarke & Co., 1970), p. 115.

25. Ibid., p. 116.

26. Ibid., p. 117.

27. Hal Lindsey, *The Road to Holocaust* (New York: Bantam Books, 1989), p. 2.

28. Ibid., p. 2.

29. Ibid., p. 3.

30. Grace Halsell, *Prophecy and Politics: Militant Evangelists on the Road to Nuclear War* (Westport, CT: Lawrence Hill & Company, 1986), p. 197–98.

31. Gary DeMar, *Last Days Madness: Obsession of the Modern Church* (Powder Springs, GA: American Vision, 1999), p. 314.

32. Grace Halsell, *Forcing God's Hand: Why Millions Pray for a Quick Rapture — And Destruction of Planet Earth* (Beltsville, MD: Amana Publications, 1999).

33. Jane Lampman, "Mixing Prophecy and Politics," *Christian Science Monitor*, July 7, 2004, Internet edition accessed July 14, 2004.

34. Lampman, "Mixing," p. 1.

35. Timothy Weber as cited in Lampman, "Mixing," p. 2.

36. Partial preterists believe most Bible prophecy has been fulfilled in the A.D. 70 destruction of Jerusalem by the Romans, but still look for a future Second Coming. Full preterists believe the second coming took place in A.D. 70 and do not look forward to any future prophetic fulfillment.

37. Full Preterists John Anderson and Don Preston regularly have scare programs on the dangers of dispensationalism on their daily radio program that can be heard on the Internet at the following: http://www.lighthouseproductionsllc.com/broadcast.htm.

38. Donald E. Wagner, *Anxious for Armageddon: A Call to Partnership for Middle Eastern and Western Christians* (Scottdale, PA: Herald Press, 1995); *Dying in The Land of Promise: Palestine and Palestinian Christianity from Pentecost to 2000* (London: Melisende, 2003).

39. Wagner, *Dying*, p. 280.

40. Stephen Sizer, *Christian Zionists: On the Road to Armageddon* (Colorado Springs, CO: Presence Media, 2004), 4 lectures.
41. "Major US Christian Denomination Backs Divestment From Israel," Arutz Sheva, Israel National News.com, July 16, 2004, Internet edition.
42. Gershom Gorenberg, *The End of Days: Fundamentalism and the Struggle for the Temple Mount* (New York: The Free Press, 2000), p. 227–28.
43. Hank Hanegraaff, *The Apocalypse Code* (Nashville, TN: Thomas Nelson, 2007), p. 166.
44. Benny Morris, *The Birth of the Palestinian Refugee Problem, 1947–1949* (Cambridge, MA: Cambridge University Press, 1987), p. 25, cited in Hanegraaff, *Apocalypse Code*, p. 167.
45. Efraim Karsh, *Fabricating Israeli History: The "New Historians"* (New York: Frank Cass, 2000), p. xvii.
46. Ibid., p. xvii–xviii.

## CHAPTER 8

# REVELATION 12 AND THE FUTURE OF ISRAEL

One of the grimmest recurrences of history has been the continuing irrational hatred and persecution of the Jewish people. . . .

I believe this chapter answers the puzzling mystery of anti-Semitism. It shows that anyone who hates and persecutes a Jew is actually doing so at the instigation of a mighty spirit-being who hates all Jews.[1] — Hal Lindsey

In the Holocaust under Hitler, one-third of the world's Jewish population died. Under the fierce persecution of the Antichrist, controlled and energized by Satan, two-thirds of the Jewish population will die. This will be the largest and most intense persecution of the Jew ever known in Jewish history.[2] — Arnold Fruchtenbaum

Some critics of our futuristic views of Bible prophecy say the New Testament does not speak prophetically about a future national Israel. "There is not a single verse in the New Testament that supports the claim that there is prophetic significance in Israel's restoration as a nation," declares replacement theologian Gary DeMar. "Beyond A.D. 70, Israel as a nation plays no prophetic role. The New Testament only addresses Israel's near destruction never its distant restoration."[3] DeMar needs to read Romans 11:25–27. While I believe there are a number of references throughout the New Testament, especially in Revelation, that clearly indicates a future nation of Israel is in existence in their land, Revelation 12 is a whole chapter dealing with national Israel during a future time.

### New Testament References to Future Israel

In order for supersessionism or replacement theology to be correct in the belief that Israel has no biblical prophetic destiny in the future, a New Testament passage would need to be located that teaches this, and then demonstrate in plain language that the Church is the new Israel. As noted elsewhere in this book, such passages do not exist. Instead, there are New Testament passages that speak prophetically or simply view national Israel existing as a nation in the future.

Michael Rydelnik gave a lecture on this very topic at the 2013 Pre-Trib Study Group Conference.[4] Rydelnik noted the following passages and categorized them as follows: the New Testament reaffirms that the promises presently belong to Israel (Acts 3:25; Rom. 9:4–5, 11:28–29); the New Testament reaffirms God gave the land to Israel (Acts 7:5, 10:37, 39; Heb. 11:8–10); the New Testament speaks of Israel in the land in the future (Matt. 24:15–20; Rev. 7:4–9, 11–12, 16:14–16); the New Testament refers to a future Temple in the land of Israel (Matt. 24:15; 2 Thess. 2:1–4); the New Testament refers to a future restoration of the Jews to the land of Israel (Matt. 23:37–39, 24:30; Luke 21:24; Rom. 11:25–27); the New Testament speaks of a future Jewish kingdom in the land of Israel (Matt. 19:28; Acts 1:6–7).

### Israel in the Tribulation

Revelation 12 is an entire chapter that speaks of a future time concerning Israel in God's plan. Robert Thomas notes the place of chapter 12 within the flow of the Book of Revelation:

> The seventh trumpet has opened the way for a reve-
> lation of the seven bowl-judgments, but for that revelation
> to be meaningful, a sketch of the hidden forces behind this
> great climax of human history and of the personages that
> play a part in that climax is necessary.[5]

Revelation 12 deals with the Jews of Israel who are in Jerusalem and the surrounding area of Judah. It speaks of events relating to the Jews of Israel in the second-half of the Tribulation. This chapter examines the angelic conflict aspect of future history and how it impacts Israel. As God pulls back the spiritual curtain, we are shown the historic struggle between the seed of the serpent and the seed of the woman being played out in history and the eventual victory of Christ over His foes, which includes the rescue of national Israel.

Revelation 12 and 13 are considered the most symbolic chapters in the entire Book of Revelation, long considered the most symbolic book in the Bible. Paul Tan defines a symbol as "a representative and graphic delineation of an actual event, truth, or object. The thing that is depicted is not the real thing but conveys a representative meaning."[6] Even though symbols are employed in Revelation, that is no reason not to interpret the book literally, as we recognize the use of symbols.[7] "Where symbols exist," notes Brian Hand, "they either have a contextual interpretation, a broader biblical interpretation, or a clear enough referent for the interpreter to grasp what is happening."[8] Literal interpreters of Revelation identify about 25 symbols in Revelation.[9] About half of those symbols are identified in the text of Revelation. For example, "As for the mystery of the seven stars which you saw in My right hand, and the seven golden lampstands: the seven stars are the angels of the seven churches, and the seven lampstands are the seven churches" (Rev. 1:20).

### The Woman and the Dragon

"A great sign appeared in heaven: a woman clothed with the sun, and the moon under her feet, and on her head a crown of twelve stars" (Rev. 12:1). Chapter 12 begins by saying, "a great *sign* appeared in heaven." Verse 3 says, "another *sign* appeared in heaven." Thus, the text itself identifies the woman and the dragon as symbols, since "sign" in this context indicates the use of a symbol. "The word 'sign' draws attention to the divine purpose behind the symbol or happening."[10] Who does the woman of Revelation 12 symbolize? Catholics and many replacement theologians believe the woman in this passage is the Church, Mary, or simply the people of God down through the ages. For example, Hippolytus in the early church (c. A.D. 200) said, "By the woman clothed with the sun, he meant most manifestly the church."[11] A more widely accepted view today advocated by contemporary replacement theologians is that "the remarkable woman of Revelation 12 symbolizes the people of God."[12] Not that the woman symbolizes Israel, but saved Jews and Gentiles down through history. Another says, "She is the people of God, both before and after the coming of Jesus, representing Israel, Mary (the mother of Jesus), and the church, all at once."[13] As J.B. Smith declares, "The woman in this text of Revelation can represent none other than Israel, as all the facts and evidence abundantly prove."[14] Even a preterist like DeMar realizes the biblical symbolism of Genesis 37:9–11 demands that it refer to Israel.[15] However, preterists err in seeing it as a reference to Israel in the past, not the future. The only other time the trio of sun, moon, and stars are grouped together in a symbolic use is Genesis 37:9–11. In Joseph's dream, the sun refers to Jacob, the moon Rachel, Jacob's wife, and the 12 stars to the sons of Jacob who are also the 12 tribes of Israel (Jacob). There should be no doubt, based upon biblical analysis, that this symbol depicts the nation of Israel.

## The Woman in Labor

Revelation 12:2 says, "and she was with child; and she cried out, being in labor and in pain to give birth." We see here the picture of Israel as a woman experiencing labor pains during the time of the birth of the Messiah at Christ's first coming. Such a picture of Israel was quite common in the Old Testament.[16] Thomas tells us: "The reference is to the birth of Jesus at His first coming, but technically speaking this historical event had already occurred when John wrote. So this is a heavenly enactment of that past historical event just as other parts of this vision are enactments of events yet to occur."[17] Since the woman refers to Israel, even though Mary is in view, it must refer to something the nation experiences in history. "Thus the real travail of the nation of Israel did not occur at the time of this actual birth but still lies ahead in the terrible anguish of the tribulation,"[18] notes Allen. This passage also makes a connection to the outworking of the struggle between the seed of the serpent and the seed of the woman in Genesis 3:15. What was introduced in the first book of the Bible is now depicted as coming to a culmination in the final book of Scripture.

This vision of the woman (Israel) giving birth to a male child (the Messiah who is Jesus) demonstrates that within the sphere of the struggle between the seed of the serpent and the seed of the woman (Gen. 3:15) down through history, that Israel plays the central role in this conflict. It is precisely because of this role in the coming of Messiah and His eventual reign over Satan and his followers, that Israel has been and will be attacked and persecuted by Satan himself, even though he uses human instrumentality (for example, King Herod at Christ's birth). "Just as the woman was seen invested with symbols of power from above which God has given her, so here Satan is clothed with the fullness of earthly authority,"[19] concludes Kelly.

The Old Testament refers to "labor" or "birth pangs" in Jeremiah 30:6–7, which says, " 'Ask now, and see if a male can give birth. Why do I see every man with his hands on his loins, as a woman in childbirth? And why have all faces turned pale? Alas! for that day is great, there is none like it; and it is the time of Jacob's distress, but he will be saved from it." Randall Price explains the birth pangs of Messiah as follows:

> The birth pangs are significant in the timing of the Tribulation, as revealed by Jesus in the Olivet discourse (Matt. 24:8). Jesus' statement of the "birth pangs" is specifically that the events of the first half of the Tribulation (vv. 4–7) are merely the "beginning," with the expectation of greater birth pangs in the second half (the "Great Tribulation"). Based on this analogy, the entire period of the seventieth week is like birth pangs. As a woman must endure the entire period of labor before giving birth, so Israel must endure the entire seven-year Tribulation. The time divisions of Tribulation are also illustrated by the figure, for just as the natural process intensifies toward delivery after labor ends, so here the Tribulation moves progressively toward the second advent (vv. 30–31), which takes place "immediately after" the Tribulation ends (v. 29). As there are two phases of the birth pangs (beginning labor and full labor), so the seven years of Tribulation are divided between the less

severe and more severe experiences of terrestrial and cosmic wrath, as revealed progressively in the Olivet discourse and the judgment section of Revelation 6–19.[20]

Birth pangs were a clear expression in rabbinic Judaism for the Tribulation. Thus, the time of birth pangs commences with the beginning of the Tribulation period and culminates with the Second Coming of Christ. The Greek word ôdinon means "the pain of childbirth, travail-pain, birth-pang." It is said to be "intolerable anguish, in reference to the dire calamities which the Jews supposed would precede the advent of the Messiah."[21] Another authority agrees and says, "of the 'Messianic woes,' the terrors and torments that precede the coming of the Messianic Age."[22] This is the picture in Revelation 12 of Israel in travail or in the midst of the birth pangs of the Tribulation period.

Raphael Patai, in his helpful book *The Messiah Texts*, has dozens of references to extra-biblical commentary from Jewish writings in a chapter entitled "The Pangs of Times."[23] Patai tells us that "the pangs of the Messianic times are imagined as having heavenly as well as earthly sources and expressions. . . . Things will come to such a head that people will despair of Redemption. This will last seven years. And then, unexpectedly, the Messiah will come."[24] This widespread Jewish idea fits exactly into the framework Jesus expresses in the Olivet Discourse and in Revelation 12. The birth pangs of Messiah, also known as "the footprints of the Messiah,"[25] supports the notion that Revelation 12 refers to a time for Israel, as depicted by the woman, during the birth pangs of the Tribulation.

Paul also uses the motif of birth pangs in 1 Thessalonians 5:3 where he says, "While they are saying, 'Peace and safety!' then destruction will come upon them suddenly like labor pains upon a woman with child; and they will not escape." The context of Revelation 12 relates to the Tribulation period, which fits the other uses of birth pangs. Isaiah 66:7 says, "Before she travailed, she brought forth; before her pain came, she gave birth to a boy." "Thus the real travail of the nation of Israel did not occur at the time of this actual birth but still lies ahead in the terrible anguish of the tribulation period."[26]

## The Great Red Dragon

Revelation 12:3 says, "And another sign appeared in heaven: and behold, a great red dragon having seven heads and ten horns, and on his heads were seven diadems." The fact that verse 3 speaks of heaven (as does verse

1) indicates that we are seeing in this vision the angelic conflict that is being played out throughout history, and its relationship and impact upon Israel, especially during the Tribulation. The past conflicts set the stage and demonstrates a trend, which is the basis for understanding the future conflict noted in verses 6 through 17. The red dragon is unmistakably Satan himself (see Rev. 12:9, 20:2). The seven heads represent "seven consecutive world empires . . . indicating that they are in the process of running their course as John writes."[27] The kingdoms or empires also include a significant king or ruler associated with each empire. The empires and rulers are Egypt and Pharaoh, Assyria and Sennacherib, Babylon and Nebuchadnezzar, Medo-Persia and Ahasuerus, Greece and Antiochus Epiphanes, Rome and Caesar, and still in the future, the Revived Roman Empire or the antichrist's kingdom during the Tribulation. Allen explains, "Under each of these kingdoms and kings there was a deliberate attempt to wipe out Israel and thus rule out any possibility of the Christ coming through the line of promise. This view of history given by God shows that Satan was behind each one of these attempts; they were neither accidents of history nor to be explained in terms of political expediency but were Satan-directed attacks on the line of Christ."[28] The "ten horns resting on the seventh head and representing a rebellious confederacy aligned with the Devil and the antichrist,"[29] during the Tribulation as indicated in Daniel 7:7–24 and Revelation 13:1–8 and 17:7–18. The seven diadems "denote seven kings and seven historic kingdoms"[30] which correspond to the seven heads mentioned earlier in the verse. The emphasis on diadems indicates rulership or kingdoms. So the focus is on the future but with linkage to the past conflict.

"And his tail swept away a third of the stars of heaven and threw them to the earth. And the dragon stood before the woman who was about to give birth, so that when she gave birth he might devour her child" (Rev. 12:4). The past conflict between the seed of the woman and the seed of the serpent (Gen. 3:15) is rehearsed in verses 4 and 5. A third of the stars having been swept away by the dragon's tail inform us that a third of the angels fell and followed Satan in his original revolt and are still loyal to him during the Tribulation period. "Satan is described as 'Lucifer' the 'day-star' (Isa. 14:12). It is therefore suggested that what is in view is the great rebellion of Satan against the Most High, a rebellion that resulted in one third of the angels being cast down to earth."[31] We learn this when we realize that the stars in this passage are symbolic of angels (compare Rev. 12:7, 9).

The statement of the dragon who, "stood before the woman" is one of confrontation, like a ravenous animal poised to pounce at the right moment on its prey. "The standing position is unusual when viewed in connection with a serpent (cf. Gen. 3:14), but this was the usual posture of ancient dragons and serpents which sought to devour children."[32] Robert Thomas summarizes the Old Testament history of the struggle between the seed of the woman and dragon's evil intent as follows:

> Instances of his hostility surfaced in Cain's murder of Abel (Gen. 4:8), the corrupting of the line of Seth (Gen. 6:1–12), attempted rapes of Sarah (Gen. 12:10–20, 20:1–18) and Rebekah (Gen. 26:1–18), Rebekah's plan to cheat Esau out of his birth right and the consequent enmity of Esau against Jacob (Gen. 27), the murder of the male children in Egypt (Ex. 1:15–22), attempted murders of David (e.g., 1 Sam. 18:10–11), Queen Athaliah's attempt to destroy the royal seed (2 Chron. 22:10), Haman's attempt to slaughter the Jews (Esther 3–9), and consistent attempts of Israelites to murder their own children for sacrificial purposes (cf. Lev. 18:21; 2 Kings 16:3; 2 Chron. 28:3; Ps. 106:37–38; Ezek. 16:20).
>
> The attack of Herod against the children of Bethlehem (Matt. 2:16) and many other incidents during Jesus' earthly life, including His temptation, typify the ongoing attempt of the dragon to "devour" the woman's child once he was born. The most direct attempt was, of course, in the crucifixion of Christ.[33]

"And she gave birth to a son, a male child, who is to rule all the nations with a rod of iron; and her child was caught up to God and to His throne" (Rev. 12:5). The male child is Jesus the Messiah, who is the seed of the woman, and the One the dragon is really at war with, although it impacts in history God's chosen nation — Israel. Jesus is identified in Revelation 2:27 as the One who "shall rule them with a rod of iron, as the vessels of the potter are broken to pieces, as I also have received authority from My Father." Perhaps the fact that the "male child" is "caught up" (the word for the rapture in 1 Thess. 4:17 for the Rapture of the Church) depicts the victorious venture of Christ's first coming. Christ, not the Church, is caught up to God the Father's throne and not yet to rule on His own throne as will be the case during the millennium. Christ is currently at the right hand of the Father (Rev. 3:21) and after His Second Coming will reign on His throne during the millennial kingdom (1 Cor. 15:24–28; Rev. 20:4).

## Petra: The Second Exodus

"Then the woman fled into the wilderness where she had a place prepared by God, so that there she would be nourished for one thousand two hundred and sixty days" (Rev. 12:6). Many Bible commentators locate this event in the middle of the Tribulation and call it the second Exodus (see also Matt. 24:15–22) where God will miraculously take care of the Jewish remnant in a manner similar to the 40-year exodus event. "He has prepared a place for His people in the wilderness — a place of protection and provision during the awful days of the tribulation which will bring much suffering to Israel."[34] "The future flight of Israel to a place of safety midway through the seventieth week is the best way to understand the reference of the prophecy of this vision,"[35] declares Thomas. While we cannot be 100 percent sure of where the place in the wilderness is, the most likely place where Israel will go is the ancient fortress city of Petra in southwest Jordan. Some Old Testament passages call that area Bozrah (Isa. 34:1–7, 63:1–6; Jer. 49:13–14; Mic. 2:12–13; Hab. 3:3) because of the village located near the city of Petra that was eventually built.

Arnold Fruchtenbaum tells us about Petra:

> Petra is located in a basin with Mount Seir, and is totally surrounded by mountains and cliffs. The only way in and out of the city is through a narrow passageway that extends for about a mile and can only be negotiated by foot or by horseback. This means the city is easy to defend. . . . Petra is shaped like a giant sheepfold, with its narrow passage opening up to a spacious circle surrounded by cliffs. . . . The city of Bozrah in Mount Seir is located in ancient Edom or southern Jordan. Since this area will escape the domination of the Antichrist, it is logical for the Jews to flee to this place. Thus, God will provide a city of refuge outside the Antichrist's domain for the fleeing Remnant.[36]

There will apparently be enough Jewish Believers by the midpoint of the Tribulation to heed Jesus' warning when He says, "Therefore when you see the abomination of desolation which was spoken of through Daniel the prophet, standing in the holy place (let the reader understand), then those who are in Judea must flee to the mountains" (Matt. 24:15–16, see also Mark 13:14). The ministry of the two witnesses in Revelation 11 in the first half of the 70th week of Daniel will have been effective in bringing many Jews to belief that Jesus is the Messiah (see Rev. 11:13). "Now the flight of the woman must be interpreted in keeping with the symbols and it shows not a remnant . . . but the nation of Israel itself fleeing into the wilderness,"[37] says Allen.

"The preparation is made prior to her flight so that the place is ready for her upon her arrival."[38] The perfect tense in the Greek indicates that this place had been prepared for some time by God, which further supports the view that it likely refers to Petra. Fruchtenbaum says, "The place in the wilderness was prepared by God in advance and therefore indicates a very adequate and preexisting place of refuge."[39] Just as Jesus said He was going to prepare (same Greek word) a place in the Father's House (heaven), so the Lord has prepared a place for Israel to flee to during the second half of the tribulation, which is said to be "one thousand two hundred and sixty days" (Rev. 12:6). Perhaps the Lord's preparation includes the unique formation of the Petra area as far back as creation and Noah's Flood, when that range of mountains was formed. Smith says, "As in the sojourn in the wilderness in the days of Moses, Israel undoubtedly will be nourished in a miraculous way in the future."[40] John MacArthur notes, "Wherever their hiding place will be, they will be nourished and defended by God (cf. v. 14–16), just as their ancestors were during the forty years of wandering in the wilderness."[41] Some call this Israel's second Exodus since they will be led by the Lord into the wilderness where they would normally perish without His supernatural intervention, just as occurred during the first Exodus.

Revelation 12:6 appears to fit the Old Testament teaching that Israel will be hidden away in the wilderness and protected at some point during the Tribulation. For example, "Come, my people, enter into your rooms, and close your doors behind you; hide for a little while, until indignation runs *its* course. For behold, the LORD is about to come out from His place to punish the inhabitants of the earth for their iniquity; and the earth will reveal her bloodshed, and will no longer cover her slain. In that day the

LORD will punish Leviathan the fleeing serpent, with His fierce and great and mighty sword, even Leviathan the twisted serpent; and He will kill the dragon who *lives* in the sea" (Isa. 26:20–27:1). Isaiah 24–27 is known as Isaiah's Apocalypse, which emphasizes the Lord's last-day judgment upon the nations. This passage clearly speaks of the Tribulation period that parallels with Revelation 12. Also, the Jewish people are hid away until the indignation passes and the passage ends with the judgment of Leviathan, which is another symbol for Satan. We see a similar scenario in the analogy of Hosea and his wife Gomer when compared to the Lord and Israel. "Therefore, behold, I will allure her, bring her into the wilderness and speak kindly to her" (Hos. 2:14). The nation of Israel will go into the wilderness and the Lord will speak kindly to her at Petra during the last half of the Tribulation. The Lord will win back the nation to Himself. "Israel will again be allured into the wilderness (in the land of Edom and the city of Bozrah)," observes Fruchtenbaum, "where God will speak to her heart in courtship, and when she responds all her vineyards will be restored."[42]

### God versus Satan

The first six verses of chapter 12 convey what John saw in the vision of the woman and the dragon. Now, starting in verse seven through the end of the chapter we see an explanation of the vision and some further details added. The historic conflict between Christ and Satan reaches a climax in heaven where Satan and his demons are cast out of heaven to the earth at the midpoint of the seven-year Tribulation period (Rev. 12:7–12). Satan's defeat is first implemented in heaven by Michael and his angels in preparation for the final defeat of the dragon on earth three and a half years later at the Second Coming (Rev. 20:1–3).

God has chosen to use angelic agents at this point in history, as opposed to the end of history and the final revolt at the end of history, where it simply says, "fire came down from heaven and devoured them" (Rev. 20:9). Apparently, elect angels through the power of God are able to defeat the once head angel (Satan) and his fellow fallen angels since the passage says of the fallen ones, "they were not strong enough, and there was no longer a place found for them in heaven" (Rev. 12:8). My guess as to why God uses angels is because this event takes place in history. The purpose of history is the stage where creatures perform. Michael is seen in Scripture as the defender of Israel. David Hocking says, "Michael has been in conflict with the devil in previous history (Jude 9) and a staunch defender of Israel (Dan. 10:13, 21)."[43] Smith rightly observes:

> The war between Michael and the dragon is in fulfill-ment of Daniel 12:1, where it is said: "At that time [season] shall Michael stand up, the great prince which standeth for the children of they people." "Thy people," that is Daniel's people are Israel. The passage continues: "And there shall be a time of trouble [Greek: tribulation], such as never was since there was a nation even to that same time: and at that time thy people shall be delivered." This points unmistak-ably to the fact that the woman of Revelation 12 is Israel and that her fleeing to the wilderness constitutes the deliv-erance spoken of by Daniel.[44]

"And the great dragon was thrown down, the serpent of old who is called the devil and Satan, who deceives the whole world; he was thrown down to the earth, and his angels were thrown down with him" (Rev. 12:9). Verse nine uses the non-symbolic references to the parties first depicted symbol-ically via the vision at the beginning of the chapter. The dragon is "the ser-pent of old who is called the devil and Satan" and the one-third of the stars thrown down to earth are Satan's angels.

## Finally Gone from Heaven

"Then I heard a loud voice in heaven, saying, 'Now the salvation, and the power, and the kingdom of our God and the authority of His Christ have come, for the accuser of our brethren has been thrown down, he who accuses them before our God day and night' " (Rev. 12:10). "The saying of the group in heaven is obviously proleptic."[45] "God is now moving to take into His own hands that government that has been so long usurped by the great enemy, and this is the first movement, to clear the heavens; this is *their* salvation."[46] The Lord is cleansing heaven of evil and will do the same with earth three and a half years later. This long-awaited fact is acknowledged by heaven with joyous praise. "Their shout of triumph seems to be a fitting conclusion to their long wait for vindication, as they realize that this action heralds a decisive step towards the ultimate defeat of Satan and the establish-ment of the kingdom," says Allen. "As so often in the book, they see in the first step the whole completed process."[47]

This passage also reveals, at least partly, what Satan has been doing in heaven as a member of the angelic counsel throughout history. The oldest book in the canon of Scripture, Job, reveals that Satan brings false accusations against God and those who serve Him (Job 1 and 2). Walvoord explains: "It seems strange that Satan should have access to the very throne of God, yet this is precisely the picture in Job 1, where Satan along with other angels presents himself before God and accuses Job of fearing God because of God's goodness to him."[48] However, the New Testament is clear that Jesus Christ is the defense lawyer who defends the elect when Satan brings charges against a believer. We see this in two passages that speak of Christ: "Therefore He is able also to save forever those who draw near to God through Him, since He always lives to make intercession for them" (Heb. 7:25). "My little children, I am writing these things to you so that you may not sin. And if anyone sins, we have an Advocate with the Father, Jesus Christ the righteous" (1 John 2:1). Satan is banished forever from God's courtroom, never again to bring frivolous lawsuits against God's children.

"And they overcame him because of the blood of the Lamb and because of the word of their testimony, and they did not love their life even when faced with death" (Rev. 12:11). Clearly, it is due to the substitutionary death by Jesus on behalf of sinners that we are able to have a righteous standing before God. But it is not enough for Christ to make this provision for sinners; we must individually trust Christ and His work on the Cross as the payment for our sins. No individual, Jew or Gentile, has been or ever will be saved without personally trusting in the Messiah in order to speak a word of their testimony. We see this demonstrated early on by the faith of Abraham. "Then he believed in the LORD; and He reckoned it to him as righteousness" (Gen. 15:6). The third factor in verse 11 relates to sanctification, that is, living the Christian life. Believers, who are willing to die for Christ, as He did for them, are the ones who are also willing to live for Him. Lindsey notes, "The greatest weapon a believer ultimately has against Satan is that he's prepared for death."[49] Jack MacArthur adds, "We shall later see in our study how these saints will refuse the mark of the beast and refrain from worship of the beast because of their loyalty to Jesus Christ, and for this they will suffer depredation and even martyrdom."[50]

"For this reason, rejoice, O heavens and you who dwell in them. Woe to the earth and the sea, because the devil has come down to you, having great wrath, knowing that he has only a short time" (Rev. 12:12). We see the second reference in this passage to the rejoicing of the "heaven dwellers," which is the opposite reaction to that of the "earth dwellers." "The heavens rejoice over the removal of Satan and his angels, but earth is warned."[51]

What is Satan's response to being cast down to the earth, knowing that he has only a short time? Just like in the movies, when the bad guys cannot defeat the superhero himself, they go after his wife and children. Since Satan cannot defeat God in direct combat, when he is cast down to the earth he attacks His children. In this case, he goes after Israel, the Jewish remnant. The nature of evil is if you cannot succeed then you desire to take down as many innocent people with you as you can. The fact that Satan only has three-and-a-half years left energizes him to redouble his efforts and cause as much havoc on God's people as possible. "And when the dragon saw that he was thrown down to the earth, he persecuted the woman who gave birth to the male child" (Rev. 12:13). This will result in the greatest time of persecution against the Jews in the history of the world, since Satan will be on planet Earth directing it himself. "The Jewish people have been persecuted longer than any other nation in history, and this last persecution will have the purpose of their complete and final destruction. God however, will once again intervene on their behalf, and they will be protected there in their place in the wilderness,"[52] states Morris. S. Lewis Johnson says, "Satan, having failed to devour the son, now turns to the woman who produced Him! This is the time of Jacob's trouble."[53]

Why is persecution of the Jews so important to Satan? Since Revelation 12 is a chapter dealing with the issue of the great struggle between God and Satan, with a focus on the future, we see the outworking of Satan's final effort to defeat God, which is to prevent the Second Coming. Since the second advent cannot occur until the Jewish nation is converted to Messiah and calls on Him to rescue them, Satan attempts to liquidate the Jewish people in his attempt to prevent it from happening. Satan believes that if He can obstruct God's predestined plan from unfolding then he will have defamed Him and defeated Him. However, it is not going to happen! "This nation is attacked because it is the nation through which Christ has come," observes Allen. Satan "plots and plans and pursues Israel with the object of exterminating her."[54]

## Head for the Hills

What is God's response to Satan's persecution of His people? "The two wings of the great eagle were given to the woman, so that she could fly into the wilderness to her place, where she was nourished for a time and times and half a time, from the presence of the serpent" (Rev. 12:14). "Satanic persecution is answered by divine intervention."[55] God will protect the remnant supernaturally as noted by the phrase "two wings of the great eagle." "The symbolism relates back to the Exodus."[56] This is a figure of speech used in the Exodus (Exod. 19:4; Deut. 32:10–11) to speak of God's divine intervention as the Jews leave Jerusalem and the surrounding areas and are protected in Petra. Once again, the persecution of Israel will last three and a half years.

Satan launches an effort to track down the Jewish people, but God's protection overcomes his efforts. "And the serpent poured water like a river out of his mouth after the woman, so that he might cause her to be swept away with the flood" (Rev. 12:15). In context, it appears that Satan's pouring out of water like a river from his mouth after the woman is a metaphor for military pursuit. He sends out his armies to search for the Jewish people who are in hiding. The intent of his pursuit is to destroy the Jews as stated in the figure of speech "so that he might cause her to be swept away with the flood." "Since the origin of this flood is a *sign* (the mouth of the great dragon) and the text says *like a flood*, it is best to take this as a figure of speech denoting the overwhelming military force of an adversary. . . . The dragon's pursuit of the woman may be a continuation of the Beast's invasion of the glorious land. If so, the flight of the woman does not take place until after the abomination is set up (Matt. 24:15). Then, the invasion of the Antichrist continues in his pursuit of the woman."[57]

In spite of Satan's great efforts, God miraculously hides and protects His people. "But the earth helped the woman, and the earth opened its mouth and drank up the river which the dragon poured out of his mouth" (Rev. 12:16). Since symbolic language is in use throughout chapter 12, this verse could simply refer to the fact that God uses the rugged and mountainous terrain of the wilderness to counteract Satan's efforts at destroying the Jewish remnant. However, I think it makes more sense, since this is the second Exodus, that we see in Scripture at the first Exodus during the rebellion of Korah when the earth opened up and swallowed the rebels, a similar act by God occurs in the future on behalf of Israel. "As he finished speaking all these words, the ground that was under them split open; and the earth opened its mouth and swallowed them up, and their households, and all the men who belonged to Korah with their possessions" (Num. 16:31–32). Morris explains what will happen during the tribulation:

> A great chasm will open in the earth, already trem-
> bling and unstable from the worldwide earth movements of
> the tribulation period, and swallow them up.
>
> Such a terrestrial miracle is quite appropriate in the
> context. The whole situation is analogous to the pursuit of
> the children of Israel by Pharaoh at the time of the Exodus.
> When the Egyptian armies were drowned in the Red Sea.[58]

Again, Morris notes a similarity to the Exodus. "As the forty years in the wilderness prepared the people of Israel in olden times to enter the land of Canaan, so these three-and-a-half years in the wilderness will make them ready to receive Christ and enter the glorious kingdom age of the millennium."[59]

Like in the coyote and roadrunner cartoon series, no matter what Wile E. Coyote does to get the roadrunner, he is never able to win. So it is with Satan and his relentless attack throughout history during the Tribulation against the nation of Israel. We see the dragon's frustration with the woman in the final verse of chapter 12. "So the dragon was enraged with the woman, and went off to make war with the rest of her children, who keep the commandments of God and hold to the testimony of Jesus" (Rev. 12:17). Satan gives up his search for the assembly of Jews in the wilderness, and in his anger attempts to pick off other individual Jewish believers, likely the 144,000 Jewish witnesses (Rev. 7:1–8, 14:1–3) who are scattered across the globe, as well as the spiritual offspring, which could include Gentile believers. Whoever these offspring are, they are clearly believers, since they "keep the commandments of God and hold to the testimony of Jesus." "Satan frustrated by divine intervention in his evil purpose to destroy the nation turns against these more accessible believers with redoubled fury."[60] Walvoord says,

> the dragon is especially angry with those within the
> nation Israel. . . . There is a double antagonism against
> those in Israel who turn to Christ as their Messiah and Sav-
> iour in those critical days and maintain a faithful witness.

Undoubtedly many of them will suffer a martyr's death, but others will survive the period including the 144,000 sealed in chapter 7.[61]

The dragon's temper tantrum is the result of his unfulfilled anger at the woman and the male child she provided, who has become the Savior of the world. Smith explains that "*the rest or remnant,* applying to groups of individuals, is used in Revelation in the following passages: 2:24, 3:2, 9:20, 12:7, 19:21, 20:5, and always in a general sense, as an examination of the passages will plainly indicate."[62] Hocking argues that this group of believers includes Jews and Gentiles. "This phrase would apply to Jewish believers in the tribulation but could also apply to Gentile believers. . . . they must be believers in Jesus Christ, either Jewish or Gentile. All Gentile believers are a part of the 'offspring' of Israel. We are sons of Abraham by faith (Galatians 3:6–9)."[63] Morris believes the offspring will be other Jewish believers.

> In any case, there will be considerable numbers of Israelis who will continue to live in Jerusalem and other parts of Israel; and these also are referred to in a number of biblical prophecies. Furthermore, there will still be many Israelites in other nations, and these too are included in the prophecies. All of these will undergo severe persecution at the end-times, by virtue of being Jews, and for refusing the mark of the beast.[64]

## Conclusion

Not only are there references to the future of Israel in the New Testament, the future destiny of the nation is outlined in great detail in Revelation 12 and also found in other passages throughout the final book of the Bible. As noted at the beginning of this chapter, there are many New Testament passages like Revelation 12 that continue to present Israel as very much part of God's future plan for history. Nothing in the New Testament supports even a hint that God has replaced Israel with the Church. When we realize Israel has already become a nation (1948) that is generally in unbelief toward Christ today and virtually the whole world is already anti-Israel, it is not hard to realize the Lord is setting the stage for Tribulation events that will focus on the tiny nation the Lord loves. Many comparisons are being made today between the conditions in the Muslim world and the mentality of the Nazis toward the Jews in the 1930s.[65] At the end of the day, Revelation 12 teaches us that it is a fight between God and Satan, which impacts the creaturely realm in real future history.

## Endnotes

1. Hal Lindsey, *There's a New World Coming: An In-Depth Analysis of the Book of Revelation*, updated edition (Eugene, OR: Harvest House Publishers, 1984), p. 158–59.
2. Arnold G. Fruchtenbaum, *Footsteps of the Messiah: A Study of the Sequence of Prophetic Events* (Tustin, CA: Ariel Press, 2003), p. 289.
3. Gary DeMar, *Last Days Madness: Obsession of the Modern Church* (Powder Springs, GA: American Vision, 1999), p. 398.
4. Michael Rydelnik, "What Does the New Testament Say about Israel?" Irving, TX, Dec. 2013, http://www.pre-trib.org/data/pdf/Rydelnik-GodsFaithful-PromiseT.pdf.
5. Robert L. Thomas, *Revelation 8–22: An Exegetical Commentary* (Chicago, IL: Moody Press, 1995), p. 121.
6. Paul Lee Tan, *The Interpretation of Prophecy* (Winona Lake, IN: Assurance Publishers, 1974), p. 152.
7. Brian Hand, *The Climax of Biblical Prophecy: A Guide to Interpreting Revelation* (Greenville, SC: Bob Jones University Press, 2012), p. 199.
8. Ibid., p. 200.
9. Hand lists 24, *The Climax of Biblical Prophecy*, p. 198–99; John Walvoord lists 26, *The Revelation of Jesus Christ: A Commentary* (Chicago, IL: Moody Press, 1966), p. 29–30.
10. J. Allen, *Revelation: What the Bible Teaches* (Kilmarnock, Scotland: John Ritchie, LTD, 1997), p. 302.
11. Hippolytus, "On the Antichrist," p. 61; cited in William C. Weinrich, *Ancient Christian Commentary on Scripture: New Testament, Vol. XII, Revelation* (Downers Grove, IL: InterVarsity Press, 2005, p. 173. More recently this view is advocated by G.H. Lang, *The Revelation of Jesus Christ: Selected Studies* (Miami Springs, FL: Conley & Schoettle Publishing, 1985 [1945]), p. 198–201.
12. Ranko Stefanovic, *Revelation of Jesus Christ: Commentary on the Book of Revelation* (Berrien Springs, MI: Andrews University Press, 2002), p. 378.
13. Darrell W. Johnson, *Discipleship on the Edge: An Expository Journey Through the Book of Revelation* (Vancouver, Canada: Regent College Publishing, 2004), p. 219.
14. J.B. Smith, *A Revelation of Jesus Christ* (Scottdale, PA: Herald Press, 1961), p. 181.
15. DeMar, *Last Days Madness*, p. 146–47.
16. See Isa. 13:8, 21:3, 26:17–18, 61:7–8, 66:7ff; Jer. 4:31, 13:21, 22:23, 30:4–8; Hos. 13:13; Mic. 4:10, 5:2–3.
17. Thomas, *Revelation 8–22*, p. 121.

18. Allen, *Revelation*, p. 305.
19. Kelly, *Revelation*, p. 257.
20. J. Randall Price, "Old Testament Tribulation Terms," in Thomas Ice and Timothy Demy, *When the Trumpet Sounds: Today's Foremost Authorities Speak Out on End-Time Controversies* (Eugene, OR: Harvest House, 1995), p. 72.
21. Joseph Henry Thayer, *A Greek-English Lexicon of the New Testament* (New York: American Book Company, 1889), p. 679.
22. William F. Arndt and F.W. Gingrich, *A Greek-English Lexicon of the New Testament* (Chicago, IL: University of Chicago Press, 1957), p. 904.
23. Raphael Patai, *The Messiah Texts: Jewish Legends of Three Thousand Years* (Detroit, MI: Wayne State University Press, 1979), p. 95-103.
24. Patai, *Messiah Texts*, p. 95-96.
25. Price, "Tribulation Terms," p. 450, f.n. 56.
26. Allen, *Revelation*, p. 305.
27. Thomas, *Revelation 8–22*, p. 123.
28. Allen, *Revelation*, p. 306.
29. Daniel Green, "Revelation" in Michael Rydelnik and Michael Vanlaningham, general editors, *The Moody Bible Commentary* (Chicago, IL: Moody Publishers, 2014), p. 2015.
30. Tony Garland, *A Testimony of Jesus Christ: A Commentary on the Book of Revelation*, 2 vols. (Camano Island, WA: SpiritAndTruth.org, 2004), Vol. 1, p. 480.
31. Allen, *Revelation*, p. 308.
32. Thomas, *Revelation 8–22*, p. 125.
33. Ibid., p. 125.
34. David Hocking, *The Coming World Leader: Understanding the Book of Revelation* (Portland, OR: Multnomah Press, 1988), p. 194.
35. Thomas, *Revelation 8–22*, p. 127.
36. Fruchtenbaum, *Footsteps of the Messiah*, p. 296-97.
37. Allen, *Revelation*, p. 311.
38. Garland, *Revelation*, vol. 1, p. 488.
39. Fruchtenbaum, *Footsteps of the Messiah*, p. 294.
40. Smith, *Revelation*, p. 190.
41. John MacArthur, *Revelation 12-22* (Chicago, IL: Moody Press, 2000), p. 12.
42. Fruchtenbaum, *Footsteps of the Messiah*, p. 592.
43. Hocking, *The Coming World Leader*, p. 196.
44. Smith, *Revelation*, p. 185.
45. Ibid., p. 186.
46. F.C. Jennings, *Studies in Revelation* (New York: Our Hope Publishers, 1937), p. 332.
47. Allen, *Revelation*, p. 315–16.
48. Walvoord, *Revelation*, p. 192.
49. Lindsey, *There's A New World Coming*, p. 165.
50. Jack MacArthur, *Expositional Commentary on Revelation* (Eugene, OR: Certain Sound Publishing, 1973), p. 259.
51. Hocking, *The Coming World Leader*, p. 198.

52. Henry M. Morris, *The Revelation Record: A Scientific and Devotional Commentary on the Prophetic Book of the End Times* (Wheaton, IL: Tyndale House Publishers, 1983), p. 228.
53. S. Lewis Johnson, "Notes on Revelation from the Greek Text" (Class notes compiled by Dan Wallace, 1976), p. 84.
54. Allen, *Revelation*, p. 319.
55. Ibid., p. 319.
56. Johnson, "Notes on Revelation," p. 85.
57. Garland, *Revelation*, Vol. 1, p. 497–98.
58. Morris, *The Revelation Record*, p. 230.
59. Ibid., p. 230.
60. Allen, *Revelation*, p. 322.
61. Walvoord, *Revelation*, p. 196.
62. Smith, *Revelation*, p. 191 (italics original).
63. Hocking, *The Coming World Leader*, p. 200.
64. Morris, *The Revelation Record*, p. 231.
65. Chuck Morse, *The Nazi Connection to Islamic Terrorism: Adolf Hitler and Haj Amin al-Husseini* (New York: iUniverse, 2003).

CHAPTER 9

# LOVERS OF ZION:
# A HISTORY OF
# CHRISTIAN ZIONISM

"The growing importance of the English Bible was a concomitant of the spreading Reformation, and it is true to say that the Reformation would never have taken hold had the Bible not replaced the Pope as the ultimate spiritual authority. With the Bible as its tool, the Reformation returned to the geographic origins of Christianity in Palestine. It thereby gradually diminished the authority of Rome."[1] — Michael Pragai, Historian

The first salient school of thought in American history that advocated a national restoration of the Jews to Palestine was resident in the first native-born generation at the close of the seventeenth century in which Increase Mather played a dominate role. The men who held this view were Puritans, . . . From that time on the doctrine of restoration may be said to have become endemic to American culture.[2]
—Carl F. Ehle, Jr., Historian

It is popular in our day to criticize and dismiss a biblical belief that the modern state of Israel is significant in light of Bible prophecy. These critics think evangelical support for Israel is a bad thing, because they view the modern state of Israel as a bad thing and totally unrelated in any way to Bible prophecy. These naysayers often like to blame John Nelson Darby and dispensationalism as the modern source of our views. The truth of the matter is that love for Israel was well entrenched by Bible-believing Christians long before 1830. Such views pretty much follow the rise of Protestantism since the Reformation.

## The Early Church

While there is some evidence that a few ante-Nicene fathers (from A.D. 100 till 325) envisioned the Jews back in the land of Israel, by and large, they did not really look for a restoration of the Jews to the land of Israel, even though premillennialism was widespread. There was a statement or two by some of these early believers that implied a Jewish return to Israel. For example, Irenaeus, writing about A.D. 185, expressed this view in the following way:

> But when this Antichrist shall have devastated all things in this world, he will reign for three years and six months, and sit in the Temple at Jerusalem; and then the Lord will come from heaven in the clouds, in the glory of the Father, sending this man and those who follow him into the lake of fire; but bringing in for the righteous the times of the kingdom.[3]

Carl Ehle has summarized the views on the early Church as follows: "What is singularly absent from early millenarian schemes is the motif of the Restoration of Israel . . . the Church Fathers from the second century on did not encourage any notion of a revival of national Israel."[4]

Even though the ante-Nicene fathers were predominately premillennial in their understanding of future things, they laid a groundwork that would not only oppose Christian Zionism, but eventually premillennialism as well. Premillennialist Justin Martyr was the first to view "the Christian church as 'the true spiritual Israel' (*Dial. 11*)"[5] around A.D. 160. Justin's views laid the groundwork for the growing belief that the Church had superseded or replaced Israel. "Misunderstanding of it colours the Church's attitude to Judaism and contributes to anti-Semitism," notes Peter Richardson.[6] Further, by the time of Irenaeus, it had become entrenched in Christian theology that "the bulk of Israel's Scriptures [are] indecisive for the formation of Christian doctrine."[7] The details about Israel's future, especially in the Old Testament, are simply not a part of the development of Christian theology. Jeffrey Siker cites this issue as the primary reason for the disinheriting of the Jews within the early Christian Church. "The first factor is the diminishing emphasis upon the eschatological dimensions of the Christian faith."[8] Lacking an emphasis upon Israel's future, it is not surprising that belief in a future restoration of the Jews to their homeland is sparse in the early and medieval Church.

## The Medieval Church

Apart from a few sporadic medieval statements, Christian belief in the restoration of Israel to her land would not surface until "the second generation Protestant reformers."[9] Normally, support for Christian Zionism appears to go hand in hand with belief in millennialism. Some forms of postmillennialism and all kinds of premillennialism make it conducive for its advocates to look for a return of the Jews to Israel. "Inhibitions about millennialism were so pronounced that for the entire time between about 400 and 1050 there is no surviving written product that displays an independent Western millenarian imagination."[10] Since millennialism was absent from the Church for about a thousand years, it is not surprising that Christian Zionism was not a topic of concern during this time. It should also be remembered that these issues need to be viewed within the backdrop of a vicious anti-Semitism that governed the thought of the Medieval Church.

Joachim of Fiore (c. 1135–1202) dominated the eschatological beliefs of the Middle Ages. Even though some think that Joachim could have been of Jewish descent,[11] his thought is typical of the non-Zionist views of the time. "The final conversion of the Jews was a common medieval theme but one of peculiar significance to Joachim,"[12] notes Joachimist scholar Marjorie Reeves. It was popular in medieval eschatology to see a future time in which "Rome was to be the temporal capital of the world, Jerusalem the spiritual."[13] "The great rulers of Jewish history — Joseph, David, Solomon, Zorobabel — were interpreted in a priestly rather than an imperial sense,"[14] notes Reeves. Thus, while medieval eschatology saw a role for the Jews in the future, it was one of subservience, having been absorbed into the Gentile Church. Medieval prophetic thought provided no real distinct future for the

Jews as a regathered nation of Israel; certainly little that could be labeled as Zionism.

In spite of the overall trend to the contrary, there is some evidence that a few stray late-medieval voices did see some kind of a future for Israel. An example of one who held to a Jewish restoration is Gerard of Borgo San Donnino (around 1255). He taught that some Jews would be blessed as Jews in the end time and would return to their ancient homeland.[15] John of Rupescissa (c. 1310–1366) could most likely be viewed as a Christian Zionist. "For him the converted Jews would become God's new imperial nation and Jerusalem would be completely rebuilt to become the center of the purified faith. For proof he drew on a literal exposition of the Old Testament prophecies, which until then had been read by Christian exegetes to apply either to the time of the incarnation or to the heavenly Jerusalem in the beyond."[16]

Recently, premillennial historian Dr. William Watson discovered a manuscript from the 1400s at the British Library in London. The manuscript is entitled: "Heare beginneth the treatise of the Comynge of Antecrist"[17] written in Middle English. In modern English it would be: "Here begins the treatise of the Coming Antichrist." Dr. Watson says it speaks of "the Jews need to rebuild Jerusalem and their temple for the Antichrist to be able to desecrate it in order to reveal himself as antichrist. It also speaks of a departure of good Christians prior to the coming of Antichrist, but seems to imply a departure from the Roman Church by good Christians rather than an actual pretrib rapture." This manuscript indicates that some were beginning to read the Bible more closely and took it more literally than many before them. For the most part, medieval European Christendom remained overwhelmingly anti-Semitic in thought, word, and deed, which would not lend itself to seeing a future for the Jews in Israel.

## The Reformation

As I have noted, the flourishing of millennialism and a belief in a future return of the Jews to their land often go hand in hand. This is evident as the second generation Reformers begin to fade. Thus, to date, I have not been able to find any reformers who supported the restoration of the Jews back to their land in Israel. Such views must await the post-reformation era. "Neither Luther nor Calvin saw a future general conversion of the Jews promised in Scripture; some of their contemporaries, however, notably Martin Bucer and Peter Martyr, who taught at Cambridge and Oxford respectively in the reign of Edward VI, did understand the Bible to teach a future calling of the Jews."[18] It appears that toward the end of the Reformation there was some movement toward a belief in the conversion of the Jews, which would then grow into the belief of a national restoration of the Jews to their land.

Calvin's successor at Geneva, Theodore Beza, in the 1560s influenced the English and Scottish exiles who produced the famed Geneva Bible that the Jews would be converted in the end times, as expressed in a note on Romans 11:15 and 26.[19] "The first volume in English to expound this conviction at some length was the translation of Peter Martyr's Commentary upon Romans, published in London in 1568," says Gruber. "The probability is strong that Martyr's careful exposition of the eleventh chapter prepared the way for a general adoption amongst the English Puritans on a belief in the future conversion of the Jews."[20] This view was then adopted by such great Reformation and Puritan theologians as William Perkins, Richard Sibbes, Thomas Goodwin, William Strong, William Bridge, George Gillespie, and Robert Baillie, to name but a few.[21]

Crawford Gribben tells us:

> This latter-day conversion of the Jews to the Christian faith was to become a staple component of subsequent puritan eschatology, but is an expectation absent from the writings of the earlier Reformers. Calvin's understanding was that the passage which appeared to teach the latter-day conversion of the Jews — Romans 9–11 — only referred to "spiritual Israel," not Jews but the elect of all ages, places, and nationalities.[22]

However, the Reformation in many ways prepared the way for the later rise of Christian Zionist views. "It marked the end of the medieval era and the beginning of the modern time."[23] The main gift of the Reformation was that of the Bible in the language of the people. "The reformation opened men's eyes to the Scriptures," notes Gruber. "Its entire thrust was to turn away from the traditions of men which had nullified the Word of God, and to examine the Word itself."[24]

Gruber declares: "Views which were 'un-Lutheran' and 'un-Calvinistic,' but thoroughly Biblical, began to emerge from the Reformation."[25] "Since Wyclif's time," notes Barbara Tuchman, "the New Learning had revived the study of Greek and Hebrew, so long ignored in the Latin-dominated Middle Ages."[26] Michael Pragai tells us the following:

> The growing importance of the English Bible was a con-
> comitant of the spreading Reformation, and it is true to say
> that the Reformation would never have taken hold had the
> Bible not replaced the Pope as the ultimate spiritual author-
> ity. With the Bible as its tool, the Reformation returned to
> the geographic origins of Christianity in Palestine. It thereby
> gradually diminished the authority of Rome.[27]

Thus, so it would come to be, that the provision of the Bible in the language of the people would become the greatest spur to the rise of Christian Zionism. The simple provision of the Bible in the native tongue of the people, which gave rise to their incessant reading and familiarization of it, especially the Old Testament, was the greatest soil that yielded a crop of Christian Zionism over time. It was a short step from a near-consensus belief in the conversion of the Jews by the end of the Reformation period to the widely held view among post-Reformation Puritans in the restoration of Israel to her covenant land.

### The English Protestant Era

The path that led to the widespread belief in the end-time restoration of the Jews to Israel started with the study of the Bible, first in the original languages, followed by the influence of the newly acquired English trans-lations.[28] When both scholars and laymen alike, for the first time in the history of the Church, had the text of Scripture (both Old and New Testaments) more readily available, it led to greater study, a more literal inter-pretation, and a greater awareness of the Israel of the Old Testament. This provided the atmosphere in which a major shift occurred in England (also on the Continent to a lesser degree) from medieval Jew-hatred, which led to the expulsion of all Jews from Britain in 1290, to their invitation under Cromwell to return in 1655. "From such a context and from among this people," notes Douglas Culver, "now growing more and more intimate with things Jewish, the early millenarian protagonists for the restoration of the Jews to their Palestinian homeland arose."[29] However, it would be a tough road to get to the point where belief in a Jewish restoration to their ancient homeland would become so widespread.

It wasn't just any group of English protestants that provided a fertile soil for Jewish Restorationist doctrines; it was out of the English Puritan movement that this belief sprang. "Starting with the Puritan ascendancy," notes Tuchman, "the movement among the English for the return of the Jews to Palestine began."[30] Why the Puritans? Puritans were not just dissenters; they were a Protestant sect that valued the Old Testament to an unprecedented degree in their day. Tuchman tells us:

> They began to feel for the Old Testament a preference that showed itself in all their sentiments and habits. They paid a respect to the Hebrew language that they refused to the language of their Gospels and of the epistles of Paul. They baptized their children by the names not of Christian saints but of Hebrew patriarchs and warriors. They turned the weekly festival by which the church had from primitive times commemorated the resurrection of her Lord, into the Jewish Sabbath. They sought for precedents to guide their ordinary conduct in the books of Judges and Kings.[31]

One of the first Englishman to put forth the view that the Jews should be restored to the land of Israel was a scholar named Francis Kett who had taken two degrees from Cambridge. In 1585 he had published a book entitled *The Glorious and Beautiful Garland of Mans Glorification Containing the Godly Misterie of Heavenly Jerusalem* (one of the shorter titles of the day). While his book primarily dealt with other matters, Kett did have a section in which he mentioned "the notion of Jewish national return to Palestine."[32] This notion, which some think was likely gaining many followers,[33] was deemed heretical to the English establishment of the day, and Rev. Kett was quickly burned at the stake on January 14, 1589, for expressing such views about the Jews' return to their land, an idea he claimed to have received from reading the Bible.[34] About the same time as Kett, strict Calvinist Edmund Bunny (1540–1619) taught the Jewish restoration to Palestine in a couple of books: *The Scepter of Ivday* (1584) and *The Coronation of David* (1588).[35]

As the 1600s arrived, a flurry of books advocating Jewish restoration to their land began to appear. Thomas Draxe released in 1608 *The Worldes Resurrection: On the general calling of the Jews, A familiar Commentary upon the eleventh Chapter of Saint Paul to the Romaines, according to the sense of*

*Scripture.* Draxe argued for Israel's restoration based upon his Calvinism and Covenant theology.[36]

Two great giants of their era were Thomas Brightman (1552–1607), (likely a Postmillennialist) and Premillennialist Joseph Mede (1586–1638), who both wrote boldly of a future restoration of Israel. Brightman's work, *Revelation of the Revelation*, appeared in 1609 and told "how the Jews will return from the areas North and East of Palestine to Jerusalem and how the Holy Land and the Jewish Christian church will become the centre of a Christian world."[37] Brightman wrote: "What, shall they return to Jerusalem again? There is nothing more certain; the prophets do everywhere confirm it."[38] Brightman went so far as to predict that the Jews would be converted to Christ in 1650.[39]

Joseph Mede's contribution was released in 1627 in Latin[40] and in 1642 in English as *The Key of the Revelation*.[41] The father of English premillennialism was also an ardent advocate of Jewish restoration to their homeland. Following Mede in many ways, Thomas Goodwin (1600–1680) also saw the Jews one day returning to Israel. In *An Exposition of the Book of Revelation* (1639), he taught that the Jews would be converted to Christ by 1656.[42] Momentum was certainly building toward widespread acceptance of English belief in Jewish restoration, but a few bumps in the road still lay ahead.

Giles Fletcher (1549–1611), a fellow at King's College, Cambridge, and Queen Elizabeth's ambassador to Russia, wrote a work advocating Restorationism. Fletcher's book, *Israel Redux: or the Restauration of Israel; or the Restauration of Israel exhibited in two short treatises* (shortened title) was published posthumously by the Puritan divine Samuel Lee in 1677.[43] Fletcher cites a letter in his book from 1606 as he argues for the return of the Jews to their land.[44] Fletcher repeatedly taught the "certainty of their return in God's due time."[45]

A key proponent for Israel's future restoration was Henry Finch (1558–1625), who wrote a seminal work on the subject in 1621, called *The World's Resurrection or The Calling of the Jewes. A Present to Judah and the Children of Israel that Ioyned with Him, and to Ioseph (that valiant tribe of Ephraim) and all the House of Israel that Ioyned with Him.*[46] Finch, at the time of the publication of his book, was a member of Parliament and one of the most highly respected legal scholars in England at the time. "The book had been published for a matter only of weeks when the roof caved in on the author's head," notes Culver. "In the persecution which ensued, Finch lost his reputation, his possessions, his health — all precipitated by his belief in Jewish national restoration."[47] "Finch's argument may be considered the first genuine plan for Restoration."[48] Finch taught that the biblical "passages which speak of a return of these people to their own land, their conquest of enemies and their rule of the nations are to be taken literally, not allegorically as of the Church."[49] King James of England was offended by Finch's statement that all nations would become subservient to national Israel at the time of her restoration.[50] Finch and his publisher were quickly arrested when his book was released by the High Commissioner (a creation of King James) and examined.[51] Finch was stripped of his status and possessions and then died a few years later. "The doctrine of the restoration of the Jews continued to be expounded in England, evolving according to the insight of each exponent, and finally playing a role in Christian Zionistic activities in the latter part of the nineteenth and in the first of the twentieth centuries."[52]

Many Puritans of the 17th century taught the restoration of the Jews to the Holy Land.[53] One of the greatest Puritan theologians in England was John Owen (1616–1683), who wrote, "The Jews shall be gathered from all parts of the earth where they are scattered, and brought home into their homeland."[54] "From the first quarter of the seventeenth century, belief in a future conversion of the Jews became commonplace among the English Puritans."[55] Many who believed in the conversion of the Jews also came to believe in Jewish restoration as well. Peter Toon, speaking of Puritans of this era, says:

> Of course, those who expected the conversion of the Jews added to Romans 11 other proof-texts from the Old and New Testament. Furthermore, a large proportion of those who took "Israel" in Romans 11:25 ff. to speak of Jews, also taught that there would be a restoration of Jews to their ancient homeland in the Near East either after, or at the same time as, their conversion to Christ.[56]

There was a similar Restorationist movement throughout Europe where the Reformation was strongest, but on a smaller scale. There were a number of Restorationists in Holland during the time of the Puritan movement. Isaac de la Peyrere (1594–1676), who served as the French Ambassador to Denmark, "wrote a book wherein he argued for a restoration of the Jews to Israel without conversion to Christianity."[57] In 1655, Paul Felgenhauever, wrote *Good News for Israel* in which he taught that there would be the "permanent return of the Jews to their own country eternally bestowed upon them by God through the unqualified promise to Abraham, Isaac and Jacob."[58] The Dane Holger Paulli (1644–1714) "believed wholeheartedly in the Jewish Return to the Holy Land, as a condition for the Second Coming."[59] He even "lobbied the kings of Denmark, England, and France to go and conquer Palestine from the Ottomans in order that the Jews could regain their nation."[60] Frenchman Marquis de Langallerie (1656–1717) schemed with the Turkish Ambassador in the Hague on a plan to defeat the pope and trade the papal empire for a return of the Jews to the Holy Land. Langallerie was arrested in Hamburg, tried and convicted of high treason, and died in prison a year later.[61] Other European Restorationists of the era include: Isaac Vossius, Hugo Grotius, Gerhard John Vossius, David Blondel, Vasover Powel, Joseph Eyre, Edward Whitaker, and Charles Jerran.[62]

The mid-1600s witnessed "the sudden explosion of millenarian publications,"[63] which predisposed the British to also consider the future fate of the Jews in the Holy Land. James Saddington lists the following 17th-century English individuals as holding to Restorationist views: John Milton, John Bunyan, Roger Williams, John Sadler, and Oliver Cromwell.[64] "The doctrine of the restoration of the Jews continued to be expounded in England, evolving according to the insight of each exponent," concludes Ehle, "and finally playing a role in Christian Zionistic activities in the latter part of the nineteenth and in the first of the twentieth centuries."[65]

## Colonial America

Since the American colonies, especially in Puritan New England, were settled primarily by Englishmen who brought with them to the New World many of the same issues and beliefs that were circulating in the motherland, it is not surprising to find many zealous advocates in America for the restoration of the Jews. Perhaps the most influential of the early Puritan ministers in New England was John Cotton, who, following the postmillennialism of Brightman, held to the restoration of the Jews to the Holy Land.[66] According to Ehle, in addition to John Cotton (1584–1652), early Restorationists included John Davenport (1597–1670), William Hooke (1601–1678), John Eliot (1604–1690), Samuel Willard (1640–1707), and Samuel Sewall (1652–1730).[67] Ephraim Huit, a Cambridge-trained early minister in Windsor, Connecticut, believed that the Jews would be regathered to their homeland in 1650.[68]

One of the standout advocates of the restoration doctrine was Increase Mather (1639–1723), the son of Richard and father of Cotton. Increase Mather wrote over 100 books in his life and was a president of Harvard. His first work was *The Mystery of Israel's Salvation*, which went through about a half-dozen revisions during his life.[69] His support of the national restoration of Israel to her land in the future was typical of American Colonial Puritans and was generally widespread. Ehle notes the following:

> The first salient school of thought in American history that advocated a national restoration of the Jews to Palestine was resident in the first native-born generation at the close of the seventeenth century in which Increase Mather played a dominate role. The men who held this view were Puritans. . . . From that time on, the doctrine of restoration may be said to have become endemic to American culture.[70]

"It was Increase Mather's view that this final and greatest reformation of the Christian world would be led by the Jewish people ensuing upon their restoration to the Holy Land."[71]

From the earliest times, American Christianity has always tilted toward support of the restoration of national Israel in the Holy Land. American Christians, when compared with Euro-Asian Christianity, has always had a philo-Semitic disposition. Thus, it is not surprising that this tradition continues today, especially in dispensational circles.

## Early American Support for Israel

With a significant number of English-speaking Christians during the last 400 years thoroughly saturated with Jewish restoration theology, it should not be surprising that many such Christians in the last two hundred years have risen up to play key roles in the establishment of the modern state of Israel.

It should not be considered strange that President John Quincy Adams expressed his desire that "the Jews again [were] in Judea, an independent Nation . . . once restored to an independent government and no longer persecuted."[72] President Abraham Lincoln, in a meeting with Canadian Christian Zionist Henry W. Monk, in 1863 said, "Restoring the Jews to their homeland is a noble dream shared by many Americans. He (the Jewish chiropodist of the President) has so many times 'put me on my feet' that I would have no objection to giving his countrymen a 'leg up.' "[73]

## 19th-Century British Restorationism

The 1800s marks a high point in British premillennialism and a corresponding apex for Christian Zionism. Many contemporary accounts critical of Christian Zionism focus their emphasis upon J.N. Darby and the rise of dispensationalism as the foundation for British Restorationism. As one examines the record, such is not the case. The real advocates of Christian Zionism in Britain were primarily Anglican premillennialists. By the mid-19th century, about half of all Anglican clergy were evangelical premillennialists. Iain Murray said, "Some seven hundred ministers of the Establishment were said to believe that Christ's coming must precede His kingdom upon earth. This was in 1845."[74] Murray went on to add that "the number almost certainly increased in the latter half of the century."[75] An example of such clergymen would be J.C. Ryle (1816–1900), who wrote a Pre-Millennian Creed.[76] The wave of premillennialism is what produced in Britain a crop of Christian Zionists that led to political activism that culminated in the Balfour Declaration.

Anthony Ashley Cooper (1801–1885), later Lord Shaftesbury, is said by Tuchman to have been "the most influential nonpolitical figure, excepting Darwin, of the Victorian age."[77] As a strong evangelical Anglican, he is said to have based his life upon a literal acceptance of the Bible and was known as the "Evangelical of Evangelicals." Shaftesbury was the greatest influence for social legislation in the 19th century. He was led into acceptance of premillennialism by Edward Bickersteth, which then gave rise to his views of Jewish Restorationism.[78] Lord Shaftesbury said concerning his belief in the Second Coming, that it "has always been a moving principle in my life, for I see everything going on in the world subordinate to this great event."[79] Because of his premillennialism, Shaftesbury became greatly involved as chairman of the London Society for Promoting Christianity among the Jews.[80] Shaftesbury spearheaded a movement that lead to "the creation by the Church of England of an Anglican bishopric in Jerusalem, with a converted Jew consecrated as its first bishop."[81]

"Oh, pray for the peace of Jerusalem" were the words engraved on a ring that he always wore on his right hand.[82] Since Lord Shaftesbury believed that the Jews would return to their homeland in conjunction with the second advent, he "never had a shadow of a doubt that the Jews *were* to return to their own land. . . . It was his daily prayer, his daily hope."[83] In 1840, Shaftsbury was known for coining a slogan that he would often repeat throughout his life, that the Jews were "a country without nation for a nation without a country."[84]

Shaftsbury greatest contribution to the Restoration movement was his attempt to accomplish something in the political realm in order to provoke England to develop a policy in favor of returning the Jews to their homeland. He succeeded in influencing England to adopt that policy, but England failed, at that time, to influence the Turks.

In 1838, in an article in the *Quarterly Review*, Shaftsbury put forth the view that Palestine could become a British colony of Jews that "could provide Britain with cotton, silk, herbs, and olive oil."[85] Next, Shaftsbury "lobbied Lord Palmerston, the Foreign Secretary, using political, financial, and economic arguments to convince him to help the Jews return to Palestine. And Palmerston did so. What was originally the religious beliefs of Christian Zionists became official British policy (for political interests) in Palestine and the Middle East by the 1840s."[86] This was primarily the result of Lord Shaftsbury's efforts. However, at the end of the day, Shaftsbury's plan failed, but it succeeded in setting a precedent for putting concrete, political legs on one's religious beliefs. This would yield results at a later time.

Lord Shaftsbury had used his great power of persuasion to sway Henry John Temple Palmerston (1784–1865), to whom he was related by marriage, to the Restorationist position.[87] Palmerston had a distinguished political career serving in government almost the entire time from 1807 till his death in 1865. He served the British government many years as war secretary and foreign minister and was a popular prime minister for about ten years. Even though Shaftsbury influenced Palmerston to hold to the Restorationist position, it appears that it was a deeply held conviction and not one of mere political expediency. While British foreign secretary in 1840, Palmerston wrote the following letter to his ambassador at Constantinople in his attempt to advocate on behalf of the Jews:

> There exists at the present time among the Jews dispersed over Europe, a strong notion that the time is approaching when their nation is to return to Palestine. . . . It would be of manifest importance to the Sultan to encourage the

Jews to return and to settle in Palestine because the wealth which they would bring with them would increase the resources of the Sultan's dominions; and the Jewish people, if returning under the sanction and protection and at the invitation of the Sultan, would be a check upon any future evil designs of Mehemet Ali or his successor. . . . I have to instruct Your Excellency strongly to recommend [the Turkish government] to hold out every just encouragement to the Jews of Europe to return to Palestine.[88]

Shaftsbury was not the only one lobbying Palmerston during this time. A wave of premillennialism had hit the Scottish, resulting in a growing sentiment toward Jewish Restoration. "In 1839 the Church of Scotland sent Andrew Bonar and Robert Murray M'Cheyne, to report on 'the Condition of the Jews in their land.' Their report was widely publicized in Great Britain and it was followed by a 'Memorandum to Protestant Monarchs of Europe for the restoration of the Jews to Palestine.' This memorandum was printed verbatim in the *London Times*, including an advertisement by Lord Shaftsbury igniting an enthusiastic campaign by the *Times* for restoration of the Jews."[89] "Three hundred and twenty citizens of Carlow, Ireland, sent a similar memorandum to Palmerston."[90]

One-time governor of Australia, Colonel George Gawler (1796–1869), was one of the most zealous and influential Restorationists, next to Shaftsbury, in the 1840s.[91] "Colonel Gawler was a senior commander at the Battle of Waterloo."[92] When he returned to England in 1841, he became a strong advocate of Jewish settlements in the land of Palestine. Gawler's Restorationism, like most of his day, was sparked by his religious convictions, but he argued for Jewish return to their land upon geopolitical grounds. Gawler stated the following:

[England] urgently needs the shortest and safest lines of communication. . . . Egypt and Syria stand in intimate connection. A foreign hostile power mighty in either would soon endanger British trade . . . and it is now for England to set her hand to the renovation of Syria through the only people whose energies will be extensively and permanently in the work — the real children of the soil, the sons of Israel.[93]

Working with Sir Moses Montefiore (a British Jew), Gawler provided an agricultural strategy for Jewish resettlement of the Holy Land. One of these Montefiore-Gawler projects resulted in "the planting of an orange grove near Jaffa, still existent today and known as Tel Aviv's 'Montefiore Quarter.' "[94]

Charles Henry Churchill (1814–1877), an ancestor of Winston Churchill, was a British military officer stationed in Damascus in 1840. "He was a Christian Zionist and he supported the Jews against the non-Zionist Christians of Damascus."[95] It was through his efforts that he helped acquit the Jews accused of the infamous charge of blood libel. Col. Churchill was honored at a banquet hosted by a grateful Jewish community where he spoke of the "hour of liberation of Israel . . . that was approaching, when the Jewish Nation would once again take its place among the powers of the world."[96] In a letter to Jewish philanthropist Sir Moses Montefiore (1784–1885), dated June 14, 1841, Churchill said,

> I cannot conceal from you my most anxious desire to see your countrymen endeavor once more to resume their existence as a people. I consider the object to be perfectly obtainable. But two things are indispensably necessary: Firstly that the Jews themselves will take up the matter, universally and unanimously. Secondly that the European powers will aid them in their views.[97]

Churchill continued to live in the Middle East, and in 1953 wrote *Mount Lebanon* and "predicted that when Palestine ceased to be part of the Ottoman Empire, it would either become an English colony or an independent state."[98]

British General Charles Warren, also known for his archeological work in Jerusalem, served in Syria on behalf of the Palestine Exploration Fund. In 1875 he wrote *The Land of Promise: or Turkey's Guarantee*.[99] Warren proposed that the land be developed with the "avowed intention of gradually introducing the Jews, pure and simple, who would eventually occupy and govern the country." He even speculated that the land could hold "a population of fifteen million."[100]

Laurence Oliphant (1829–1888) was an evangelical "British Protestant, an officer in the British Foreign Service, a writer, world-traveler and an unofficial diplomat."[101] Oliphant was passionate about the Jewish Restoration to their land that came from his intense religious convictions. "He tried to conceal them behind arguments based on strategy and politics."[102] In 1880, he published a book, *The Land of Gilead*, "proposing Jewish resettlement, under Turkish sovereignty and British protection, of Palestine east of the Jordan."[103] Even then, he foresaw the agricultural potential and the possibilities of developing the resources of the Dead Sea.

> All the fruits of Southern Europe, such as apricots, peaches, and plums, here grow to perfection; apples, pears, quinces, thrive well on the more extreme elevation . . . while the quick-growing Eucalyptus could be planted with advantage on the fertile but treeless plains.
>
> The inclusion of the Dead Sea within its limits would furnish a vast source of wealth, by the *exploitation* of its chemical and mineral deposits. . . . The Dead Sea is a mine of unexplored wealth, which only needs the application of capital and enterprise to make it a most lucrative property.[104]

There were many other British Restorationists during the 19th century that created a momentum that would pay off later in British control of Palestine and the Balfour Declaration. Restorationism found a voice in one of the most popular novelists of the 19th century, as George Eliot penned the influential Restorationist novel *Daniel Deronda*.[105] "Among the advocates we may include Lord Lindsay, Lord Shaftsbury, Lord Palmerton, Disraeli, Lord Manchester, Holman Hunt, Sir Charles Warren, Hall Caine, and others."[106] Among the 19th-century British, one observes the "gradual drift from purely religious notion to the political."[107] These two influences, the Bible and the sword (religion and politics), as Tuchman has put it,[108] would merge into a powerful team that led to the Balfour Declaration, and the eventual founding of the Jewish state in the 20th century.

## J.N. Darby and Restorationism

There is no doubt that John Nelson Darby (1800–1882) believed in a future for national Israel, which would make him a Restorationist or Christian Zionist in theory.[109] However, anyone familiar with Darby and the Brethren know that they were not involved politically in any way and their distinctive dispensational views did not penetrate Anglican Evangelicals.[110] Yet a number of critics of Christian Zionism say that Darby is a major source of Christian Zionism. Donald E. Wagner appears to be the biggest culprit in this matter.[111] "If Brightman was the father of Christian Zionism," declares Wagner, "then Darby was its greatest apostle and missionary, the apostle Paul of the movement."[112] Wagner continues this theme when he says, "Lord Shaftsbury, was convinced of Darby's teachings."[113] Fellow anti-Christian Zionist, Stephen R. Sizer, echoes Wagner's misguided views when he says of Shaftsbury: "He single-handedly translated the theological positions of Brightman, Henry Finch, and John Nelson Darby into a political strategy."[114]

I have never found, within the writings of the specialists on Christian Zionism, anyone who makes more than a brief mention of Darby.[115] No one includes him among those who could be considered even a quasi-significant Restorationist. In fact, Barbara Tuchman, whose work *Bible and Sword* is considered the most significant and comprehensive treatment of British Christian Zionism, does not even mention Darby at all.

When it comes to the alleged influence of Darby upon Lord Shaftsbury, this is most unlikely. One of Shaftsbury's biographers makes it clear that it was Anglican premillennialist Edward Bickersteth[116] (who was not even a futurist, but an historicist) who influenced him toward premillennialism. Battiscombe, speaking about the year 1835, says the following:

> In that year he first met the man who was to be one of the chief influences in his life, and through that man he in all probability first came in contact with a mode of belief which was to be all-important to his view of religion. The man was Edward Bickersteth, a leading Evangelical; the belief was that curiously explicit teaching about the end of the world and the Last Judgment usually known as Millenarianism.[117]

Even though Darby was not really a player in British Restorationism, there is no doubt that his dispensationalism, once imported to the United States, would eventually become the staple for current Christian Zionism. "Most dispensationalists were satisfied to be mere observers of the Zionist movement," notes Weber. "They watched and analyzed it." Weber notes that American William Blackstone "was one exception to the general pattern." The fact that Blackstone would become one of the first dispensational activists on behalf of Zionism (after the Civil War) proves the main point that dispensationalists, especially Darby, were generally not active in the Jewish Restoration movement until more recent times. Current realities should not cloud a clear view of the past.

## Restorationist on the Continent

Even though the English-speaking world led the way when it came to Christian Zionism, there were important contributions from continental Europe. While Napoleon's attempt at Jewish Restoration lacked religious motivation,[118] there were many Europeans who were smitten with religious Restorationism. "The Enlightenment in 18th-century France and Germany, by its very nature of questioning the past" notes Epstein, "questioned the Jews' status as separated from the rest of society because of religious differences."[119] Such a development made the public, free expression of ideas more common. As a result of the new openness some began advocating the return of the Jews to their homeland. The rise of nationalism was another trend of the day. "Nationalism actually initially had an unusual effect on the restorationist movement: it increased Christian support and decreased Jewish support."[120]

A German Lutheran, C.F. Zimpel, who "described himself as Doctor et Philosopiae, member of the Grand Ducal Saxon Society for Mineralogy and Geognosy at Jena," published pamphlets in the mid-1800s entitled "Israelites in Jerusalem" and "Appeal to all Christendom, as well as to the Jews, for the Liberation of Jerusalem."[121] He addressed a number of geographical issues and warned that if the Jews were not allowed to return to Palestine then it would lead to their persecution and slaughter.[122] Unfortunately Zimpel proved correct on this prediction.

Frenchman Charles-Joseph Prince de Ligne (1735–1814) advocated Jewish Restorationism. He called upon the Christians of Europe to lobby the Turkish sultan so that the Jews could return to their homeland. De Ligne's appeal was used by Napoleon in his efforts to establish a Jewish homeland in Palestine. "Among those French Restorationists were theologians and authors, but also, increasingly, politicians."[123] Some of them included Ernest Laharanne, Alexandre Dumas, and Jean-Henri Dunant (1828–1910), who was also the founder of the International Red Cross.[124]

Restoration proposals were put forth by a number of Europeans in the 19th century. A Swiss theologian named Samuel Louis Gaussen wrote a book advocating a Jewish return to their land in 1844.[125] Italian Benedetto Musolino (1809–1885) wrote a book, after a visit to the Holy Land, in which he argued "that the restoration of the Jews would allow European culture into the Middle East."[126]

## 20th-Century British Christian Zionism

Even though the momentum of over 300 years of British Restorationism was beginning to fade, there was enough activity to carry through World War I, which saw England finally gain control of the Holy Land. The early 1900s saw some of the most devout Christian Zionists arise and give birth to the Balfour Declaration and the British Mandate for Palestine.

Author James Balfour (1848–1930) was born in Scotland and reared in a strong Christian home, which instilled in him a love for the Jews based upon a biblical interest. Balfour, a life-long bachelor, even wrote a book on Christian philosophy and theology.[127] Lord Balfour served much of his life within the highest offices of British government, including prime minister. His interest in Jewish Restoration "was Biblical rather than imperial."[128] His sister and biographer said the following:

> Balfour's interest in the Jews and their history was lifelong. It originated in the Old Testament training of his mother, and in his Scottish upbringing. As he grew up, his intellectual admiration and sympathy for certain aspects of Jewish philosophy and culture grew also, and the problem of the Jews in the modern world seemed to him of immense importance. He always talked eagerly on this, and I remember in childhood imbibing from him the idea that Christian religion and civilization owes to Judaism an immeasurable debt, shamefully ill repaid.[129]

In 1906, a time in which he had just lost the office of prime minister of England, Lord Balfour met Dr. Chaim Weizmann, the foremost proponent of early Zionism next to Theodor Herzel. Balfour's sister said, "Balfour for his part told me often about the impression the conversation made on him." "It was from the talk with Weizmann that I saw that the Jewish form of patriotism was unique," noted Lord Balfour. "Their love for their country refused to be satisfied by the Uganda scheme. It was Weizmann's absolute refusal even to look at it which impressed me."[130]

After many starts and stops, Balfour was finally able to persuade all of the British War Cabinet that the time had come to issue a declaration of

British support for Jewish Restoration to their homeland. The declaration is dated November 2, 1917, and was addressed to Lord Rothschild as follows:

> His Majesty's Government view with favour the establishment in Palestine of a national home for the Jewish people, and will use their best endeavors to facilitate the achievement of this object, it being clearly understood that nothing shall be done which may prejudice the civil and religious rights of existing non-Jewish communities in Palestine, or the rights and political status enjoyed by Jews in any other country.[131]

Before the Balfour Declaration was finally issued, much discussion with allies and behind-the-scene discussion took place. Prime Minister Lloyd George wanted to make sure that the United States was fully on board before it was issued. President Woodrow Wilson would support it and on October 1918 issued the following statement of acceptance:

> I welcome an opportunity to express . . . satisfaction . . . in progress . . . since the Declaration of Mr. Balfour on . . . the establishment in Palestine of a National Home for the Jewish People, and his promise that the British Government would use its best endeavors to facilitate the achievement of that object . . . all America will be deeply moved by the report [on the founding] of the Hebrew University at Jerusalem with the promise that bears of spiritual rebirth.[132]

The impact of the Balfour Declaration was a tremendous event within the Zionist movement. Since Britain was on the verge of controlling Palestine, it provided a great step on the road to the founding of the nation of Israel in 1948. This great declaration was spearheaded, not just by British geopolitical concerns, as important as that was within their thinking, but by Christian sympathies that were formed by biblical beliefs. Lord Balfour does not appear to have been moved by his views of eschatology, although it may have been a factor, "but simply exiles who should be given back, in payment of Christianity's 'immeasurable debt,' their homeland."[133]

David Lloyd George (1863–1945) was British Prime Minister (1916–1922) when the Balfour Declaration was issued. Balfour and Lloyd George were both life-long friends. From Wales, Lloyd George was steeped in the Bible in which he was trained as a youth. This clearly predisposed him to view with favor the Zionist movement. Saddington says:

> It was Lloyd George's decision that was primarily responsible for the British launching a large-scale offensive to conquer all of Palestine despite the risks. As a Christian Zionist he was determined to gain control of Palestine without the French to interfere. He also wanted his country to carry out what he regarded as God's work in Palestine.[134]

Lloyd George made a number of statements concerning his biblical upbringing that influenced him throughout his life. "Lloyd George recalled how in his first meeting with Chaim Weizmann in December 1914, place names kept coming into the conversation that were 'more familiar to me than those of the Western front,' " notes Tuchman. "Lord Balfour's biographer says that his interest in Zionism stemmed from his boyhood training in the Old Testament under the guidance of his mother."[135] On another occasion, when speaking about the Balfour Declaration, Lloyd George said:

> It was undoubtedly inspired by natural sympathy, admiration and also by the fact that, as you must remember, we had been trained even more in Hebrew history than in the history of our own country. I could tell you all the kings of Israel. But I doubt whether I could have named half a dozen of the kings of England![136]

Undoubtedly, God put men like Lord Balfour and Lloyd George into positions of power at this crucial time in history to aid the eventual founding of the modern Jewish state. This appears more clearly when one realizes that there were not many men within British government of that era who held the biblically molded views of Christian Zionism, yet these were the men who were in power at that time. Christian Zionist William Hechler said, "Lloyd George and Arthur Balfour accepted Zionism for religious and humanistic reasons; they saw it as fulfillment of the Biblical prophecies, not just as something suiting British Imperial interests."[137] Tuchman tells us the following:

> Lloyd George's afterthoughts on the motivation of the War Cabinet in issuing the Balfour Declaration have

bewitched and bewildered all subsequent accounts of this episode. Unquestionably he doctored the picture. Why he did so is a matter of opinion. My own feeling is that he knew that his own motivation, as well as Balfour's, was in large part a sentimental (that is, a Biblical) one, but he could not admit it. He was writing his Memoirs in the 1930s when the Palestine trouble was acute, and he could hardly confess to nostalgia for the Old Testament or to a Christian guilty conscience toward the Jews as reasons for an action that had committed Britain to the painful, expensive, and seemingly insoluble problem of the Mandate. So he made himself believe that the Declaration had been really a reward for Weizmann's acetone process or alternatively, a propagandist gesture to influence American and Bolshevik Jews — an essentially conflicting explanation, neither so simple nor so reasonable as the truth.[138]

Irishman John Henry Patterson (1867–1947) grew up in a conservative Protestant home in which he was intensely taught the Bible throughout his youth. "His familiarity with the Bible, its stories, laws, geography, prophecies, and morals, stood him in good stead when his army superiors chose him to take the Zion Mule Corps."[139] The Zion Mule Corps was a Jewish military unit made up of volunteers from Palestine in the British Army during World War I. Lieutenant Colonel Patterson wrote about his experiences in *With the Judeans in the Palestine Campaign*, which he had published in the 1930s.[140] Patterson's views of Bible prophecy are evident in the following:

> Britain's share towards the fulfillment of prophecy must . . . not be forgotten and the names of Mr. Lloyd George and Sir Arthur Balfour, two men who were raised up to deal justly with Israel, will, I feel sure, live for all time in the hearts and affections of the Jewish people. It is owing to the stimulus given by the Balfour Declaration to the soul of Jewry throughout the world that we are now looking upon the wonderful spectacle unfolding itself before our eyes, of the people of Israel returning to the Land promised to Abraham and his seed forever. In the ages to come it will

always redound to the glory of England that it was through
her instrumentality that the Jewish people were enabled to
return and establish their National Home in the Promised
Land.[141]

As a Christian, Patterson describes the events of his day relating to the Jews
as "the fulfillment of prophecy." There were many others from this era who
believed similarly, and who played some kind of role in seeing that the Jews
would return to their homeland, but space prohibits their mention.[142]

### Herzel's Number One Advisor

The modern Jewish founder of Zionism is recognized to have been Theodor
Herzl. His earliest and closest advisor just happened to have been the Chris-
tian minister William Hechler (1845–1931), who was a zealous Christian
Zionist. Rev. Hechler was a pastor who was born in India of German missionary parents. He attended college in Basel, Switzerland,[143] which is where
Herzl was living when he first met him. "Hechler, bilingual in English and
German from childhood . . . was like his father, a member of the Church of
England."[144] He studied theology in London and then in Tubingen, which
was the center of the liberal approach to the Scripture. However, "he was
not persuaded by the key arguments of the liberals and retained a distinctly
creedal, doctrinal, even literalist theology."[145] This makes sense, since anyone
holding to a liberal view of Scripture would not have come to love Israel, as
did Hechler.

"Upon recommendation of the British court, he became private tutor
to Prince Ludwig, son of Frederick, the Grand Duke of Baden," says Pragai.
"At the time he met the Grand Duke's nephew, the future Emperor William
II of Germany. After the Prince's premature death, Hechler served in the
ministry in England."[146] "At Hechler's behest, the Grand Duke built up a
massive library of biblical eschatology, biblical history, and archeology. At
the Grand Duke's request, Hechler presented sermons and scholarly papers
on these themes before the Court and it's visitors."[147] Hechler was one of the
most zealous Christian Zionists of all time. He seemed consumed with the
goal of Jewish restoration to their homeland.

In 1882 he had published a book entitled *The Restoration of the Jews to
Palestine according to Prophecy.*[148] In 1885, "Hechler was appointed Chaplain
to the British Embassy in Vienna."[149] In 1896, Hechler introduced himself

to Herzl and thus became his most important aide, advisor, and advocate. It was said, "William Hechler would prove to be 'not only the first, but the most constant and the most indefatigable of Herzl's followers.' "[150] Hechler's connections in both Germany and England proved helpful to Herzl, as Hechler often arranged meetings for Herzel with the highest officials of each nation. Hechler often told the secular Herzl that what they were doing was "fulfilling prophecy."[151] Merkley tells us that Herzl "grew to trust Hechler more and more. Indeed, frequently, for brief but crucial periods, he virtually entrusted the whole Zionist enterprise to William Hechler, and, though Hechler frequently annoyed and embarrassed him, he never failed him."[152] Herzl said in his diary of Hechler the following:

> Of all the people who have been drawn to me by the "movement," the Rev Hechler is the finest and most fanciful. . . . He frequently writes me postcards, for no particular reason, telling me that he hasn't been able to sleep the previous night because Jerusalem came into his mind.[153]

What did Hechler mean when he would say that he and Herzl were helping to fulfill prophecy? We get a glimpse from his writings:

> Every detail of this remarkable Movement is of interest to us . . . clergy, who stand as watchmen on the spiritual walls of Zion. . . .
>
> We are now seeing the stirrings of the bones in Ezechiel's valley: oh! may we soon see the glorious outpourings of spiritual life predicted in Ezechiel 36: The religious element is, according to God's Word, to become the inspiring force, and, I think I can see that it is the religious faith in Zionism, which is now already influencing the whole nation of the Jews. . . . What food for reflection to every thoughtful student of the Bible and of history!
>
> The Jews are beginning to look forward to and believe in the glorious future of their nation when, instead of being a curse, they are once more to become a blessing to all.[154]

Hechler was a true friend and supporter of Herzl and was at his side when he died in 1904. Later Hechler wrote, "I was with him at the beginning of his dreams, and I was with him almost at the last moment of his earthly death."[155] Christian Zionist William Hechler continued to work hard for the cause that almost solely possessed his mind by trying to convince Gentile Christians of the worthiness of this cause. He died in 1931.

## Blackstone and American Christian Zionism

No doubt, one of the most outstanding examples of a Christian Zionist is that of American William E. Blackstone (1841–1935). Blackstone was born in Adams, New York, and reared in a pious Methodist home, where he became a Christian at age 11.[156] When he married he moved to Chicago and became a very successful businessman. Even though he was Methodist, he had become motivated by his dispensational view of Bible prophecy to work for the re-establishment of national Israel.

Blackstone, a tireless, self-taught student of Bible and theology, became very interested in what the Bible had to say about Israel. Like many Christians with similar interests, this led to attempts to evangelize Jewish people with the gospel. He founded in 1887 the Chicago Hebrew Mission for the evangelization of the Jews. Blackstone wrote the best-selling book *Jesus Is Coming* in 1908, which sold over a million copies in three editions. "Probably no dispensational Bible teacher of his time had a larger popular audience."[157] Concerning the restoration of the Jews to their homeland, Blackstone said in his book:

> But, perhaps, you say: "I don't believe the Israelites are to be restored to Canaan, and Jerusalem rebuilt."
>
> Dear reader! have you read the declarations of God's word about it? Surely northing is more plainly stated in the Scriptures.[158]

He then proceeds to list almost 14 pages of virtually nothing but scriptural citations supporting his belief. Then he concludes:

> We might fill a book with comments upon how Israel shall be restored, but all we have desired to do was to show that it is an incontrovertible fact of prophecy, and that it is intimately connected with our Lord's appearing, and this we trust will have satisfactorily accomplished.[159]

Even though widely known throughout evangelicalism for a number of things, he is best known for his tireless work on behalf of re-establishing the Jewish nation in Israel. Timothy Weber says the following of Blackstone and dispensationalism:

> Most dispensationalists were satisfied to be mere observers of the Zionist movement. They watched and analyzed it. They spoke out in favor of it. But seldom did they become politically involved to promote its goals. There is one exception to the general pattern, however, in the person of William E. Blackstone, one of the most popular dispensational writers of his time.[160]

By 1891, Blackstone, the activist, had obtained the signatures of 413 prominent Americans and sent this document to President Benjamin Harrison advocating the resettlement of persecuted Jews in Russia to a new homeland in what was then called Palestine.[161] Part of the petition read as follows:

> Why not give Palestine back to them again? According to God's distribution of nations it is their home — an inalienable possession from which they were expelled by force. Under their cultivation it was a remarkably fruitful land, sustaining millions of Israelites, who industriously tilled its hillsides and valleys. They were agriculturists and producers as well as a nation of great commercial importance — the center of civilization and religion. . . .
>
> We believe this is an appropriate time for all nations, and especially the Christian nations of Europe, to show kindness to Israel. A million of exiles, by their terrible suffering are piteously appealing to our sympathy, justice, and humanity. Let us now restore to them the land of which they were so cruelly despoiled by our Roman ancestors.[162]

Ehle had the following to say about the signers:

> Among the 413 signers listed by their cities — Chicago, Boston, New York, Philadelphia, Baltimore, and Washington — were the opinion makers of the day: the editors and/or publishers of the leading newspapers and

religious periodicals (at least ninety-three newspapers in all), the mayors of Chicago, Boston, New York, Philadelphia, and Baltimore, as well as other officials, leading churchmen and rabbis, outstanding businessmen, and in Washington, Speaker of the House of Representatives, T. B. Reed, Chairman of the House Committee on Foreign Affairs, Robert R. Hitt, and William McKinley, of Ohio, who later became president.[163]

Even though it accomplished little politically, Blackstone's petition was said to have had a galvanizing impact upon Americans as a whole. The petition received widespread coverage in newspapers and generated a great amount of discussion and acceptance. It sparked great interest among the Jews as a whole.[164]

Blackstone later made a similar appeal to President Woodrow Wilson, a Presbyterian minister's son who became a Christian Zionist, which influenced his acceptance of the Balfour Declaration of 1917.[165] It is not surprising that there is today a forest in Israel named the "Blackstone Forest" in his honor. Neither should it be surprising to learn that "William E. Blackstone [was] once dubbed the 'father of Zionism' for his political activities on behalf of the Jews."[166] Like Hechler, Blackstone spent the rest of his life working for his beloved cause until his death in 1935. While he was thrilled with the developments of the Balfour Declaration and the British Mandate after World War I, he basically died disappointed that Israel had not yet become a nation. However, that would indeed take place 13 years later.

### Harry Truman and Recognition of Israel

President Harry S. Truman (1884–1972) grew up in Missouri in a devout Christian home. When Harry was born, his parents attended a Southern Baptist church that both sets of grandparents helped establish in Grandview. "His father, John Anderson Truman was also a strong Baptist. Both his father and mother, Martha, raised him in the conventional Baptist tradition."[167] However, when Harry was six they moved to Independence, and they attended the First Presbyterian Church at Lexington and Pleasant every Sunday until Harry was 16. When Harry turned 18 and moved to Kansas City, he joined the Baptist church by baptism and remained a Southern Baptist the rest of his life. Truman said, "I'm a Baptist because I think that sect gives the common man the shortest and most direct approach to God."[168]

While growing up, Truman read the Bible through twice by age 12 and two more times by the age of 14. "From Sunday School and his own reading of the Bible, he knew many Biblical passages by heart and could quote many Bible verses at random."[169] Young Harry was an avid reader and remained so throughout his entire life. The Truman family owned a set of *Great Men and Famous Women*, edited by Charles Francis Horne. "According to Truman's daughter, Margaret, the book Truman preferred most after Horne's biographies was the Bible. There is even an indication that Truman considered entering the ministry for a time."[170] Every indication reveals that Harry and his sister Mary were very active in the church throughout their late teens and early 20s.

What about Truman's Christian beliefs? "Truman had little interest in theological issues, although he had an almost fundamentalist reverence for the Bible."[171] Blending Truman's great interest in history and the Bible, he once stated the following about the United States:

> Divine Providence has played a great part in our history. I have the feeling that God has created us and brought us to our present position of power and strength for some great purpose.
>
> It is not given to us to know fully what that purpose is, but I think we may be sure of one thing, and that is that our country is intended to do all it can, in cooperating with other nations to help create peace and preserve peace in the world. It is given to defend the spiritual values — the moral code — against the vast forces of evil that seek to destroy them.[172]

"While premillennial eschatology dominated the Southern Baptist denomination, the church into which Truman was born and to which he returned when he was eighteen," observes Saddington, "Truman never expressed his acceptance of premillennialism. It is even doubtful that he ever adequately understood it."[173] Truman's Christian focus was on the ethics of everyday living and tended to shy away from theological systems. Truman's Christian Zionism was a combination of his attraction to the people of the Bible (the Jews) that grew out of his familiarity of biblical details with humanitarian concern for a persecuted people. "The stories of the Bible," said Truman, "were to me stories about real people, and I felt I knew some of them better than *actual* people I knew."[174] His Christian Zionist beliefs were well developed and deeply rooted long before he became president of the United States. Presidential Counsel Clark Clifford described Truman's

> own reading of ancient history and the Bible made him a supporter of the idea of a Jewish homeland in Palestine, even when others who were sympathetic to the plight of the Jews were talking of sending them to places like Brazil. He did not need to be convinced by Zionists. . . . All in all, he believed that the surviving Jews deserved some place that was historically their own. I remember him talking once about the problem of repatriating displaced persons. "Every one else who's been dragged away from his country has someplace to get back to," he said. "But the Jews have no place to go."[175]

Truman's Christian Zionism came into play during two of the greatest decisions that he would have to make during his presidency: First, how should the United States vote on the partition of Israel, which would result in the creation of the new Jewish state, during the United Nations vote in late November of 1947? Second, should the United States diplomatically recognize the newly formed nation when David Ben-Gurion declared the birth of Israel on May 14, 1948?

On both issues, virtually all of Truman's personal advisors, the State Department, and the military establishment were opposed to him. Saddington notes:

> Truman's most trusted foreign policy advisers, almost to a man, were dead-set against the establishment of a Jewish state in Palestine. The president faced the formidable front of General Marshall, Under Secretary of State Robert Lovett, Secretary of the Navy James Forrestal, Policy Planning Staff's George Kennan, State Department Counsel Charles Bohlen, and Marshall's successor as secretary, Dean Acheson. Loy Henderson, director of NEA, who arrived at the State Department just three days after FDR's death, also opposed the Zionist aims. William Yale, also at the State Department, said that the creation of a Jewish state in Palestine would be "a major blunder in statesmanship." When

Secretary Forrestal reminded the president of the critical
need for Saudi Arabian oil in the event of war, Truman said
he would handle the situation in light of justice, not oil.[176]

Truman dealt with both issues by applying his "the buck stops here" approach
with tough, responsible decisions. "Truman instructed the American dele-
gate at the U. N., Herschel Johnson, to announce U. S.'s endorsement of the
UNSCOP partition plan on 11 October 1947."[177] Then, 17 minutes after
David Ben-Gurion's declaration of the new state of Israel, a cable was sent
to Israel and a message went to the press from the White House announcing
the following:

> This government has been informed that a Jewish
> State has been proclaimed in Palestine, and recognition has
> been requested by the provisional government thereof.
> The United States recognizes the provisional govern-
> ment as the *de facto* authority of the new State of Israel.[178]

Clark Clifford said of President Truman's decisions to favor Israel the following observation:

> As a student of the Bible, he believed in the historic
> justification for a Jewish homeland, and it was a conviction
> with him that the Balfour Declaration of 1917 constituted
> a solemn promise that fulfilled the age-old hope and dream
> of the Jewish people.[179]

After his presidency, his longtime Jewish friend Eddie Jacobson introduced
Truman to a group of professors by saying, "This is the man who helped
create the state of Israel," but Truman corrected him: "What do you mean
'helped to create'? I am Cyrus. I am Cyrus."[180] Truman was comparing himself to Cyrus in the Old Testament who enabled the Jews to return to their
land in the 6th century B.C. from their 70-year captivity. Perhaps his response
indicates that Truman had indeed found the main reason as to why God's
providence placed him into the presidency at the time in which he arrived.
In fact, many who have sifted through the data believe that had Franklin
Roosevelt remained president, he would not have made the same decisions
as those made by the cussing Baptist from Missouri.[181] It appears to my biblically informed, evangelical mind that God raised up Harry S. Truman and

put him in the White House for the purpose of providing a key human agent whom He used, as He did Cyrus centuries ago, to restore Israel to her land.

## Conclusion

God has greatly used many Gentile Christians during the last few hundred years who have prepared the way for Israel's return to their land. God will continue to use believers in the future who believe His prophecies about a national future for His people Israel. Yet today there are a growing number of voices saying that we are dangerous and heretical, and our influence should be resisted.[182] "The danger isn't going away," declares Gershom Gorenberg. "Not as long as people think they know what God has to do next and where He has to do it, and are terribly impatient for Him to begin."[183] After suggesting elsewhere in his book that dispensational, Christian Zionists could set into motion a self-fulfilling prophecy,[184] Timothy Weber oddly concludes the opposite when he says:

> Since the end of the Six-Day War, then, dispensationalists have increasingly moved from observers to participant-observers. They have acted consistently with their convictions about the coming last days in ways that make their prophecies appear to be self-fulfilling. It would be too easy — and completely unwarranted — to conclude that American prophecy believers are responsible for the mess the world is in, that their beliefs have produced the current quagmire in the Middle East. Given the history of the region, the long-standing ethnic and religious hatreds there, and the attempt of many nations, both Western and Arab, to carry out their own purposes in the Holy Land, it is easy to imagine the current impasse even if John Nelson Darby and his views had never existed.[185]

With such a conclusion I have to ask, "Why the fear-mongering?"

As demonstrated in this chapter, Christian Zionists have not always had it easy. Nevertheless, like those who have gone before us, we will stand on biblical conviction as we constantly watch for the further outworking of God's historical plan, revolving around His people Israel and His any-moment return.

## Endnotes

1. Michael J. Pragai, *Faith and Fulfillment: Christians and the Return to the Promised Land* (London: Vallentine, Mitchell, 1985), p. 10

2. Carl F. Ehle Jr., "Prolegomena to Christian Zionism in America: The Views of Increase Mather and William E. Blackstone Concerning the Doctrine of the Restoration of Israel," Ph.D. Dissertation at New York University, 1977, abstract.

3. Irenaeus, *Against Heresies*, Book V, chapter 30, paragraph 4.

4. Ehle, "Prolegomena," p. 31.

5. R. Kendall Soulen, *The God of Israel and Christian Theology* (Minneapolis, MN: Fortress Press, 1996), p. 35.

6. Peter Richardson, *Israel in the Apostolic Church* (Cambridge: At The University Press, 1969), p. 2. Richardson contends: "In spite of the many attributes, characteristics, prerogatives of the latter which are applied to the former, the Church is not called Israel in the NT. The continuity between Israel and the Church is partial; and the discontinuity between Israel B.C. and its continuation A.D. is partial," p. 7.

7. Soulen, *God of Israel*, p. 50. Soulen adds: "In addition to narrowing the thematic focus of the Hebrew Scriptures to the problem of sin and redemption, the standard model also foreshortens the Hebrew Scriptures into a temporal sense. As perceived through the lens of the standard model, the Hebrew Scriptures do not relate a story that extends indefinitely into the future," p. 53.

8. Jeffrey S. Siker, *Disinheriting The Jews: Abraham in Early Christian Controversy* (Louisville, KY: Westminster/John Knox Press, 1991), p. 194.

9. Ehle, "Prolegomena," p. 32.

10  Robert E. Lerner, "Millennialism," in John J. Collins, Bernard McGinn, and Stephen J. Stein, editors, *The Encyclopedia of Apocalypticism*, 3 vols. (New York: Continuum, 2000), Vol. 2, p. 356.

11  Marjorie Reeves, *The Influence of Prophecy in the Later Middle Ages* (London: Oxford University Press, 1969), p. 14.

12  Reeves, *Influence of Prophecy*, p. 6, f.n. 2.

13  Ibid., p. 382.

14  Ibid., p. 304.

15  Ehle, "Prolegomena," p. 41–42.

16. Lerner, "Millennialism," p. 353.

17. William C. Watson, e-mail quote (Oct. 11, 2016) relating to manuscript research on "Heare beginneth the treatise of the Comynge of Antecrist." For more great material from Watson see his *Dispensationalism Before Darby: Seventeenth-Century and Eighteenth-Century English Apocalypticism* (Silverton, OR: Lampion Press, 2015).

18. Daniel Gruber, *The Church and the Jews: The Biblical Relationship* (Springfield, MO: General Council of the Assemblies of God, 1991), p.301–02.

19. Ibid., p. 302.

20. Ibid., p. 302.

21. Ibid., p. 302.

22. Crawford Gribben, *The Puritan Millennium: Literature & Theology, 1550–1682* (Dublin: Four Courts Press, 2000), p. 39–40.

23. James A. Saddington, "Prophecy and Politics: A History of Christian Zionism in the Anglo–American Experience, 1800–1948," PhD Dissertation at Bowling Green State University, 1996, p. 32.

24. Gruber, *The Church and the Jews*, p. 299.

25. Ibid., p. 300.

26. Barbara W. Tuchman, *Bible and Sword: England and Palestine from the Bronze Age to Balfour* (New York: Ballatine Press, 1956), p. 93.

27. Pragai, *Faith and Fulfillment*, p. 10

28. See Douglas J. Culver, *Albion and Ariel: British Puritanism and the Birth of Political Zionism* (New York: Peter Lang, 1995), pp. 51–70.

29. Ibid., p. 60.

30. Tuchman, *Bible and Sword*, p. 122.

31. Ibid., p. 125.

32. Culver, *Albion and Ariel*, p. 73.

33. Ibid., p. 73.

34. Ibid., p. 71–73; Ehle, "Prolegomena," p. 47–48.

35. Lawrence J. Epstein, *Zion's Call: Christian Contributions to the Origins and Development of Israel* (Lanham, MD: University Press of America, 1984), p. 7

36. Culver, *Albion and Ariel*, p. 75–78; Ehle, "Prolegomena," p. 49.

37. Peter Toon, "The Latter-Day Glory," in Toon, editor, *Puritans, the Millennium and the Future of Israel: Puritan Eschatology 1600 to 1660* (Cambridge: James Clarke & Co., 1970), p. 30.

38. Malcolm Hedding, "Christian Zionism," essay on the website of the International Christian Embassy Jerusalem, February 18, 2001, p. 4.

39. Gribben, *Puritan Millennium*, p. 43.

40. Culver, *Albion and Ariel*, p. 79–82; Ehle, "Prolegomena," p. 53–56; enlarged second edition in 1632, Gribben, *Puritan Millennium*, p. 43.

41. Robert G. Clouse, "The Rebirth of Millenarianism," in Toon, *Puritans*, p. 56.

42. Gribben, *Puritan Millennium*, p. 46–47.

43. Culver, *Albion and Ariel*, p. 89–93; Ehle, "Prolegomena," p. 51–52.

44. Culver, *Albion and Ariel*, p. 94.

45. Cited in Culver, *Albion and Ariel*, p. 93.

46. Culver, *Albion and Ariel*, p. 101.

47. Ibid., p. 101.

48. Epstein, *Zion's Call*, p. 8.

49. Toon, "The Latter-Day Glory," p. 32.

50. Culver, *Albion and Ariel*, p. 102-03.

51. Ibid., p. 116-17.

52. Ehle, "Prolegomena," p. 61.

53. Culver provides the most detailed information concerning the 17th-century British Puritan development of Restorationism in *Albion and Ariel*. Tuchman's *Bible and Sword* also provides deep insight into this movement.

54. Martha Lou Farmer, "They Believed the Scriptures — The Story of Christian Zionism," Bridges For Peace website, May 21, 2004, p. 2; see also Ehle, "Prolegomena," p. 79.

55. Iain Murray, *The Puritan Hope: Revival and the Interpretation of Prophecy* (Edinburgh: Banner of Truth, 1971), p. 42.

56. Toon, "Conclusion," in Toon, *Puritans*, p. 126.

57. Hedding, "Christian Zionism," p. 4.

58. Grace Halsell, *Prophecy and Politics: Militant Evangelists on the Road to Nuclear War* (Westport, CT: Lawrence Hill & Company, 1986), p. 135.

59. Pragai, *Faith and Fulfillment*, p. 15.

60. Saddington, "Prophecy and Politics," p. 38.

61. Epstein, *Zion's Call*, p. 14.

62. Saddington, "Prophecy and Politics," p. 38.

63. Gribben, *Puritan Millennium*, p. 48.

64. Saddington, "Prophecy and Politics," p. 34–38.

65. Ehle, "Prolegomena," p. 61.

66. Ehle, "Prolegomena," p. 66; Toon, "The Latter-Day Glory," p. 34–36.

67. Ehle, "Prolegomena," p. 67.

68. Le Roy Froom, *The Prophetic Faith of Our Fathers: The Historical Development of Prophetic Interpretation*, 4 vols. (Washington, DC: Review and Herald, 1950), Vol. III, p. 60, 66.

69. Ehle, "Prolegomena," p. 67, 80.

70. Ibid., abstract.

71. Ibid., p. 186.

72. Pragai, *Faith and Fulfillment*, p. 49.

73. Farmer, "They Believed," p. 4.

74. Murray, *The Puritan Hope*, p. 197. See also Froom, *Prophetic Faith*, Vol. III, p. 706, and Grayson Carter, *Anglican Evangelicals: Protestant Secessions from the Via Media, c. 1800–1850* (New York: Oxford University Press, 2001), p. 155, 157.

75. Murray, *Puritan Hope*, p. 197.

76. J.C. Ryle, *Are You Ready for the End of Time?* (Guernsey, Scotland: Guernsey Press [1867] 2001), p. 8–10.

77. Tuchman, *Bible and Sword*, p. 176.

78. Georgina Battiscombe, *Shaftesbury, a Biography of the Seventh Earl: 1801–1885* (London: Constable, 1974), p. 100-03.

79. Tuchman, *Bible and Sword*, p. 178.

80. Battiscombe, *Shaftesbury*, p. 103.

81. Tuchman, *Bible and Sword*, p. 202.

82. Pragai, *Faith and Fulfillment*, p. 45.

83. Tuchman, *Bible and Sword*, p. 178.

84. Wagner, *Anxious for Armageddon*, p. 92.

85. Saddington, "Prophecy and Politics," p. 62.

86. Ibid., p. 62.

87. Battiscombe, *Shaftesbury*, p. 119–20.

88. Tuchman, *Bible and Sword*, p. 175.

89. Ami Isseroff, "British Support for Jewish Restoration," (www.mideastweb.org, 2003), p. 1.
90. Epstein, *Zion's Call*, p. 35.
91. Ibid., p. 37.
92. Pragai, *Faith and Fulfillment*, p. 22.
93. Tuchman, *Bible and Sword*, p. 216–17.
94. Pragai, *Faith and Fulfillment*, p. 23.
95. Saddington, "Prophecy and Politics," p. 62–63.
96. Pragai, *Faith and Fulfillment*, p. 48.
97. Tuchman, *Bible and Sword*, p. 209.
98. Saddington, "Prophecy and Politics," p. 63.
99. Ibid., p. 63.
100. Pragai, *Faith and Fulfillment*, p. 70.
101. Ibid., p. 53.
102. Tuchman, *Bible and Sword*, p. 270.
103. Ibid., p. 272.
104. Pragai, *Faith and Fulfillment*, p. 55.
105. See Epstein, *Zion's Call*, p. 48–50; Pragai, *Faith and Fulfillment*, p. 23; Tuchman, *Bible and Sword*, p. 236–40.
106. Isseroff, "British Support," p. 1.
107. Epstein, *Zion's Call*, p. 26.
108. Hence the title of her book, *Bible and Sword*; Tuchman said, "The origins of Britain's role in the restoration of Israel, which is the subject of the following pages, are to be found in two motives, religious and political." p. xiii.
109. For an overview of Darby's teachings on this matter see Weber, *Armageddon*, p. 20–23.
110. See Carter, *Anglican Evangelicals*, p. 195–248.
111. Wagner, *Anxious for Armageddon* (Scottdale, PA: Herald Press, 1995).
112. Ibid., p. 89.
113. Ibid., p. 91.
114. Stephen R. Sizer, *Christian Zionists: On the Road to Armageddon* (Colorado Springs, CO: Presence Ministries International, 2004), p. 14
115. Pragai, *Faith and Fulfillment*, p. 20; Epstein, *Zion's Call*, p. 39; Saddington, "Prophecy and Politics," p. 64–65; Ehle, "Prolegomena," p. 231–32.
116. Bickersteth wrote a number of books on prophecy, including *The Restoration of the Jews to Their Own Land, in Connection with Their Future Conversion and the Final Blessedness of Our Earth*, 2nd edition (London: L. Seeley, 1841).
117. Battiscombe, *Shaftesbury*, p. 99. Carter makes the same observation, *Anglican Evangelicals*, p. 157.
118. For an account of Napoleon's Restoration efforts see Tuchman, *Bible and Sword*, p. 147–174.
119. Epstein, *Zion's Call*, p. 16.
120. Ibid., p. 17.
121. Pragai, *Faith and Fulfillment*, p. 49–50.
122. Ibid., p. 51.
123. Epstein, *Zion's Call*, p. 40.

124. Ibid., p. 41; see also Pragai, *Faith and Fulfillment*, p. 75–77.

125. Epstein, *Zion's Call*, p. 40.

126. Ibid., p. 40.

127. Arthur James Balfour, *The Foundations of Belief Being Notes Introductory to the Study of Theology* (London: Longmans, Green, and Co., 1895).

128. Tuchman, *Bible and Sword*, p. 311.

129. Blanche E.C. Dugdale, *Arthur James Balfour: First Earl of Balfour, 1848–1906* (New York: G.P. Putnam's Sons, 1937), p. 324.

130. Dugdale, *Balfour*, p. 325.

131. Photocopy in *Encyclopaedia Judaica* (Jerusalem: Keter Publishing House, n.d.), Vol. 4, p. 132.

132. Cited by Pragai, *Faith and Fulfillment*, p. 123.

133. Tuchman, *Bible and Sword*, p. 312.

134. Saddington, "Prophecy and Politics," p. 176–77.

135. Tuchman, *Bible and Sword*, p. 83.

136. Pragai, *Faith and Fulfillment*, p. 87.

137. Ibid., p. 271.

138. Tuchman, *Bible and Sword*, p. 337.

139. Pragai, *Faith and Fulfillment*, p. 80.

140. Ibid., p. 80.

141. Ibid., p. 88.

142. For more detail about these individuals see Pragai, *Faith and Fulfillment*; Tuchman, *Bible and Sword*; Epstein, *Zion's Call*; Paul C. Merkley, *The Politics of Christian Zionism: 1891–1948* (London, Frank Cass, 1998); Saddington, "Prophecy and Politics;" Bruce R. Crew, "A Structural Framework For British Geo-Political Perceptions Toward Land as Sacred Place: Christian Zionism and the Palestine Question, 1917–39," (Ph.D. Dissertation, The University of Wisconsin-Milwaukee, 1995).

143. Merkley, *Politics of Christian Zionism*, p. 11.

144. Ibid., p. 11.

145. Ibid., p. 12.

146. Pragai, *Faith and Fulfillment*, p. 58.

147. Merkley, *Politics of Christian Zionism*, p. 12.

148. Ibid., p. 3.

149. Pragai, *Faith and Fulfillment*, p. 59.

150. Merkley, *Politics of Christian Zionism*, p. 25.

151. Ibid., p. 17.

152. Ibid., p. 23.

153. Ibid., p. 23.

154. Pragai, *Faith and Fulfillment*, p. 60–61.

155. Cited by Saddington, "Prophecy and Politics," p. 128.

156. Weber, *Road to Armageddon*, p. 102.

157. Ibid., p. 103.

158. William E. Blackstone, *Jesus Is Coming*, 3rd edition (New York: Fleming H. Revell, 1932), p. 162.

159. Ibid., p. 176.

160. Weber, *Road to Armageddon*, p. 102.
161. Ehle, "Prolegomena," p. 240–44.
162. Ibid., p. 241–42.
163. Ibid., p. 242–43.
164. Ibid., p. 243.
165. Ibid., p. 290-93.
166. Ehle, "Prolegomena," abstract. This fact is recognized by Benjamin Netanyahu in his book, *A Place Among the Nations: Israel and the World* (New York: Bantam, 1993), p. 16–17.
167. Saddington, "Prophecy and Politics," p. 362.
168. Merkley, *Politics of Christian Zionism*, p. 160.
169. Saddington, "Prophecy and Politics," p. 363.
170. Ibid., p. 363.
171. Merkley, *Politics of Christian Zionism*, p. 161.
172. Ibid., p. 162–63.
173. Saddington, "Prophecy and Politics," p. 364.
174. Merkley, *Politics of Christian Zionism*, p. 159.
175. Cited in Saddington, "Prophecy and Politics," p. 372–73.
176. Saddington, "Prophecy and Politics," p. 436.
177. Ibid., p. 448.
178. Merkley, *Politics of Christian Zionism*, p. 190.
179. Cited in Saddington, "Prophecy and Politics," p. 464.
180. Merkley, *Politics of Christian Zionism*, p. 191.
181. See Saddington, "Prophecy and Politics," p. 347–54; Merkley, *Politics of Christian Zionism*, p. 149–54; John Goodall Snetsinger, "Truman and The Creation of Israel," (Ph.D. dissertation, Stanford University, 1969); Earl Dean Huff, "Zionist Influences Upon U.S. Foreign Policy: A Study of American Policy Toward the Middle East from the Time of the Struggle for Israel to the Sinai Conflict," (Ph.D. dissertation, University of Idaho, 1971).
182. James Solheim, "Jerusalem Conference Calls Christian Zionism a 'Heresy,' " in *Episcopal News Service*, April 28, 2004, accessed on the Internet.
183. Gershom Gorenberg, *The End of Days: Fundamentalism and the Struggle for the Temple Mount* (New York: The Free Press, 2000), p. 232.
184. Weber, *Armageddon*, p. 249–68.
185. Ibid., p. 266.

## Tommy Ice
Executive Director
Pre-Trib Research Center

**WWW.PRE-TRIB.ORG**

*Looking for the blessed hope and the appearing of the glory
of our great God and Savior, Christ Jesus*

— Titus 2:13.

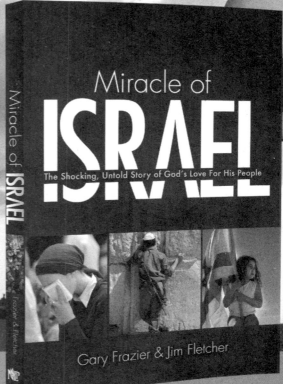